THE STURGILL BOOK

The Ancestors of
Angela Marie Sturgill

Compiled and Edited by
Stanton Darnbrook Colson

THE STURGILL BOOK

The Ancestors of
Angela Marie Sturgill

Compiled and Edited by
Stanton Darnbrook Colson

ISBN 13: 978-1517556716
ISBN 10: 1517556716

Published by AAS White Heron Press
1623 Soundneck Road, Elizabeth City, NC 27909
White Heron Press and associated logos are trademarks
and/or
registered trademarks of American Artists' Studios

Printed in the U.S.A.

Cover Design by Kim Colson

This Book
Chronicles the
Sturgill Families
The Ancestors of
Angela Marie Sturgill

[Additional photographs, documents
and research for this book are on file
with Stanton Darnbrook Colson]

Please feel free to send any corrections,
changes and/or updates to the editor
at the email address provided below.

Stanton Darnbrook Colson
cwaveofobx@yahoo.com

Acknowledgments

Thanks to those who assisted in providing information for this book, including Angela Marie Colson, Pat Croson, George Sturgill and Peggy Comer Walker, etal

Dedicated to
Joyce Dell Sturgill

The Sturgill Family

Joyce Dell Sturgill — Age 18

The Life and Times of
Joyce Dell[10] Sturgill

PATERNAL ANCESTRY: [STURGILL: Stevenson Conley[9], James Estil[8], Joshua[7], Francis[6] Jr., Francis[5] Sr., James[4], James[3], John[2], John[1] {of North Petherton Parish, Somersetshire, England}, Richard[1a], George[2a]]

MATERNAL ANCESTRY: [LAMB: Emma Rosetta[11], George Harvey[10], Hiram Jackson[9], Pemberton B.[8], Matthew William[7], Richard[6], John[5], Anthony[4], John[3], Landerous Anthony[2], Robert[1] {of Newcastle-Upon-Tyne, Northumberland, England}, Percy[1a]]

JOYCE DELL[10] was born at 3:54 p.m. on July 11, 1945 in the Arlington Hospital at Arlington, Arlington County, Virginia. She died from complications of the lungs due to acute leukemia on August 3, 1978 in the Fairfax Hospital [now Inova] at Falls Church, Fairfax County, Virginia. She was buried in the Lamb family cemetery on Pocoson Mountain in Green County, Virginia. Her father was Stevenson Conley[9] Sturgill of Rugby, Grayson County, Virginia [Editor's Note: The surname STURGILL was originally found as STOG-DELL, STODGHILL and STODGILL before generally becoming STURGILL with Francis[5] Sr.]. Her mother was Emma Rosetta[11] Lamb of McMullen, Green County, Virginia.

Joyce & Stan

JOYCE DELL[10] of Aldie, Loudoun County, Virginia married Stanton Darnbrook[10] Colson on September 24, 1964 at St. Albans Episcopal Church at Annandale, Fairfax County, Virginia. The ceremony was performed by the Reverend John Frizzel, with Marcus Winfield Todd [Stanton[10]'s friend] as the best man and Patricia Ann[10] Sturgill Croson [Joyce[10]'s sister] as maid of honor. Stanton[10] and Joyce[10] were separated on March 1, 1975 and divorced on August 13, 1976 at Fairfax, Fairfax County, Virginia. His father was Douglas Herman[9] [Henry Wilson[8], Stanton E(phraim)[7], Theophilus T.[6] 2nd, Ephraim[5], Ichabod Downs[4], Hatevil[3], Samuel[2] {Corson of Dover, Strafford County, New Hampshire}, Cornelius[1] {Cursonwhitt of New Amsterdam/later known as New York City}, Jan[1a] Cornelisen van Rotterdam {of Rotterdam, Zud-Holland, The Netherlands}, Cornelius Jonkers[2a]] Colson of Brooklyn, Queens County, New York City, New York. His mother was Mary Elsie[2] [William Irving[1], Morris[1a] {of Canada} Franklin[2a] {of France}] Quebec of Manhattan, New York City, New York.

JOYCE DELL[10] lived in Arlington, Arlington County,

Virginia the first several years of her life, then moved with her parents to Arcola, Loudoun County, Virginia where she attended the first through the eighth grades at the Arcola Elementary School. She continued her schooling in the ninth through the twelfth grades at Loudoun County High School at Leesburg, Loudoun County, Virginia. After graduation, she continued living at home and helped support her mother, who at that time was separtated from her father, by working in several secretarial positions.

JOYCE DELL[10] was baptized on the Sunday next before Advent on November 23, 1945 at the Chapel of Epiphany Diocese of Virginia in McMullen, Green County, Virginia. Attending were her parents Steve Conley[9] Sturgill, Sr. and Rosetta[11] Lamb Sturgill, and sponsors, Rosser Lamb, Ethel Lamb Shifflette and Sevilla Lamb Powell.

JOYCE DELL[10] and her husband and daughter resided at Sterling Park, Loudoun County, Virginia for four years. While there she worked as a secretary for the Three Chef's Corporation of Annandale, Fairfax County, Virginia and then with the Mount Vernon National Bank, also in Annandale, Fairfax County, Virginia. In 1969 the family moved from Sterling Park to Annandale, Fairfax County, Virginia and remained there until 1975. During that time, she worked as a secretary for American Furniture Rentals in Arlington, Virginia and then for Parsons, Brinker-hoff, Quade and Douglas, an engineering firm in Fairfax, Fairfax County, Virginia. In March 1975, after she separated from Stanton[10], she moved to Centreville, Fairfax County, Virginia where she resided until her death.

What follows are the residential address where Joyce Dell[10] lived:

to September 23, 1964	5611 N. 8th Street, Arlington, & Rte 1, Box 103 Aldie, Loudoun County, Virginia
September 24, 1964 to August 31, 1969	127 East Poplar Street, Sterling, Loudoun County, Virginia
September 1, 1969 to October 31, 1972	7427 Little River Tpke Annandale, Fairfax County, Virginia
November 1, 1972 to February 28, 1975	3551 Marvin Street, Annandale, Fairfax County, Virginia
March 1, 1975 to October 31, 1976	14220 Saguaro Place Centreville, Fairfax County, Virginia

November 1, 1976   14351 St. Germaine Drive
to August 3, 1978   Centreville, Fairfax County,
                          Virginia

The following is from a newspaper obituary in Green
County, Virginia:

Colson
Standardsville

A funeral for Joyce Dell Sturgill Colson,
33, of Centreville was held at the Baker
Funeral Home in Manassas on August 4.
Burial followed at the Lamb family cemetery here.

The Reverend Tom Seltz and the
Reverend McClannon presided at the
funeral service.

Mrs. Colson died on August 3, at the
Fairfax Hospital. She was an administra-
tive assistant with Parsons-Brinkerhoff of
Tyson's Corner.

Survivors include a daughter, Miss
Angela Marie Colson; a sister, Mrs.
Patricia Croson of Manassas; and two
brothers, Steve C. Sturgill, Jr. of Bailey's
Cross Roads and George Sturgill of

Loudoun County.

Mrs. Colson was the daughter of Steve C. Sturgill of Baltimore, Maryland and the late Rosetta Lamb Sturgill. She was a member of the Albany Episcopal Church of Annandale.

The Children of
Joyce Dell[10] Sturgill

[EDITOR'S NOTE: Stanton Darnbrook[10] Colson adopted the following child of Joyce Dell[10] Sturgill]

1. Angela Marie[11] Sturgill
   born 4 pounds, 8 ounces at 4:11 pm on August 9, 1965 in the Fairfax County Hospital [now Inova] at Falls Church, Fairfax County, Virginia.

   Angela[11] married, first, Dirk Handley[9] Hinkle on September 24, 1983 in the front yard of the home of her uncle George[10] Sturgill at Arcola, Loudoun County, Virginia, the Reverend Stanley Wherry officiating. Dirk[9] was born on July 16, 1964 at the City of Petersburg, Dinwiddie County, Virginia. He committed suicide [shot himself between the eyes with a 22 calibre rifle] on July 3, 1985 and died while in route by medivac helicopter to Fairfax County Hospital [now Inova] at Falls

Joyce and Angela

Church, Fairfax County, Virginia and was buried in the Union Cemetery at Leesburg, Loudoun County, Virginia. His father was Roger Lee[8] [Harold Glenn[7], Isaac Newton[6] {of Grant County, West Virginia}, Miles[5], Nobel[4] {of Virginia}, Abraham E.[3] {of German Valley, Pendleton County, Virginia}, Abraham[2] {Henckel of upper Milford, Bucks County, Pennsylvania, Johan Justus[1] {of Mosbach, Neckar-Odenwwald, Baden-Wuerttemberg, Germany}, Anthony Jacob[1a] {Henkel}, Georg[2a] {Henckel of Allendorf, Ad-Lumda, Germany}, Mattias[3a], Casper[4a], Ludwig[5a] {of Darmstadt, Hessen, Germany}, Anthony[6a], Georg[7a] {of Leutschau, Germany}, Johann I.[8a] {of Breslav, Germany}, Jacob[9a] {of Schleswig-Holstein, Germany}, Petrius[10a] {born circa 1378}] Hinkle of Hardy County, West Virginia. His mother was Susan[7] [Charles Breathed[6], Charles Isaac[5], Abraham W.[4] {of Pennsylvania}, Isaac[3], Rudolph[2] {of Pennsylvania}, Jacob[1] {Schaub of Wittensburg, Bassel, Switzerland}, Jacob[1a], Jacob[2a], Sebastian[3a], Jacob[4a], Sebastian[5a] {born on May 30, 1704}] Shobe of Hardy County, West Virginia. Angela[11] and

9

Dirk[9] had no issue.

Angela[11] married, second, Martin Guillermo[1] Carrazco of San Salvadore, El Salvadore. Martin[1] was born on February 14, 1961 at San Salvadore, El Salvadore. His father was Juan B.[1a] Carrazco of San Salvadore, El Salvadore. His mother was Ana Mirian[1a] Fuentes of El Salvadore. Angela[11] and Martin[1] were divorced on February 17, 1998 at Leesburg, Loudoun County, Virginia. Angela[11] and Martin[1] had no issue.

Angela[11] graduated from Loudoun County High School and the Charles S. Monroe Vocational School at Leesburg, Loudoun County, Virginia in May 1983. She obtained her Virginia State license as a hair stylist and began her career with the Hair Port at Sterling, then Countryside, and finally Ashburn, Loudoun County, Virginia where she was still working in 2015. As of 2015 she resided, with her cat Avry at Ashburn, Loudoun County, Virginia.

After Joyce and Stan were separated and before she died, she wrote two short works of non-fiction. What follows are *Come Fly With Me!* by Joyce D. Colson, November 1974 and *Work vs. Woman* by Joyce D. Colson, September 8, 1976. The editor has transcribed these works from the original manuscripts. With the exception of changing *underlined* words and phrases to *italics*, there are no edits or changes:

Come Fly With Me!
A Short Non-Fictional
by Joyce D. Colson
November – 1974

CHAPTER ONE

"Anxiety"

Thanksgiving day and I've got to prepare dinner for thirteen people, clean house and, most important of all, *pack*. How on earth can I concentrate on a turkey and worry about how the house is going to look when the very next morning I'm going to be doing something that I had always dreamed about and after twenty-nine years, had yet to do? Joyce Colson, tomorrow morning you are going to go on your very first plane trip—no, I still don't believe it. *Me*? No, it can't be, I'm afraid of flying—always wondered about it, but never had the guts to try it—and, still don't. But, here are the tickets, so, we must be going—*plane tickets*—so, that's what those little devils look like!

Let's get the turkey in before the guests arrive and find no dinner. Keep busy and you won't think about it. I got the bird in the oven, cleaned the house and got the tables set up. They'll never know that's two tables put together — just because one's round and the other one is square — na, they'll be so hungry, they'll never notice. I'm scared. Keep busy. O.K., let's see now, I need salt and pepper shakers — the nice ones, of course. Mmmm, the nice ones need cleaning. Can't keep everything up, I work in an office, too, you know. Gee, that was really nice of the office gang to give me a going away card with "Experimental" written across the little plane, but, their gift idea — a barf bag — really topped it off. Are they trying to tell me something? Probably are, most of them have flown many times. Na, everybody says once I've flown, I'll never want to go any other way — now wait just a minute, what the hell did they mean by *that*? I always thought going in my sleep would be the less painful way of going. How many napkins do I need? Oh, yes, glasses on the table would be nice, too. And, plates — my gosh, Joyce, get your head together. Hey, I'm really getting into the dinner scene now, and they'll be here soon. You're doing O.K., kid. Where's the can opener? What was that — A PLANE CRASH?? Oh, no, where? How? What kind of plane — *a 747??* My God, I'm gonna be sick. That's one in a hundred, says my happy-go-lucky husband. Yes, but a 747? That's what we're flying back on — I don't want to go. *You're going.* Get the door, they're here. But, I'm not ready. Get the door. Hi! How are you? Yea, I'm fine, thank you, just fine. Excuse me, won't you, I was just on my way to the bathroom.

Hey, Joyce, your lima beans are running over—oh, no, and look at your gravy! Where in the world is your head??? High, sweetheart, very high. Come on, let's get all this on the table so we can eat. Mommy, the dog just threw up in the living room! Now, wait just a minute, Angie, I know you're just saying that because you saw it on a cartoon. The dog *did* throw up, mommy, and I'm getting sick from looking at it. *She's* sick—oh, God, give me strength. Wow, the table(s) look great, sure wish I had a picture of it. George—where's George? He isn't here yet. Let's eat. I'm hungry. But, honey, George isn't here. *Let's eat.* Thank you, Heavently Father for this Thanksgiving Day and for giving us the opportunity to share it with our friends and family. (Where *is* George?) Let's eat. Pass your plates and ya'll help yourselves. Bet you're really excited about flying off tomorrow, huh? Now, why do they have to talk about that at the table? Well, George, it's about time—why didn't you just stay away until it was time for dessert? Gee, is this all that's left??? Well, the nerve of you. Glad you're spending the night, George, otherwise, we'd never make the plane on time. Now, George, tell the truth, have you *ever* been on time for *anything*??? Listen, why don't you just go back home tonight and meet us at the airport—that way, if you don't meet us on time, we'll just have to cancel our trip! (Thinking to myself, now, that was good, JC!) Not too funny, dear. Oh.

You sound like you don't want to go to Atlanta. I hear it's really great, especially the Underground City. Yea, I want to go and I'm excited about it — I'm just not that crazy about flying there. You'll love it — there's just no other way to go. I don't believe they just said that — excuse me, I'm off to the John again.

Joyce and Stan, thank you so much for inviting us and the dinner was just delicious. Oops, Angie wasn't kidding about the dog throwing up, was she??? Sorry 'bout that. Well, thanks agin and try to relax on the plane; you really will love it. Yea, thanks for coming over and ya'll be careful going home. We'll call you when we get back from the trip. Whew, God, am I glad they're gone. Well, that's not very nice. I know, but, it's just that I've got so much on my mind and still have to pack and besides that, I feel sick. You're gonna ruin the whole trip by being sick — now, shape up. And, pack. Yes, dear, I'll do that right now. Let's see now, make-up, tooth brush, deodorant, night-gown — nightgown, who in the hell needs a night-gown — we're going on vacation and staying in a nice hotel — oh, yea, George is sharing our room — take the nightgown. And, what's this at the bottom of my list — and, bring Angie something back. Bless her heart, she must of written that on there before she left. Gosh, I hope she has a good time at Peggy's. That cute little thing didn't even tell us to have a good time, just to bring her something! She'll be O.K. and Peggy will take good care of her — just in case something does happen. I *did* tell Angie that I loved her, didn't I? Yes, I did. I wouldn't let her go away without telling her that. Oh, no, did I forget to pack her toothbrush that's right, she got it. She'll be alright. She's getting so big now. Can you imagine, she'll be a teenager soon. Joyce, you're not packing. It would help if I didn't have a bad case of diarrhea. Long gown, heels, camera — where on earth is the camera — oh, here it is. Well, I think that's everything. Yep, everything's been checked off. No, that isn't everything — what about Stan's clothes??? Yea, I guess he would like to have a change of clothes! Now, that's everything — oh, no, you know what that means??? That means we're packed — packed to go on a trip — *a plane trip*. My gosh, what a time to run out of toilet paper. Damn. Now, I'll do my nails and then I can finally hit the sack. If I go to bed now, the time will pass by faster — maybe I'll just stay up a little longer — a lot longer. I really am excited about it, but it's just that I'm, well, you know. Gee, wonder if I'll dream about it. Hell, I won't even be alseep long enough to dream about anything. Upset stomach, excited, nervous, scared, diarrhea — sleep — what's that??? Dear God, let us have a safe trip and please don't let me be afraid. I'm too tired to be afraid. Yea, that's good. I'm too tired to be afraid . . . .

CHAPTER TWO

"Take-Off"

Mmmm, looks mighty light out there. Couldn't be morning already. Nah, couldn't be bird day already. Hey, honey, get up—IT'S BIG BIRD DAY!!! Yep, it's bird day alright. Oh, no, there's that funny feeling in my tummy again, and, oops, did anybody get toilet paper last night? I get the bathroom first. Am I *really* going to fly today? In one of those things I've always wondered where they were bound and wondered how on earth they were able to, stay up in the air? How do they stay up in the air??? George, aren't you scared yet? Heck no, man, I'm really looking forward to it—it's the biggest thing I've ever done. Yea, me too, that's exactly why I'm scared. That's pretty neat, though, we're both going to fly for the very first time and together. You two quit yakking and get your things together, we'll be leaving soon. Leaving soon? Gulp. Oops, Dad Colson is here. Toothbrush, make-up, food left out for the dogs. Are you sure we have everything? Come on, quit making excuses to delay things. You're gonna be just fine. Oh, no, did you lock the door already? Yea, why? I've really got to go to the bathroom in a real bad way. Well, it can just wait til' we get to the airport. Airport. You shouldn't have said that, you know. Oh, come on, for Pete's sake, we'll miss the plane for sure. Hey, think there's a chance??? Well, kids, you've got a beautiful day for flying. Dad, I'd really appreciate it if you didn't mention that word unless you absolutely have to. You're gonna love it, really love it. Why, I can remember the first time I flew . . . .

It's 10:00, we'll be at the airport in just a few minutes. Can you believe it—me, Joyce Colson, going to the airport, and not to watch the planes take off either—but, to actually take off in one. Just think, they'll be somebody else at the airport watching *me* take off this time. Take-off, gee, that kinda sounds important. Oh, no, we're here—we're actually here. All of a sudden, it doesn't sound important at all—sounds more like "scarey". Well, you kids have a great time and enjoy yourselves and I'll be sure to take care of the dogs for you. Thanks, dad, I love you.

Now, look, George, what you have to do is just act like you've been flying all your life. Oh, sure, look who's talking. You're the one half scared out of your wits, not me. Heck, I'm not scared anymore. I'm excited now. It's now time for me to start acting like I know what the hell I'm doing. WOW—look at the size of that plane—gotta be the biggest one I've ever seen. Take a good look, honey, I'm sure that's the one we're taking off in. No, it can't be—it's too big. How can it stay up in the air—and, my gosh, where are the propellers??? Propellers—are you kidding—they don't have propellers on these babies. George, get a picture of it—hurry up, get a picture, get several—

that's *our* plane! O.K., our baggage has been checked in and the tickets are alright. Now, let's go have a light breakfast. BREAKFAST??? Who in the hell can eat at a time like this? I can — I'm hungry, so, come on. I'll just have a coke; my stomach's kinda upset. Well, go to the bathroom then. Thanks, I think I will — gee, I hope *they* have toilet paper.

Come on, drink your coke, we've gotta get going. Just as I'm taking my last gulp, I overhear a woman saying how she hates to fly — *fly* — am I really going through with this? Guess so, here's the waiting room. Sure is full of people. Now's the time to act all big — like there's nothing to it. Just think, I'm at National Airport — all ready to go on a trip. At least, I think I'm ready. I'm doing pretty good, so far. Maybe it really won't be so bad — yea, I'll probably love it — just like they said I would.

Did you hear that, that woman just said she absolutely hates to fly Eastern — aren't we flying Eastern??? Calm down, look at a magazine. I can't. Ladies and gentlemen, I'm sorry to announce that the flight to Atlanta, Georgia will be delayed about an hour. WHAT??? YOU'RE KIDDING??? Honey, we're not even on the plane and already, there's something wrong. There's nothing wrong, most flights are delayed for some reason or another. Yep, that's what they said, there's a malfunction with the plane's brakes. My God, did you hear that? Well, look at it this way, you don't need brakes once you're up in the air. (My husband should be a comedian, right?) I just know something is going to happen. Will you just settle down. George, are you sure you're not afraid? No, Joy, I'm not afraid. Come on, we're boarding. Oh, please let everything be alright. Are we on the plane yet? No, silly, we're still walking through the waiting room. Oh. Are we on, *now*? Yep, we sure are. Oh, gosh, where's the bathroom—quick. Look, here we are, yea, these are the seats—good, right by the window. Good, he says. Ha. George, you can sit next to the window. No, Joy, you can. Are you kidding, that's the last place I want to sit. Are you sure this plane is safe? Well, I guess we won't know that until we get to Atlanta! (He's definitely a born comedian). Oh, that was real cute, dear, real cute. Sometimes, you're not funny at all. Is that the motor??? What do you mean, we're moving, they haven't even announced it yet. Sweetheart, they don't announce anything until we're at least off the ground. Well, if there's something *really* wrong, then they usually annouce that. There you go again, *trying* to be funny. I can't stop shaking—honey, I'm really scared. Hang on, cause here we go! Oh, God, I'm scared—I can't stop shaking. Will ya'll lplease quit lauging at me? As I'm holding on for dear life, my brother is sitting back actually enjoying this and begging me to look out the window.Come on, Joy, look, what a beautiful sight. Just look how tiny everything is from up here—look, Joy. I can't, I just can't. As much as I wanted to, I just couldn't look out and continued to cling on to Stan with all my might. He was convinced his hand was broken by now—I just couldn't let go and I was shaking like a leaf. Man, what a weird feeling. I think I'm gonna be sick. Weill you *please* stop shaking and let go of my hand? I can't help it, I'm petrified. Relax, we're way up there, now. And, all of a sudden, things got better. Just like that. The noise was gone and it seemed kinda still. George was still begging me to look out the window. I very slowly looked out . . . wow, look out there, honey, isn't it just beautiful??? Look at those clouds; we're really up there, aren't we? And, I actually leaned back and stopped shaking— what a great relief to Stan. His hand was actually red. As I turned to look at George, the look on his face was unforgetable. He was leaning back in his seat and grinning from ear to ear, replying, man, this is really the life, isn't it—I can't believe it, this is really great! Bless his heart, I was just so happy that he'd been able to come along. He just never really has a chance to do much of anything and has never gone on a real vacation. This was the life, he kept saying, and, I was happy knowing he was happy. So, then, I just kinda leaned back myself and half grinned and replied, and ya'll thought I wouldn't make it—boy, you guys just don't have any faith at all!

Oh, how neat, here comes our lunch, and, I actually feel—now, *that's* a good feeling—think just maybe I'll like flying after all! The lunch was delicious and we even had drinks. Man, this *was* the life! *What was that*? What's wrong with the plane? Why are we rocking back and forth? Settle down, we just went through turbulance, that's all. Turba who??? Hey, we're going to land in a few minutes. My gosh, are you shaking again? What's going on — why are things so bumpie? I feel sick — really sick this time. I just know something was going to happen — something bad. But, it didn't. We were landing!!! All of a sudden, the announcement came on that we were now landing in Atlanta, Georgia. It was bumpie and loud and I could hear the wheels and everything. George, weren't you afraid at all? Hell, I'm an experienced flier, now — and, now, I'm out to see Atlanta! Boy, wish I had his confidence. Oh, thank you, dear God, for getting us here safely, thank you.

As we stood up to start getting off, I found myself, surprisingly enough, getting half way back to normal and convinced myself I could act big getting *off* the plane! And, what a show I put on! As I came to the door of the plane, I looked out, realized we really were on ground, and, believe it or not, I walked down the steps waving to everybody! You know, just like the President does! Boy, was I acting big or what??? And, who'd ever guess what I had just been through! George and Stan both just smirked and replied that my attitude sure did change once we hit ground — and, how right they were! As we were walking into the airport, I just couldn't get it through my head that

I had actually flown in one of those big birds. Looking back for one last glance at that gigantic "wonder", I had a few seconds of mixed feelings: sick, nervous, excited, scared. I'd done it and lived through it. My very first flight was all over. I felt strange — Joyce had flown to Atlanta, Georgia. And, with that, I smiled and remembered George's remark, "and, now, I'm off to see Atlanta"!!!

CHAPTER THREE

"Atlanta"

We picked up our luggage, rented a car and headed for the Holiday Inn. Boy, was I excited now — being here in Atlanta, my first flight was actually over with and my God, the ground never looked so good! And, at this time, I was actually convinced that I would thoroughly enjoy the flight back. That, my dear people is a whole new chapter all its own!

Now that we've gotten unpacked and looked out of our balcony at the beautiful view and chatted about the flight, we decided we'd better get changed into some comfortable clothes and start making the best of our three-day vacation. And, now, I'm completely normal again (if that's possible for me!), and I'm completely filled with excitement of seeing a whole new and different city. Naturally, our very first stop was at that fabulous place called "Underground City" and what a place it turned out to be. I, of course, was just astounded of the fact that most parts of the City were the remains of the Underground from many, many years ago and got even more excited when I stood in the middle of one of the "streets" and realized that it really was a city underground. I just loved the whole idea! We didn't know where to begin and just started walking around and browsing around in the different shops. My immediate thought was "buy, buy, buy" and Stan's immediate thought was "no, no, no"! I talked him into buying me this gigantic book about the Civil War and which was printed just like the newspaper articles back in those days. I just loved it and thanked him for it and realized we had just blown a mere $27.00 on my first souvenir and within the first hour we were there — now, *that's* exciting! George said he was going to be smart and wait awhile before he started spending his money — now, what kind of fun is that and who on earth wants to be "smart" on a vacation??? We continued looking around and stopping here and there for cokes and ice cream. As the evening began to wear on, we started hitting the night clubs — oh, boy, that meant dancing, crazy mixed drinks and good music! Well, most of it was good music and some of it sounded like it should of been further down than the Underground! The drinks were really good and when we learned that we could keep the glasses when we ordered certain drinks, well, naturally, we just had to try some of those particular drinks—whoopee! The more I danced and drank, the more I realized I was wearing down and decided I'd better turn in for the night. The boys were still quite awake, so, I told them that if they took me back to the hotel, they could go and gallivant by themselves if they wanted to. They didn't have to give me an answer—I was back at the hotel in five short minutes and they were off! I was very glad to be back in my room and enjoyed the time to gather my thoughts on the day's events. It was nice to just relax and enjoy the beautiful scenery from the 18th floor overlooking the city. And, that ended my first day in Atlanta—what a day and what excitement. I fell asleep feeling very happy—and, very tired—and, for once, I felt like I didn't have a worry in the world.

Our second day there was a very wet one—the rain was just coming down and it certainly didn't help us any as tired as we were from the previous day, but, we didn't let it get us down. We got dressed and had breakfast in the hotel and before long, we were off again for the Underground. We did all of our sourvenir shopping for everybody and especially something for little Angie. I honestly believe we hit every shop that existed and trying to decide exactly what to buy was a real strain, but, of course, we managed O.K. Although we were under ground, so to speak, the rain managed to seep down to where we were and it was getting terribly cold and we were very lightly dressed. George and I were doing an awful lot of walking—especially since we had lost Stan for almost two hours! He had gone back to the hotel for the camera and left strict instructions with George and me to meet him at a particular place. Well, George and I walked and walked and saw everything there was to see—and, many times over—in our search for Stan. He was long overdue since the hotel was only about five minutes away. We were quite cold and the rain was dripping down harder and harter. He and I were ready to give up. George and I both were quite disusted to say the least, but he was keeping very quiet as usual, while I was saying a few choiced words under my breath. All of a sudden, the lost soul finally shows up. Well, where in the hell have you been and do you realize just how long George and I have been looking for you and I just can't tell you how damn cold and tired we are, etc., etc., etc.—me being the typical wife and not waiting for an explanation. Well, the poor thing had only made it as far as the car—only to find out that he had left the lights on, and thus, had a dead battery. He had spent his entire time trying to find a place open and to come out to the car to get it started again—bless his heart. God forgive me for complaining.

We were all cold and our feet were just killing us, so, we found a place to have a drink and to catch our breath. We took some pictures and relaxed for awhile and had fun talking about the older parts of the city and how neat it was. And, believe it or not, we actually got up enough strength to go bar-hopping and dancing again, but, this time, there was a lot less dancing and lots more drinking! At 11:45 p.m., we were feeling crazy and decided to go back to the hotel, get all dressed up and go to the revolving restaurant that overlooked the entire city. I think we all decided that we had our fill of the Underground! We arrived at the restaurant at about 12:30 a.m., and, what a sight! It was located on top of the Regency Hotel—we noticed right away at entering that this place was obviously for the very rich. Boy, was I ever glad I had brought a long gown on the trip. The hotel was about twenty-two stories high and quite elaborate to say the least. The women were dressed in furs and what I assumed were diamonds (probably just rhinestones!) and the men were in tuxes. We were thinking just maybe we weren't even dressed well enough for the occasion, but, we passed. The well-to-do people probably just figured we were tourists and just overlooked us—well, pooh-pooh on them! We were just enjoying the fact that *we* were there! The mighty fancy dome-shaped elevatgors just absolutely amazed us; their tinted glass and being able to see in and out of them and the bright lights that surrounded them. There were four of these beauties and we just stood there awhile and watched them go up and down twenty-two flights and *inside* the lobby no less — we were like kids in Disneyland for the first time! We waited in line for about half an hour to go up in one of these babies and what fascinated us was the fact that they actually had a bar and bartender serving you drinks while you waited in line — now, this is what I call living! Our turn for going up finally arrived and my tummy almost felt as weak as it did on the plane — we just flew right up to the twenty-second floor — hey, far out!

We stepped into the revolving lounge and the sight from up there, and, especially at night, was absolutely breathtaking. It was a clear night, in spite of the earlier rainfall, and all of Atlanta was in plain view with all its splendor and bright lights. It was quite lovely sitting there having drinks while we revolved around the beauty of the city. And, what a neat way to end our second day in Atlanta. We turned in that night at about 3:00 a.m., and I believe we all felt that even though we might not of been as rich as all those other people money-wise, we were much richer than they were in so many other ways.

CHAPTER FOUR

"Homeward Bound"

On this third and final day in Atlanta, we woke up quite exhausted, but for good reason and memories.

And, on this day, we woke up not to rain, but to snow — I could of sworn that Atlanta was in the south! It was a light snow and again, we didn't let it bother us. We felt very lazy and just lounged around the room for awhile and as I got up to look out of our eighteenth floor window, I thought maybe the snow just might give us reason to think twice, about the road conditions — cars were sliding everywhere and crashing right into one another! It was unbelievable! I told the boys to come and look and we all grabbed a chair right in front of the window and watched with amusement — every time another car came around the bend it would crash right into the car in front of him until there were about five cars lined up. The line was getting longer and longer and what made it so funny was that these idiots that had already crashed were just standing around outside their cars and sliding on the ice just looking at one another — not one of them had the brains to start waving the oncoming cars to warn them to at least start slowing down when they came to that particular area. It was actually geting funny and we sat there laughing our heads off — as long as it looked like everyone was alright! After about an half an hour of that, we got bored with it and decided we'd better start packing our gear. We all agreed that we all were returning with a lot more than we came with and very easily could have used about two more suitcases!

We rearranged our packing so many times that we

didn't know what was where and just threw it anywhere it would fit. We looked around the room to make sure we weren't forgetting anything and took one last look out the window at the Atlanta demolition derby and headed out the door. We ordered a big breakfast in the hotel restaurant and talked of our adventures in Atlanta and laughing about our first flight (ha-ha) and even talked about where we would fly to on our next trip—boy, was I talking it up big! Yea, sure, I'll fly again, where do we go next? Nah, I'm not afraid anymore—that's for amateurs! Sure, Joy, that's what you say now, but, just wait til our flight back home. No, sir, I'm really gonna enjoy this one and I'll show you guys just how relaxed I can be—no more of the kid stuff like squeezing the hand and not looking out the window—in fact, *I'll* sit by the window this time! O.K., George, you heard her and we're gonna hold you to your word. I was laughing, but, I think they both saw right through me!

After breakfast, we still had a few hours before flight time and decided to venture off to go see Stone Mountain. The roads really didn't seem to be too bad, but, then, being northerners, we knew how to drive in it. We got to the mountain and my gosh, it was just a beautiful sight all its own and quite massive. The brochure stated that it was the largest one solid rock in the world—and, we believed it! It was bigger and higher than any mountain we had seen. And, on the front of this massive stone was a carving of Jefferson

Davis, General Robert E. Lee and General Thomas "Stonewall" Jackson on their horses. We read that it took fifty years to carve this to its completion. There was a ski-lift ride people could take to the top of this mountain and George, without any hesitation, wanted to go up. Stan, on the other hand, took one look and said there was *no way* he was going to go that far up in such a little car that hung only by a cable wire—and, this is the big tough guy that isn't afraid of anything! And, for myself, I really debated about going up—wanting to, even though it did look shakey, but knew I probably couldn't handle that and the flight back all in the same day—so, I didn't go. I thought maybe George would chicken out at the last minute, but, by golly, he got on that thing and very secretly, I said a quick prayer for him! When he finally returned he said he wasn't sorry that he went up, but admitted that it *was* shakey and that the sight from way up there was just breathtaking. I was very thankful to have my brother back on ground with us! We looked around for awhile longer and George took our picture with the hugeht mountain behind us.

Our adventurous three-day trip was coming to an end as we got in our car and headed back towards the airport. We were feeling good and had a lot of super memories to take back with us and *all* of us were looking forward to our flight back in a 747!

CHAPTER FIVE

"Prayer for Survival"

It was still snowing lightly when we drove closer to the Atlanta Airport and oddly enough, it didn't bother me—I would always panic whenever I'd see the very first snowflake. My immediate thoughts were slipping on the sidewalks, wrecking the car, etec. etc. But, it sure wasn't bothering me now, until . . . . "We interrupt this broadcast for this bulletin— news of a 747 headed for Dulles Airport has crashed killing all ninety-three passengers aboard". We were flying back on a 747 and landing at Dulles—we hoped.

After hearing that ungodly news bulletin, we just looked at one another and this time there were no funny remarks coming from any of us. All of a sudden it hit me—oh, my dear God, what on earth are the people back home gonna be thinking? As I slowly began to quietly cry, I kept all my thoughts to myself: Dear God, *please* don't let our families and friends hear this news, and, for God's sake, please, please comfort them; oh, Jesus, please be with little Angie and don't let her cry. I began to get quite sick to my stomach as we hear more about the terrible storm that has hit Virginia. Oh, God, I can't take this—all of this and we're not even on the plane yet. As we went to the ticket counter, I was praying like hell that our flight would be cancelled, as so many of them already had been—but, no such luck, our flight was scheduled to take off in less than half an hour. All I could hear among the crowd was talk of the severe storm that had hit Virginia and certain flights being cancelled—oh, please God, let ours be one of those certain flights. "Flight 120 now boarding at Gate 3". Well, that's us, guys, let's go. Oh, honey, I'm scared to death, do we *have* to go? Yep, let's go.

We got on the plane and to help take some of my thoughts off my mind, Stan and George get me to look around and realize the size of this bird. And, it was truly something else and very hard for me to believe that 400 some people can actually fit in one of these things without being crowded. The seating arrangement was just like inside a movie theater. Once again, we found our seats and got somewhat settled. As usual, George and Stan both seemed to be quite a bit more relaxed than I was—I was shaking again and praying in hopes that our flight would still be cancelled. We came close to it, but, not quite. Everybody was seated and fastening their seatbelts when the Captain announced that we'd be delayed due to a fuel line problem, but, we were to remain on the plane and seated. My, God, what *next*??? Someone seated behind me replied, "don't ask". I just sat there speechless and wondering if this was really happening to us; everyone else was stirring in their seats and commenting that they could of gone all night without hearing the Captain's announcement.

George somehow got seated by the window again and while we were waiting, he looked out and remarked how high up we were to be still on the ground. And, since I knew we were still on the ground, I thought I'd be brave and look out—my God, we *are* high, aren't we??? Stan, of course, had to remind me that we were on a 747—far from being a small plane. I told him I'd appreciate it if he didn't remind me. We also notice how cloudy it was getting and having high hopes of it clearing up—and, *soon*.

The Captain came on again and announced that all was well and that we were ready for takeoff—now, *I* could of gone all night without hearing *that*! But, off we went, and, what seemed to be about five seconds time, we were off the ground. As I took a big gulp and holding on to both George *and* Stan, I remarked that I thought a plane was suppose to circle around the runway for awhile before it took off. Not on these babies—you're on a 747—they're off the ground before you know it. I thought I told you not to remind me of that. Well, you might as well sit back and enjoy it now, we're definitely up there. Enjoy? *ENJOY*! Just what the hell am I suppose to enjoy??? George and Stan obivously had forgotten their fear of "the crash" and the storm—they were once again thoroughly enjoying man's invention of flying—I was sitting straight back and holding on to anything I could get my hands on. The only parts of my body not shaking were my hands — the pressure of them holding on so tightly was the only thing keeping them from performing this way. We were flying high — my God, were we ever flying high! And, *fast*. I saw George look out the window, being the brave soul he is, and heard him reply that that just had to be the most beautiful sight he'd ever seen and begged me to look out just this once or I'd be sorry I didn't. Well, for some reason I believed him and I wasn't afraid to look out — for some odd reason. And, when I did look out, I knew the reason right away — it had to be the nearest thing to Heaven that I'd ever seen — it was absolutely breathwaking and I felt closer to God than ever before. He was very near and I truly felt it. We were complete above all the clouds and it was definitely a sight I shall never, never forget. It was like the biggest field in the world covered with cottonballs. It was almost dark when we had left the airport, but, way above the clouds as we were, it was much lighter and we even got a glimpse of the sun — something we hadn't seen for two days! It was truly amazing and while looking out at the Heavens, I forgot all my fears and felt somewhat safer — being closer to God, I guess.

And, then, just as I was beginning to really relax and "enjoy" the flight, the sky turned pitch black. I looked out and got a very strange feeling all over — like maybe something *was* going to happen. And, it did. The plane started rocking back and forth with great force. Something fell off the wall on the inside of the plane and the stewardesses could just barely stand up—one of them fell to her knees. I know my eyes just about fell out of their sockets and I couldn't honestly tell if I was breathing or not—were we to be the next victims of a second 747 crash? George took my hand and said nothing. Then, the unexpected happened. We heard a very, very loud explosion-like sound and saw a large flash of fire just outside *our* window—we were seated next to the wing and it had been struck by lightning—oh, my God, please, please spare us all. I was just plain sick and couldn't even throw it up. The plane was rocking more and more and for the first time in my life, I knew death was just minutes away. I told George and Stan that I loved them and then hid my head behind Stan's back and froze. I couldn't move a muscle and couldn't say a word—just praying with all my might and waiting for the end—I just wanted it to be over with as quickly as possible. I could hear people rumbling with fright and it was quite hard to remain seated under the circumstances. The person in front of us replied that the rain had put the fire out. For the first time in three days, we were ever so thankful for rain. I still couldn't move or speak—just praying—please God, let it be over with.

Things got real bumpie again and I remained hidden behind Stan's back. I was crying and at the same time saying, "are we landing, are we landing

—please tell me it's over, *please*." Stan put his arm around me and said yes that we were landing and indeed, it was all over with. The Captain came on and assured us that we had made a safe landing at Dulles Airport and the sound of everyone's applause was music to our ears. "Thank you, God, thank you, for sparing our lives." The plane came to a halt, but skidding quite a bit while doing so—Dulles was practically flooded from the rain. We'd never seen it rain quite so hard—but, being ever so thankful. We all got off the plane—most of us moving as though we were in shock.

We went in the restaurant to settle our nerves —I personally had none left. I was definitely walking around like I was in a trance and felt very, very numb. Still in tears, I sat down and looked out at the plain view of the runway—looking into space, wondering how we survived it, wondering if it really happened, wondering if we were really back on ground and wondering what state of mind our families were in.

We caught a cab for home and the driver didn't speak hardly a word of English and didn't know where the hell he was—it all just seemed to fit in with the rest of the program—you know? Nevertheless, we arrived safely home. Safely home—have you ever heard more beautiful words?

AUTHOR'S NOTE

This little story is dedicated to me — the author — in hopes that years from now I will be able to sit down and read this and enjoy it as a short story on the memories — good and bad — of this trip. And, hope that after reading it, I will someday realize, even though it was my first flight, that not all "first flights" turn out this way — but, you'll never convince me of that!

It will also serve as a reminder of how close I came to facing death and how very, very thankful I am to be alive.

And, finally, for all of you who told me that I'd love flying and once I'd done it I wouldn't want to travel any other way — TO HELL WITH ALL OF YOU!!!

Joyce D. Colson

WORK vs. WOMAN
by Joyce D. Colson
September 8, 1976

I was fresh out of highschool at the tender "I know it all" age of eighteen, threw away my books and celebrated the fact that my struggle in life was over. I then thought all I had to do was go out into the business world, get a job and live happily ever after without another worry. "Little Miss Know it All" couldn't have been more wrong. I definitely was not prepared for what life had in store for me.

I immediately began seeking employment so I could help mom with the bills and help my younger brother through school. It took only a couple of weeks to realize what a challenge it was to even land a job—having no college or previous experience. I'd had it with "don't call us, we'll call you" and was ready to give up when a girlfriend put in a good word for me where she was then employed. I became a clerk typist making $60.00 a week. I proudly gave mom $50.00 and saved $10.00 a week for myself. It took me quite awhile to adapt to my new schedule and geting home at six o'clock made me realize that maybe school had had its good points after all. The days were more tiring, but I was proud to be helping out at home. Unfortunately, my first job came to an end after a year when I got layed off due to a reduction in force. Needless to say, I was upset and immediatly accused myself as being a failure so early in life. I got my head together and was again ready to meet the challenge of the world. But, the next year was spent job-hopping and I became quite distressed. Mom wasn't well and the bills were mounting, and my brother had another year left in school My next job was as a receptionist, making $10.00 more a week, and I felt confident that I was "moving up" in the world. During the course of that job, I met "Prince Charming" and was convinced I was ready for married life. I told mom I would gladly help out until my brother got through school and my husband realized I wanted to do this. I now faced a whole new challenge as a working wife. And, that wasn't a bed of roses either.

My husband and I started out as the well-to-do newlyweds with a brand new house, furniture and two new cars. Blindly, we had put ourselves right out front for a financial disaster. He was working in a bank at the time, thus, hired me as one of his employees. I was very proud at this point; I was not only working for my husband in a big bank, but I was also earning more pay. But, having my husband as my boss all day at work and again at home wasn't quite working out, especially since he couldn't show partiality, so, I was soon transferred to another department. We still saw each other all day long and soon started disagreeing on certain procedures at work, and when he had to work late, I'd always have to stay. By the day's end, we were at each other's throats and not speaking during dinner. And, maybe it wasn't so unfortunate that I had to take a leave of absence for surgery. Once I got home from the hospital, my mini-vacation had its advantages and disadvantages. While I was enjoying being able to keep the house clean and actually having dinner on the table when my husband got home, we were quickly getting into debt at the same time, and I soon returned to work — but, not for long.

We were blessed with a beautiful daughter, who this time, gave me happier reasons for leaving work. I only had a couple of months of full-time motherhood when I regretfully had to go back to work. And, the pain I felt that first day I had to leave our daughter with a sitter is the same pain I feel now, eleven years later, and still leaving her with a sitter.

While our marriage was growing, the bills were growing as well, and we were finding it harder and harder to keep them all paid. And, at the same time, my husband had decided to go into his own business. I wanted to stand behind him, but, knew all to(o) well it was a bad time for making such a big step. To make ends meet, we had to sell our house and move in with his father, who wasn't exactly ready for us. He had recently lost his wife and still in mourning. We tried to make the best of the situation, but it wasn't working. None of us were in the best of moods and my having to work didn't help any. My job was becoming more demanding and called for longer hours. This interrupted everybody's schedule by getting a late dinner, getting our daughter to bed too late and trying to clean house at odd hours. Nobody was happy and my cranky attitude didn't help any. I wasn't proud of the fact that I wasn't exactly the most patient and understanding wife, mother and daughter-in-law, but, I was working full-time, trying to please dad with the cooking and cleaning, trying to explain to our daughter why we weren't living in a not-so-natural environment, and in addition, I was cleaning for my mother on weekends. After almost a year of this tearing schedule, we got an apartment of our own.

Though the housing proved better, our problems and finances continued to grow. I returned to the hospital for a month's stay. I not only needed more surgery, but the doctor stressed how important it was for me to get a good rest. Surgery, I got—rest, I did not. My husband and daughter needed this and needed that and while heavily sedated, I was answer-ing the demands of my office by telephone. By the time I got home, my nerves were anything but good. My husband had quit his job to start his own business, which meant I had to return to work sooner than anticipated. Doctors orders were to work half days for awhile, but, then, are doctors really human? My work was terribly behind and for the time being I faced being the full-time breadwinner for the family.

And, having to return to work when I wasn't quite recuperated from surgery made my job at the office and at home a little bit harder to handle.

My nerves finally cracked and I admitted I was no miracle-worker. My husband and I separated until we could get our feet back on the ground. Oddly enough, we saw more of each other during that time, he was able to get his business going, and our mental attitudes seemed to be far better than what they were. Seeing a brighter future, we were reunited after a year. And, I guess we should of left well enough alone. Once back together, we were all busier than ever. My husband was hardly home due to the business and had early plans for expansion, our daughter was now involved in sports, and my new job as administrative secretary was more demanding than ever before. Being able to concentrate totally on my work was becoming almost impossible. Instead of concentrating on the report sitting in my typewriter, I'd be wondering what time my husband would get home, why he never had time to listen to me and my problems, wondering if I'd get home in time to fix dinner and get our daughter to soccer practice, and, wishing our company would cancel out because I didn't have time to clean the house and just plain didn't feel like doing it at that point. I'd come home late, my husband was even later, dinner was getting later every night and my good housekeeping was going to the dogs.

Fearfully, I saw the nightmare returning—conflicting schedules, too tired to be husband and wife, and not enough time to be a family. I tried talking to my husband about what was happening; he simply called it constantly complaining—I called it crying for help—unsuccessfully. Our marriage ended in divorce without another effort of trying to make it work.

In summary, I might not of been the "Little Miss Know It All" I thought I was thirteen years ago, but I feel I've worked and suffered hard for paying the debt of growing up and for not being the "cool, calm and collected" working wife and mother that was expected of me. My having to work full-time, and my illnesses since the inception of my working career, have both contributed to a "rocky" marriage, home life, and motherhood. But, on the same token, I feel proud I was able to work and help my brother through school, and I'd like to feel that by working, I contributed to making my husband's dream of a successful business become a reality. I also feel that by working for thirteen years I've gained the experience and knowledge which hopefully, will enable me to face my new challenge in life as a single working woman and mother. And, even though our daughter can never understand why I can't just up and leave the office every time she wants me to, I hope my experience will help me to better prepare my own "Little Miss Know It All" for the challenge she will some day have to meet.

1931

Stevenson Conley Sturgill, Sr.

The Life and Times of
Stevenson Conley[9] Sturgill

PATERNAL ANCESTRY: [STURGILL: James Estil[8], Joshua[7], Francis[6] Jr., Francis[5] Sr., James[4], James[3], John Daniel[2], John[1] {of North Petherton Parish, Somersetshire, England}, Richard[1a], George[2a]]

MATERNAL ANCESTRY: [INGRAM: Ella Naomi[11], John Calvin[10] William[9], John W.[8], William[7], Abraham[6] III {of Sussex County, Delaware}, Abraham[5] II, Abraham[4], James[3], Robert[2] {of Northampton County, Virginia), Joseph[1] {of England}]]

STEVENSON CONLEY[9] was born on April 7, 1915 at Rugby, Grayson County [another family member says Ashe County, North Carolina], Virginia. He died, age 89, on Friday, May 28, 2004 in the Hugh Chatham Hospital at Elkin, Surry County, North Carolina. He was cremated and his ashes were spread around his mountain home in Ashe County, North Carolina. His father was James Estil[8] Sturgill of Sturgills, Ashe County, North Carolina and Rugby, Grayson County, Virginia. His mother was Ella Naomi[11] Ingram of Rugby, Grayson County, Virginia.

STEVENSON CONLEY[9] married, first, Emma[11] "Rosetta" Lamb on November 12, 1939 by the Reverend Alton B. Altfather of the Falls Church

Rosetta and Steve

Presbyterian Church at the City of Falls Church, Virginia. Mrs. A. B. Altfather and Mrs. J. R. Naffziger were witnesses. Emma[11] was born on April 23, 1915 at McMullen, Greene County, Virginia. She died on June 2, 1973, age 58, at the University of Virginia Hospital at Charlottesville, Albemarle County, Virginia and was buried in the family cemetery on Pocoson Mountain. Her father was George Harvey[10] [Hiram Jackson[9], Pembrose B.[8] "Pemberton", Mathew William[7], John Richard[6], Jr. {of Orange County, Virginia}, John Richard[5], Sr., Anthony[4] {of Charles Parish, York County, Virginia}, John[3], Anthony[2] {of Poquoson Parish, York County, Virginia}, Robert[1] {of New Castle-Upon-Tyne, Northumberland, England}, Percy[1a]] Lamb of McMullen, Greene County, Virginia. Her mother was Emma Capitolla[10] "Annie" [Henry[9] "Hiram", Thomas W.[8] {of Rockingham County, Virginia}, "Dr." James[7] {of Orange County, Virginia}, Francis[6], Thomas[5] {of Essex County, Virginia}, Thomas[4], John[3] {Meador of Charles Parish, York County, Virginia}, Thomas[2], Thomas[1] {of Bristol, Suffolk, England}]] Meadows of Page County, Virginia.

Emma[11] "Rosetta" was born and raised along the Skyline Drive area of Greene County, Virginia. When Dulles International Airport took their land [by eminent domain], the family moved out to Arcola. After her husband left her, she scrimped and scrounged to raise her four children and got them all through high school. She was a strong-willed woman. However, her weight [300+ pounds] and poor eating habits overworked her heart and ultimately killed her.

The following tribute was published in *The Daily Progress*, Charlottesville, Albemarle County, Virginia on June 4, 1973:

Mrs. Rosetta Sturgill

Mrs. Rosetta Sturgill, 58, of Aldie, Loudoun County, formerly of Greene County, died at a Charlottesville hospital.

A native of Greene County, she was the daughter of the late George and Emma Lamb. She was a member of Chantilly Episcopal Church at Chantilly. Survivors include her husband, Steve C. Sturgill, Sr. of Baltimore, Md; two sons, George Sturgill of Aldie and Steve C. Sturgill, Jr. of Manassas; two daughters, Mrs. Patricia

Croson of Manassas and Mrs. Joyce Colson of Annandale; two brothers, H. Rosser Lamb and George Elmer Lamb of Standarsville; six sisters, Mrs. Ethel Irene Shifflett of Standardsville, Mrs. Mamie R. Taylor of Woftown, Mrs. Lucy Elizabeth Monroe of Annandale, Mrs. Laura E. Breeden and Mrs. Polly Ann Perryman of Culpeper; and four grandchildren.

Funeral services will be Tuesday at 2 p.m. at Ryan-Estes Funeral Home at Quinque with burial in the family cemetery, Pocosan Mountain, the Rev. Claude McDaniel officiating. Pallbearers will be George Sturgill, Steve C. Sturgill, Jr., Stanton D. Colson, Eugene Croson, Charles E. Perryman and H. Rosser Lamb.

STEVENSON CONLEY[9] had a long term relationship but never married Elizabeth "Chic" (Unknown). "Chic" was born circa 1920. Her place of birth is not known. She died of cancer, age 60, on July 20, 1980. Her place of death is not known. Stevenson[9] and Elizabeth had no issue.

STEVENSON CONLEY[9] married, second, Valma Hill[8] Stonestreet on April 2, 1983 at Elkin, Surry County, North Carolina. She was born in 1921 in Wilkes

County, North Carolina. She died on January 18, 2013 at Elkin, Surry County, North Carolina. Her father was Joseph Harding[7] [Jediah[6] {of Davie County, North Carolina}, Benjamin[5] {of Rowan County, North Carolina}, Edward[4] {of King Georges Parish, Prince Georges County, Maryland}, Edward[3], Thomas[2] {of Newport Hundred, Charles County, Maryland}, Thomas[1] {of Withyham, Sussex, England}, Edward[1a]] Stonestreet of Surry County, North Carolina. Her mother was Mary "Molly" Caroline[10] [Abel Columbus[9], Ephraim L.[8], Eli William[7], John M.[6], William[5] {of St. Georges Parish, Herford County, Maryland}, William[4], Francis[3], William[2] {of Northampton County, Virginia}, Richard[1] {of Westminster, London, England}, Richard[1a] {of Lincolnshire, England}, Edward[2a], John[3a]}]] Hamby of Surry County, North Carolina. Stevenson[9] and Valma[8] had no issue.

Valma[8] had married, first, James Wilbur[8] Shepherd on January 22, 1941 at Wilkes County, North Carolina. James[8] was born on July 10, 1913 in Ashe County, North Carolina. He died on September 27, 1977 at Winston-Salem, Forsyth County, North Carolina. His father was Grover Cleveland[7] [John Calvin[6] {of Ashe County, North Carolina}, James Wilburn[5] {of Reddie River, Wilkes County, North Carolina}, Larkin[4], John James[3] {of Spotsylvania County, Virginia}, John[2], George[1] {of Banff, Scotland}] Shepherd of North Carolina. His mother was Ethel Isabelle [Willis Milton {of Wilkes County, North Carolina}, John Franklin, John Willis, Josiah {of Maryland}] Walker of Wilkes County, North Carolina. Valma[8] and James[8] had four children: James Wilbur[9], Jr., Martha Anna[9], Lynn[9] and Jane[9].

Valma[8]'s obituary, as published in the *Elkin Tribune*, Surry County, North Carolina follows:

Valma Shepherd Sturgill

Valma Shepherd Sturgill looked forward to family reunions. They were a joy to her as she anticipated reuniting with relatives whom she had not seen for some time. On Saturday, January 18, 2013 she departed this life for her greatest family reunion.

Valma was born in Surry County in 1920 to Joseph Hardin and Mary Caroline Stonestreet. She grew up on a farm in State Road, NC with her six brothers and five sisters. At home, she learned the skills necessary to live during that time: cooking, preserving, sewing and gardening to name a few. She attended Mountain Park Schools and while there, she played basketball for the school team. After school, she continued her education by reading and taking classes. She married Wilburn Shepherd in 1942 and reared four children. She and Wilburn were longtime residents of Elkin.

Her fondest memories were seeing her children for the first time, watching them grow up and seeing them enjoy their school days. She also loved summer vacations, seeing us taking part in Girl and Boy Scouts (especially Jim when he was at Raven Knob), our dates, cheer-leading, participating in sports, going to proms, getting married and having children and grandchildren. She smiled through most of it, being a "burr" under our saddle when we needed it, and always encouraging us to behave prop-erly and to "remember who we are." Her grandson, Wil, once said that his "Grand-mother manners" had been a great help to him throughout his life. And so it is for us all.

In 1977 Valma lost her husband, the love of her life. She found courage and went on, fell in love and married Steve Sturgill in 1983. She and Steve merged families and created more happy memories with many family events and their travels to places they had always dreamed of going. In 1995, Valma lost her daughter, Martha Anne Shepherd Lusk, to breast cancer. She managed to get through that and she and Steve had twenty-one wonderful years together living part of the time in Elkin and part of the time in Ashe County. After Steve died, she had quite a few years of life by herself, during which she lost a step-son, Steve Sturgill.

She enriched her life being a member of The Golden Friends Women's Group, the Elkin Garden Club, Jonathan Hunt Chapter of DAR, the Elkin Women's Club and the Grassy Creek Homemaker's Club. She also was a Brownie and a Girl Scout leader for many years, affecting the lives of quite a few young girls.

Surviving are her daughters Lynn Shepherd Bolts of Elkin and Jane Shepherd Eaton (Butch) of Winston-Salem; her son, Jim Sheperd (Mary) of Elkin; a step-daughter, Pat Croson of Manassas, VA; a step-son, George Sturgill of Aldie, VA. Also surviving are her nine grandchildren and great grandchildren.

A visitation will be held on Saturday, Jamuary 26, 2013 at 2:00 p.m. at First Baptist Church Chapel with a memorial service following at 3:00 p.m. A private burial will be held at a later date.

In lieu of flowers, memorials to honor Valma may be made to the charity of the donor's choice or as follows: First Baptist Church General Fund, 110 Gwyn Avenue, Elkin, NC 28621; Jonathan Hunt Chapter of DAR, c/o Ann Merlo, 773 Brookwood Drive, Elkin, NC 28621; Girl Scouts Carolinas Peaks to Piedmont, Inc., 8818 W. Market Street, Colfax, NC 27235-9419.

The family would like to thank family members, Church family and friends who visited, provided special treats, and sent flowers and cards to Valma while she was at Hugh Chatham Nursing Center. Your thoughtfulness and love will not be forgotten. We would also like to thank the staff at Hugh Chatham Nursing Center for their tender care and concern. The staff of Mountain Valley Hospice provided loving care to Valma and her family during the end stage of her life. For that, we are eternally grateful.

STEVENSON CONLEY[9] migrated from Grayson County, Virginia in his late teens or early twenties to the Washington, D.C. area. He enlisted as a Private in the U. S. Army on November 9, 1944 at Richmond, Virginia, then spent several years in the service during World War II. He later worked for Greyhound Systems as a bus driver. In the early 1950s he separated from his wife, Rosetta, and moved to Baltimore, Maryland. There he was employed at and retired from Westinghouse Corporation, where he worked in public relations.

STEVENSON CONLEY[9]'S obit read as follows:

Elkin, NC
April 7, 1915 — May 28, 2004

Mr. Steve C. Sturgill, age 89 of West Main St., passed away Friday, May 28 at Hugh Chatham Memorial Hospital. He was born April 7, 1915 in Ashe County to Estel and Ella Ingram Sturgill.

Mr. Sturgill was retired from Westinghouse in Baltimore, Md. where he worked in public relations. He was a member of Elkin First Baptist Church where he served as an usher. He was a veteran of the U.S. Army where he served in the Pacific during WWII. He also held memberships with VFW Post 7794 and the Lions Club both of Elkin. In addition to his parents, Mr. Sturgill was preceded in death by one brother, Bill Sturgill; three sisters, Cora Frasier, Lannie Spencer and Ersa Dell Sturgill; one daughter, Joyce Colson and one step daughter, Martha Shepherd Lusk.

Survivors include: his wife, Valma Shepherd Sturgill of the home; two sons, George Sturgill and Steve Sturgill Jr., both of Aldie, Va.; one daughter, Patricia Croson of Manassas, Va.; one stepson, James "Jim" Shepherd and his wife Mary of Elkin; two stepdaughters; Lynn Shepherd Bolls and her husband Bobby of Shelbyville, Ind. and Jane Shepherd Eaton and her husband Ray of Winston Salem; 15 grandchildren, Sarah Sturgill, Jennifer Lloyd, David Croson, Debbie Campbell, Angie Colson, Vince Eaton, Crystal Mendenhall, Elizabeth Lusk, Wil Lusk, Kivlina Block, Isaac Shepherd, Joseph Shepherd, Nicholas Shepherd and Sampson Shepherd; six great-grand-children, Brittany Campbell, Kayla Lloyd, Alec Lloyd, Liam Block, Drew Menden-hall and Solomon Shepherd.

A memorial service was held Sunday, May 30 at 5 p.m. at Elkin First Baptist Church by Dr. Bill Johnson. The family received friends one hour prior to the service in the church fellowship hall.

Memorials may be made to the Hugh Chatham Memorial Hospital Chapel Fund at Hugh Chatham Memorial Hospital, PO Box 560 Elkin, NC 28621 or to the donor's choice. Hodges Funeral Home of Elkin was in charge of the arrangements.

The Children of
Stevenson Conley[9] Sturgill
and Emma Rosetta Lamb

1. Patricia Ann[10] Sturgill
   born on February 19, 1941 at Arlington, Arlington County, Virginia. She married Claudis Eugene "Gene" Crosen of Arcola, Loudoun County, Virginia on February 18, 1961. They were divorced in October 1981 at Manassas, Prince William County, Virginia. He was born on June 30, 1937 at Herndon, Fairfax County, Virginia. He died, age 75, of cancer on Friday, April 12, 2013 at Warrenton, Fauquier County, Virginia. His father was Walter Jennings [Emmett Filmore of Mouth of Wilson, Grayson County, Virginia}, James H. {of Prince William County, Virginia}] Croson of Loudoun County, Virginia. His mother was Lilley May[4] [Noah Simon[3] {of Shenandoah County, Virginia}, Simon, Adam[2] {of Loudoun County, Virginia}, Johann Adam[1] {of Rhineland-Palitinate, Westerwald Kreis, Rhineland-Pfalz, Germany}, Johann Jacob[1a], Wigand[2a], Hans Jacob[3a]] Barb of Ashley Springs, Tucker County, West Virginia. Patricia[10] and Claudis had two children:

   a. David Eugene Croson
      born on November 2, 1963 at Manassas, Prince William County, Virginia.

b. Deborah Ann Croson
born on March 19, 1965 at Manassass, Prince William County, Virginia. She married Gerry Lynn Campbell in April 1987 in Virginia. They divorced in 1991 in Virginia. He was born on March 1, 1956. His place of birth is not known. Deborah and Gerry had one child: Brittany Lynn [born February 28, 1988].

2. Stevenson Conley[10] Sturgill, Jr.
born on April 24, 1943 at Arlington, Arlington County, Virginia. He died, age 67, after a long illness, including complications of diabetes, heart disease and blood clots, on March 16, 2010 at the home of his brother George[10] at Aldie, Loudoun County, Virginia. He donated his body to the University of Richmond Medical School at Richmond, Virginia. He married, first, Margaret Ellen[10] "Peggy" Comer of Arcola, Loudoun County, Virginia on September 7, 1966 at the parsonage across from Loudoun County High School, Leesburg, Loudoun County, Virginia. They divorced in 1976. She was born on December 15, 1949 at 11:56 p.m. in Havre de Grace, Hartford County, Delaware. Her father was Ralph Lee[9] [Lert Vernon[8], Stephen Thomas[7], John M.[6], Jonathan R.[5], John C.[4] {of Caroline County, Virginia}, Thomas R.[3] {of Halifax County, Virginia}, John[2] {of Lunenburg County, Virginia}, Thomas[1] {of Ireland}] Comer of

Bridle Creek, Grayson County, Virginia. Her mother was Hazel Mae[4] [Henry "Harry" Milton[3] Jr., Henry "Harry" Milton[2] Sr., William[1] {of England}] Tate of Washington D.C. and later of Norfolk, Hampton Roads, Virginia. Stevenson[10] and Margaret[10] had two children:

a. Stevenson Conley[11] Sturgill III
   born in June 1967 in the Loudoun County Hospital at Leesburg, Loudoun County, Virginia. He died at birth in June 1967 in the Loudoun County Hospital at Leesburg, Loudoun County, Virginia.

b. Jennifer Monique[11] Sturgill
   born on July 21, 1970 in Prince William Hospital at Manassas, Prince William County, Virginia. She married Coleman Worth Lloyd III. His date and place of birth is not known. His father was Coleman Worth [Van Buren, John William, Lewis {of Virginia}, Edward J. {of Granville County, North Carolina}, Edward Frederick] Lloyd II of North Carolina. His mother was Debra Jean [Tuck] Tucker. Jennifer[11] and Coleman had two children: Kayla Dey and Jacob Alecsander.

Margaret[10] "Peggy" married, second, Lloyd Larry Walker, Sr. on August 19, 1955 in the Dumfries

Church of Christ at Dumfries, Prince William County, Virginia, Pastor Larry E. Craddock presiding. It was a family-only wedding. The bride's maids were girls in the family under age seven, wearing multicolored summer dresses. Everyone else but the bride came casual. The groom was in jeans and a short-sleeve shirt.

Stevenson[10] married, second, Mary Katherine "Kathy" Dunn of Utica, Oneida County, New York on November 25, 1978. The place of their marriage is not known. She was born on August 14, 1953 at Utica, Oneida County, New York. The name of her father and mother is not known. Stevenson[10] and Kathy had one child:

c. Sarah Elizabeth[11] Sturgill
born 8 $1/3$ lbs 21 $1/2$ inches at 3:37 pm on May 27, 1982 in the Alexandria Hospital at Alexandria, Virginia.

3. **Joyce Dell[10] Sturgill**
born at 3:54 pm on July 11, 1945 in the Arlington Hospital at Arlington, Arlington County, Virginia. She died from complications of the lungs due to acute leukemia on August 3, 1978 in the Fairfax Hospital [now Inova] at Falls Church, Fairfax County, Virginia. She was buried in the Lamb family cemetery on Pocosin Mountain in Green

County, Virginia. She married Stanton Darn-brook[10] Colson on September 24, 1964 at St. Albans Episcopal Church at Annandale, Fairfax County, Virginia. The ceremony was performed by the Reverend John Frizzel, with Marcus Winfield Todd [Stanton[10]'s friend] as the Best Man and Patricia Ann[10] Sturgill Croson [Joyce[10]'s sister] as Maid of Honor. Stanton[10] and Joyce[10] were separated on March 1, 1975 and divorced on August 13, 1976. Joyce[10] had a child by (Unknown): Angela Marie[11]. Stanton[10]'s father was Douglas Herman[9] [Henry Wilson[8], Stanton E(phraim)[7], Theophilus T.[6] 2nd, Ephraim[5], Ichabod Downs[4], Hatevil[3], Samuel[2], Cornelius[1] {Cursonwhitt of New Amsterdam/later known as New York}, Jan[1a] Cornelisen van Rotterdam {of Rotterdam, Zud-Holland, The Netherlands}, Cornelius Jonkers[2a]] Colson of Brooklyn, Queens County, New York City, New York. His mother was Mary Elsie[2] [William Irving[1], Morris[1a] {of Canada}, Franklin[2a] {of France}] Quebec of Manhattan, New York City, New York. Joyce[10] and Stanton[10] had no issue: Stanton[10] adopted Angela Marie[11].

4. George Estil[10] [also found as Estel] Sturgill born on January 16, 1949 at Arlington, Arlington County, Virginia. He married Velma Ann[8] Walker Simmons on June 15, 2013 in the Little River Baptist Church at Aldie, Loudoun County,

Virginia, the Reverend Malcom, Pastor, presiding. His niece, Angela Marie[11] Colson, was the "Best Man." Velma[8] was born on March 5, 1938 at Danville [city of], Virginia. Her father was Sterling Thomas[7] [Thomas Webb[6], James Webb[5], Thomas Jackson[4], James L.[3] "Jamey," Elijah[2] {of Franklin County, Virginia}, Moses[1] {of Ireland}] Walker of Brown, Summit County, North Carolina and later of Clifton Forge, Allegheny County, Virginia. His mother was Annie Velma[6] [John William[5] {of Pittsylvania County, Virginia}, Elijah Franklin[4], Jonathan[3] {of Wirtz, Franklin County, Virginia}, Eljiah[2] {of Franklin County, Virginia}, Moses[1] {of Ireland}] McGuire of Dyers Store, Henry County, Virginia. George[10] and Velma[8] lived at Aldie, Loudoun County, Virginia [2015].

Velma[8] married, first, Bobby Elwood Simmons on April 16, 1960 at Clifton Forge, Alleghany County, Virginia. He was born on September 6, 1936 at Nimrod Hall, Bath County, Virginia. He died on June 14, 2005 in the Inova Loudoun Hospital, Landsdowne, Loudoun County, Virginia. His father was Robert Lee [George Washington] Simmons of Bath County, Virginia. His mother was Gwendlyn St. Clair "Duck" [Samuel Owens, Joseph] Matheney of Virginia. Velma[8] and Bobby had three children: names unknown.

James Estil Sturgill
at home at Wolf Knob
Grayson County, Virginia

The Life and Times of
James Estil[8] Sturgill

PATERNAL ANCESTRY: [STURGILL: Joshua[7], Francis[6] Jr., Francis[5] Sr., James[4], James[3], John Daniel[2], John[1] {of North Petherton Parish, Somersetshire, England}, Richard[1a], George[2a]]

MATERNAL ANCESTRY: [WEAVER: Phoebe Marilda[9], Andrew[8] [Isaac Vance[7], William[6], Joshua[5], Samuel[4], Samuel[3], William[2], Samuel[1] {of England}, Thomas[1a], William[2a], Griffith[3a], Jenkin[4a], John[5a], Thomas[6a], Walter[7a], Thomas[8a], Walter[9a], Walter[10a], Walter[11a], Humphrey[12a], Ieuan[13a] {of Wales}, Madoc[14a], Hywel Vychan[15a]]

JAMES ESTIL[8] [afa Estel] was born on December 22, 1878 at Sturgills, Ashe County, North Carolina. He died on May 30, 1955 at Rugby, Grayson County, Virginia and buried there at Mouth of Wilson in the Haw-Orchard Baptist Cemetery. His father was Joshua[7] Sturgill of Sturgills, Ashe County, North Carolina and Rugby, Grayson County, Virginia. His mother was Phoebe Marilda[8] Weaver of Ashe County, North Carolina.

JAMES ESTIL[8] married Ella Naomi[10] Ingram on March 6, 1897 at Sturgills, Ashe County, North Carolina. She was born on July 18, 1878 at Rugby,

Grayson County, Virginia. She died on August 2, 1915 at Rugby, Grayson County, Virginia and was buried there at Mouth of Wilson in the Haw-Orchard Baptist Church Cemetery. Her father was John Calvin[9] [William[8], John W.[7], William[6] {of Augusta County, Virginia} Abraham[5] III {of Sussex County, Delaware}, Abraham[4] {of Worchester County, Maryland} Abraham[3] {Ingraham of Somerset County, Maryland} James[2], Robert[1] {of England and later of Northampton County, Virginia}, Joseph[1a]] Ingram of North Carolina. Her mother was Charity Ann [John Wilson {of Ashe County, North Carolina}, David {of Virginia}] Farmer of Grayson County, Virginia.

JAMES ESTIL[8] was a farmer who owned his own farm at Wolf Knob, Grayson County, Virginia. He and his wife moved from Sturgills, Ashe County, North Carolina to Wilson Creek, Grayson County, Virginia. In 1930 he was listed as a widower, farming in the Rugby Precinct, Wilson Creek District, Grayson County, Virginia.

The Children of
James Estil[8] Sturgill
and Ella Naomi[10] Ingram

1. Charity Ann[9] Sturgill
born in 1899 at Rugby, Grayson County, Virginia. She died in 1899 at Rugby, Grayson County, North Carolina.

2. Lanta Mae[9] "Lantie" Sturgill
born on July 2, 1901 at Rugby, Grayson County, Virginia. She died, age 80, on March 3, 1982 in Grayson County, Virginia. She married William Marvin[7] Spencer in 1919 in North Carolina. He was born on May 25, 1899 in North Carolina. He died in November 10, 1970 in Wise County, Virginia and was buried in the Haw-Orchard Baptist Cemetery in Ashe County, North Carolina. His father was David Emory[6] [William[5], Isaac[4], Isaac[3], Joseph Charles[2], William D.[1] {of England or Wales}, Alexander[1a] {of England}, Nicholas[2a] {of Cople, Bedfordshire, England}] Spencer of Ashe County, North Carolina. His mother was Frances[6] "Frankie" [Nelson[5] {of Wilkes County, North Carolina}, Reuben[4], Humphrey[3] {of Culpeper County, Virginia}, William Humphrey[2], John[1] {of England}] Kilbey of Virginia. Lanta Mae[9] and William Marvin had four children:

69

a. James[8] Spencer
date and place of birth in Grayson County, Virginia is not known. In 2006 he was living at Mouth of Wilson, Wilson Creek, Grayson County, Virginia.

b. Lorraine[8] Spencer
date and place of birth in Grayson County, Virginia is not known. In 2006 she was living at Colorado Springs, El Paso County, Colorado. She married Gene Williams [they apparently both died at Colorado Springs, El Paso County, Colorado]. Loraine[8] and Gene had a child: name unknown.

c. Thelma[8] Spencer
born on March 3, 1922 in Ashe County, North Carolina. She died, age 84, on May 15, 2006 in the Ashe Memorial Hospital at Jefferson, Ashe County, North Carolina and was buried in the Haw-Orchard Baptist Cemetery at Mouth of Wilson, Grayson County, Virginia. She married William Allen[8] McCraw [also found as McGraw]. The date of their marriage, presumably in Ashe County, North Carolina, is not known. He was born on November 18, 1915 in Virginia. He died on August 22, 1983 at Greensboro, Guilford County [another researcher says West Jefferson, Ashe County],

North Carolina. His father was Worthey Seymour^7 [Gabe^6, James^5 {of Patrick County, Virginia}, William^4 "Buck" {of Surry County, North Carolina}, Frances^3 {of Henry County, Virginia}, William^2 {of Goochland County, Virginia}, William^1 {of Isle of Skye, Scotland}] McCraw of Surry County, North Carolina. His mother was Mary Sue^{11} [Samuel Austin^{10} {of Patrick County, Virginia}, Peter S.^{9}, John Thomas^8 {of Cunningham Creek, Fluvania County, Virginia), Benjamin^7, John D.^{6} {of New Kent County, Virginia}, Benjamin^5, William^4, John^3 {of Lower Norfolk, Prince William County, Virginia}, William^2, Simon^1 {of Devonshire, England}, William^{1a}, Thomas^{2a} {of St. Mary Woolnoth, London, Middlesex, England}] Hancock of Floyd, Floyd County, Virginia. Issue, if any, is not known.

d. Ella L.^{8} Spencer
born on March 25, 1925, presumably in Ashe County, North Carolina. She married Gene Williams.

e. James E.^{8} Spencer
born on June 26, 1939, presumably in Ashe County, North Carolina. He married, first, Nadine Campbell. He married, second, Maria Cave.

f. William Mack[8] Spencer
born on April 12, 1941 in Grayson County, Virginia. He died on November 8, 1993 in Grayson County, Virginia and was buried there in the Haw-Orchard Baptist Cemetery. He married Bea Coldiron. It is believed that William[8] and Bea had a child William Michael [born 1970 in Wilkes County, North Carolina].

3. Nancy Emaline[9] Sturgill
born on March 27, 1903 at Rugby, Grayson County, Virginia. She died on January 26, 1926 at Whitetop, Grayson County, Virginia. She married Arthur Fred[10] Weaver on May 25, 1921 at Rugby, Grayson County, Virginia. He was born on September 25, 1895 at Rugby, Grayson County, Virginia. He died on November 27, 1975 at Jefferson, Ashe County, North Carolina and was buried in the Pleasant Home Baptist Hill Church Cemetery at Grassy Creek Township, Ashe County, North Carolina. His father was Clayborn Monroe[9] [Andrew W.[8], Isaac Vance[7] {of Weaver's Ford, Ashe County, North Carolina}, William[6] {of Lunenburg County, Virginia}, Joshua[5] {of New Kent County, Virginia}, Samuel[4], Samuel[3], William[2] {of Charles River Shire, Virginia}, Samuel[1] {of Cardington Parish, Shropshire, England}, Thomas[1a], William[2a], Griffith[3a], Jenkin[4a], John[5a], Thomas[6a], Walter[7a], Thomas[8a], Walter[9a], Walter[10a],

Walter[11a], Humphrey[12a], Ieuan[13a] {of Wales}, Madoc[14a], Hywel Vychan[15a]] Weaver of Grayson County, Virginia. His mother was Martha Lutitia[7] [James Harvey[6] {of Buddle Creek, Grayson County, Virginia}, John[5], Benjamin[4] "Preacher Ben" {of Guilford County, North Carolina}, Joseph[3] {of Philadelphia, Pennsylvania}, Isaiah[2] {of Chester County, Pennsylvania}, Isaiah[1] {of Reading, Berkshire, England}, Joseph[1a], John[2a] {of Worcester, Worcestershire, England}, John[3a], William[4a]] Phipps of Old Field Creek, Ashe County, North Carolina. Nancy[9] and Arthur[10] had two children:

a. Mary Ellen[11] Weaver
born circa 1922 at White Top, Grayson County, Virginia. Her date and place of birth and death is not known.

b. Clarence Edward[11] Weaver
born on March 27, 1924 at White Top, Grayson County, Virginia. He died, age 58, on March 10, 1982 at Jefferson, Ashe County, North Carolina and was buried on March 13, 1982 at Grassy Creek, Ashe County, North Carolina. He married Sue Lee Phipps on February 11, 1951 at Helton, Ashe County, North Carolina. She was born on September 16, 1929 at Wilkesboro, Wilkes County, North Carolina. Her father was Benjamin Franklin Phipps of Mouth of Wilson,

Wilson Creek, Grayson County, Virginia. Her mother was Cora Lee Richardson of Piney Creek, Allegheny County, North Carolina and later of Troutdale, Grayson County, Virginia. Clarence[11] and Sue had a son: Jeffrey Craig[12].

Arthur[10] married, second, Fanny Quintenella Blevins on November 15, 1926 at Helton, Ashe County, North Carolina. She was born on August 14, 1903 at Crosby Creek, Ashe County, North Carolina. She died on August 3, 1985 at Avery, Ashe County, North Carolina. Her father was "Elder" Jeter C. ["Dr." David L.] Blevens of Grassy Creek, Ashe County, North Carolina. Her mother was Martha Rose "Mattie" Sage of Grassy Creek, Ashe County, North Carolina. Arthur[10] and Fanny had nine children: Arthur Jackson[11], Mattie Lou[11], Carol Judson[11], Alzina May[11] and five others whose names are not known.

4. John William[9] "Bill" Sturgill
born on October 29, 1905 at Rugby, Grayson County, Virginia. He died, age 80, on February 22, 1986 at Grayson County, Virginia. He never married. He lived in Rugby, Grayson County, Virginia. There was a family saying that "People say his mother was scared by a cow and he [Bill] looks like a bull." He lived at his parents' farm at Wolf Knob.

5. Ersa Dell[9] "Ersie" Sturgill
   born in 1908 at Wilson's Creek, Rugby, Grayson County, Virginia. She died, age 61, in 1969 in Chester County, Pennsylvania. She married Carl Gambill [afa Gamble], he probably of Silas Creek, Ashe County, North Carolina. The date and place of their marriage is not known. His date and place of birth and death is not known. The name of his father and mother is not known. They moved to Chester County, Pennsylvania. Ersa Dell[9] and Carl had two children: names not known.

6. Cora Faye[9] Sturgill
   born on November 30, 1909 at Wilson's Creek, Rugby, Grayson County, Virginia. She died, age 84, on December 17, 1993 in a nursing home in Ashe County, North Carolina. Cora Fay[9] married Arthur Morrell Frazier on December 24, 1929 in Ashe County, North Carolina. He was born in 1885 in Ashe County, North Carolina. He died, age 77, in 1962 in Virginia. The name of his father and mother is not known. He was the President of Kraft Cheese Company. He later became crippled and spent the rest of his life in a wheelchair. Cora[9] and Arthur's issue, if any, is not known.

   She married, second, John Roscoe Weaver on August 9, 1979 in Smyth County, Virginia. He was born on December 3, 1906 in Virginia. He died on

February 22, 1993 at Capitol Heights, Prince George's County, Maryland. His father was Howard S. Weaver of Virginia. His mother was Fannie Leona Wiles of Virginia. Cora[9] and John had no issue.

John Roscoe had married, first, Ruby Dollinger and was divorced in 1974. She was born on February 27, 1911 in Ashe County, North Carolina. She died on November 19, 2001 at Charleston, Kanawha County, West Virginia. Her father was Benjamin Ortie Dollinger of Ashe County, North Carolina. Her mother was Emma Ester Perry of Ashe County, North Carolina. John and Ruby had three children: Jerry, John and Carolyn.

7. John F.[9] Sturgill
    born on May 1, 1910 at Rugby, Grayson County, Virginia. He died as an infant on August 22, 1911 at Rugby, Grayson County, Virginia.

8. Guida Rose[9] Sturgill
    born on October 18, 1911 at Rugby, Grayson County, Virginia. She died in August 1985 in Dover, Kent County, Delaware. She married William Worth[5] [also found as Worth R.[5]] Weaver on September 24, 1929 in Ashe County, North Carolina. He was born on July 11, 1911 in Ashe County, North Carolina. He died in June 1986 at

Dover, Kent County, Delaware. His father was Martin Luther[4] [Eli[3], Joshua[2] {of Lee County, Virginia}, William[1] {of England}] Weaver of North Carolina. His mother was Ollie Lavina[7] [Roby James[6] {of Virginia}, Thornton[5], Reuben[4], Humphrey[3], William Humphrey[2] {of Reddies Rivere, Wilkes County, North Carolina}, John[1] {of England}] Kilby of Ashe County, North Carolina. Worth[5] and Guida[9] moved from Ashe County, North Carolina to Lancaster, then Chester County, Pennsylvania. At their death, they were found at Dover, Kent County, Delaware. Guida[9] and Worth[5] had seven children, one not known, and:

a. Glenna Faye[6] Weaver
   born circa 1929/1930 in Ashe County, North Carolina. Her date and place of death is not known.

b. Rose[6] Weaver
   born in 1932 at West Grove, Chester County, Pennsylvania. She died, an infant, in 1932 in Chester County, Pennsylvania.

c. Jacob James[6] Weaver
   born on June 2, 1933 West Grove, Chester County, Pennsylvania. He died on September 28, 1997 at Winston-Salem, Forsyth County, North Carolina and was buried there in the

Parklawn Memorial Gardens. He served in the U. S. Army as a PFC during the Korean War.

d. Lee Morrel[6] Weaver
born on July 28, 1836 West Grove, Chester County, Pennsylvania. He died circa 1989 in Dover, Kent County, Delaware.

e. Robert Bruce[6] Weaver
born on February 4, 1938 West Grove, Chester County, Pennsylvania. He died on December 31, 1997 in Chester County, Pennsylvania. He married, first, (Unknown) Sullivan. He married, second, (Unknown) Blevins. Bruce[6] and (Unknown) Blevens had at least one child: name not known.

f. William Worth[6] "Buck" Weaver
born circa 1940 at West Grove, Chester County, Pennsylvania. He died on January 9, 1977 in his home at Defiance, Bedford County, Pennsylvania. He married Caroline Padgett on September 1, 1967 in Pennsylvania. William[6] and Caroline had four children: William Mark[7], Lana Ann[7], Lorna Lynn[7] and Gregory Wayne[7].

9. (child)[9] Sturgill
born and died on September 9, 1912 at Rugby, Grayson County, Virginia.

10. Vesta Blaine[9] Sturgill
   born in 1913 at Rugby, Grayson County, Virginia.
   She died, four days old, in 1913 at Rugby, Grayson
   County, Virginia.

11. Ernest T.[9] Sturgill
   born on October 16, 1914 at Rugby, Grayson
   County, Virginia. He died, age 6, on January 9,
   1920 at Rugby, Grayson County, Virginia.

12. **Stevenson Conley[9] Sturgill**
   born on April 7, 1915 at Rugby, Grayson County,
   Virginia. He died, age 89, on May 28, 2004 in the
   Hugh Chatham Memorial Hospital at Elkin, Surry
   County, North Carolina. He was cremated and his
   ashes were spread around his mountain home in
   Ashe County, North Carolina. He married, first,
   Emma Rosetta[11] Lamb on November 12, 1939 by
   the Reverend Alton B. Altfather of the Falls
   Church Presbyterian Church at the City of Falls
   Church, Virginia. Mrs. A. B. Altfather and Mrs. J.
   R. Naffziger were witnesses. Emma[11] was born on
   April 23, 1915 at McMullen, Green County,
   Virginia. She died on June 2, 1973, age 58, at the
   University of Virginia Hospital at Charlottesville,
   Albemarle County, Virginia and was buried in the
   family cemetery on Pocoson Mountain. Her father
   was George Harvey[10] [Hiram Jackson[9], Pembrose
   B.[8] "Pemberton", Mathew William[7], John Richard[6],

Jr. {of Orange County, Virginia}, John Richard[5], Sr., Anthony[4] {of Charles Parish, York County, Virginia}, John[3], Anthony[2] {of Poquoson Parish, York County, Virginia}, Robert[1] {of New Castle-Upon-Tyne, Northumberland, England}, Percy[1a]] Lamb of McMullen, Greene County, Virginia. Her mother was Emma Capitolla[10] "Annie" [Henry[9] "Hiram", Thomas W.[8] {of Rockingham County, Virginia}, "Dr." James[7] {of Orange County, Virginia}, Francis[6], Thomas[5] {of Essex County, Virginia}, Thomas[4], John[3] {Meador of Charles Parish, York County, Virginia}, Thomas[2], Thomas[1] {of Bristol, Suffolk, England}] Meadows of Page County, Virginia. Stevenson[9] and Emma[11] had four children: Patricia Ann[10], Stevenson Conley[10], Jr., Joyce Dell[10] and George Estil[10].

Stevenson[9] had a long term relationship but never married Elizabeth "Chic" (Unknown). "Chic" was born circa 1920. Her place of birth is not known. She died of cancer, age 60, on July 20, 1980. Her place of death is not known. Stevenson[9] and Elizabeth had no issue.

Stevenson[9] married, second, Valma Hill[8] Stonestreet on April 2, 1983 at Elkin, Surry County, North Carolina. She was born in 1921 in Wilkes County, North Carolina. She died on January 18, 2013 at Elkin, Surry County, North Carolina. Her father was Joseph Harding[7] [Jediah[6] {of Davie County, North Carolina}, Benjamin[5] {of Rowan County, North Carolina}, Edward[4] {of King Georges Parish, Prince Georges County, Maryland}, Edward[3], Thomas[2] {of Newport Hundred, Charles County, Maryland}, Thomas[1] {of Withyham, Sussex, England}, Edward[1a]] Stonestreet of Surry County, North Carolina. Her mother was Mary "Molly" Caroline[10] [Abel Columbus[9], Ephraim L.[8], Eli William[7], John M.[6], William[5] {of St. Georges Parish, Herford County, Maryland}, William[4], Francis[3], William[2] {of Northampton County, Virginia}, Richard[1] {of Westminster, London, England}, Richard[1a] {of Lincolnshire, England}, Edward[2a], John[3a]}] Hamby of Surry County, North Carolina. Stevenson[9] and Valma[8] had no issue.

Valma[8] had married, first, James Wilbur[8] Shepherd on January 22, 1941 at Wilkes County, North Carolina. James was born on July 10, 1913 in Ashe County, North Carolina. He died on September 27, 1977 at Winston-Salem, Forsyth County, North Carolina. His father was Grover Cleveland[7] [John Calvin[6] {of Ashe County, North Carolina}, James Wilburn[5] {of Reddies River, Wilkes County, North Carolina}, Larkin[4], John James[3] {of Spotsylvania County, Virginia}, John[2], George[1] {of Banff, Scotland}] Shepherd of North Carolina. His mother was Ethel Isabelle [Willis Milton {of Wilkes County, North Carolina}, John Franklin, John Willis, Josiah {of Maryland}] Walker of Wilkes County, North Carolina. Valma[8] and James[8] had four children: James Wilbur[9], Jr., Martha Anna[9] and two others (names unknown).

Back row: left to right. Isom Sturgill, Bowman Pennington, Isaac Sturgill, James Estil Sturgill, John Andrew Sturgill, Francis Lee Sturgill. Front row: Lanta Ingram Sturgill, Laura Sturgill Pennington, Phoebe Marilda Weaver Sturgill, Lulu Stuart Sturgill, Charity Ann Farmer Sturgill. This photo was made after Joshua Sturgill's death in 1894. Family lore says that Joshua Sturgill would never allow his photograph to be made.

The Life and Times of
Joshua[7] Sturgill

PATERNAL ANCESTRY: [STURGILL: Francis[6] Jr., Francis[5] Sr., James[4], James[3], John Daniel[2], John[1] {of North Petherton Parish, Somersetshire, England}, Richard[1a], George[2a]]

MATERNAL ANCESTRY: [WEAVER: Phoebe[7], William[6] Joshua[5], Samuel[4], Samuel[3], William[2], Samuel[1] {of Cardington Parish, Shropshire, England}, Thomas[1a], William[2a], Griffith[3a], Jenkin[4a], John[5a], Thomas[6a], Walter[7a], Thomas[8a], Walter[9a], Walter[10a], Walter[11a], Humphrey[12a], Ieuan[13a] {of Wales}, Madoc[14a], Hywel Vychan[15a]]

JOSHUA[7] was born on December 9, 1816 in Ashe County, North Carolina. He died on August 30, 1894 in Ashe County, North Carolina. His father was Francis[6] Sturgill Jr. of North Carolina. His mother was Phoebe[7] Weaver of Weaver's Ford, Ashe County, North Carolina.

JOSAHUA[7] married Phoebe Marilda[9] Weaver on November 30, 1865 in Ashe County, North Carolina. She was born on July 14, 1849 at Weaver's Ford, Ashe County, North Carolina. She died on March 15, 1936 at Sturgills, Ashe County, North Carolina and was buried there on March 17, 1936. Her father was Andrew[8] [Isaac Vance[7], William[6], Joshua[5], Samuel[4], Samuel[3], William[2], Samuel[1] {of Cardington Parish, Shropshire, England}, Thomas[1a], William[2a], Griffith[3a], Jenkin[4a], John[5a], Thomas[6a], Walter[7a], Thomas[8a], Walter[9a], Walter[10a], Walter[11a], Humphrey[12a], Ieuan[13a] {of Wales}, Madoc[14a], Hywel Vychan[15a]] Weaver of Weaver's Ford, Ashe County, North Carolina. Her mother was Malinda[8] [Isaac[7], Isaac[6], Joshua[5], Samuel[4], Samuel[3], William[2], Samuel[1] {of Cardington Parish, Shropshire, England}, Thomas[1a], William[2a], Griffith[3a], Jenkin[4a], John[5a], Thomas[6a], Walter[7a], Thomas[8a], Walter[9a], Walter[10a], Walter[11a], Humphrey[12a], Ieuan[13a] {of Wales}, Madoc[14a], Hywel Vychan[15a]] Weaver of Ashe County, North Carolina.

The Children of
Joshua[7] Sturgill
and Phoebe Marilda[9] Weaver

1. John Andrew[8] Sturgill

   born on March 15, 1867 at Sturgills, Ashe County, North Carolina. He died on September 4, 1935 in Helton, Ashe County, North Carolina and is buried there in the Sturgill's Cemetery. He married Charity Ann Farmer on March 11, 1885 at Helton, Ashe County, North Carolina. She was born on May 16, 1869 in Ashe County, North Carolina. She died on July 15, 1957 in Ashe County, North Carolina and is buried there in the Zion Hill Baptist Church Cemetery. Her father was John "Coonrod" Wilson [John Wilson, David] Farmer of Grayson County, Virginia [Editor's Note: Another sources believes John Coonrod Wilson ancestry was through Alfred, son of David Farmer]. Her mother was Elizabeth "Bett" [Wilborn, Washington {whose surname was Hart}, William {Hart}, James {Hart}] Blevins of North Carolina. John[8] and Charity had nine children:

   a. Joshua[9] Sturgill

      born on December 10, 1885 in Ashe County, North Carolina. He died, age 3 years, 1 month,

25 days, on February 4, 1888 in Ashe County, North Carolina.

b. James Thomas[9] Sturgill

born on September 27, 1887 in Ashe County, North Carolina. He died on July 6, 1966 in Ashe County, North Carolina and was buried there in Ashelawn Memorial Gardens at Jefferson Township. He married Mary Eunice Kelly circa 1910 in Ashe County, North Carolina. She was born on May 29, 1893 in Ashe County, North Carolina. She died, age 72, of a cerebral hemorrhage on March 17, 1969 at Jefferson, Ashe County, North Carolina was buried there in Ashelawn Memorial Gardens. Her father was Richard [Christopher Columbus {of Huntsville, Surry County, North Carolina}, Thomas Sater, John Davis {of Maryland}, John] Kelly of Ashe County, North Carolina. Her mother was Charity E. [Isaac James] Hudler of Ashe County, North Carolina. James[9] and Mary had three children: Charles Ray[10], Zollie Mable[10] and May[10].

c. Lester Mathes[9] "Jack" Sturgill

born on February 3, 1889 in Ashe County, North Carolina. He died on January 4, 1970 at Jefferson, Ashe County, North Carolina. He married Ida Mae Plummer in Ashe County, North Carolina. She was born on February 24, 1889 in Ashe County, North Carolina. She died on September 7, 1969 in Ashe County, North Carolina. Her father was Samuel Cicero [John C. {of Virginia}, Samuel] Plummer of Ashe County, North Carolina. Her mother was Cora Evelyn [Jackson B., John {of Montgomery County, Virginia}] Hash of Virginia. Lester[9] and Ida had eight children; Thelma Louise[10], Edward Lee[10], Edith[10], Kathryn[10], Jack Hash[10], Walter H.[10], Wave[10] and John C.[10].

d. Charles L.[9] "Charlie" Sturgill

born on July 26, 1890 in Ashe County, North Carolina. He died, age 16, on November 30, 1905 in Ashe County, North Carolina.

e. Ida Mae[9] Sturgill

born on May 23, 1892 in Ashe County, North Carolina. She died on August 9, 1987 in Ashe County, North Carolina. She married John Wilson Sullivan on October 28, 1908 in Ashe County, North Carolina. He was born on April 9, 1891 in either Ashe or Wilkes County, North Carolina. He died on October 21, 1980 in Ashe County, North Carolina. His father was Jordan G. [William] Sullivan of Ashe County, North

Carolina. His mother was Mary J.[8] [David[7] {of Lincoln County, North Carolina}, James Abraham[6] {of Dinwiddie County, Virginia}, Richard[5] {of Richmond, Virginia}, William[4], William[3], Thomas[2] {of Gloucester County, Virginia}, Thomas[1] {of Stow-on-the-Wold, Gloucestershire, England}, Thomas[1a], George[2a], John[3a], John[4a]] Hanks of Wilkes County, North Carolina. Ida[9] and John had five children [another researcher says ten children but offers no names]: Orlie Hampton, Mamie Faye, Charles T., Dee C. and John Ancil.

f. Elizabeth[9] "Bettie" Sturgill

born on May 7, 1894 in Ashe County, North Carolina. She died on September 30, 1968 at Jefferson [another researcher says Lansing], Ashe County, North Carolina. She married Samuel Herbert Yearick sometime before 1916 [when their first child was born], presumably in Ashe County, North Carolina. He was born on November 3, 1873 in Snyder County, Pennsylvania. He died on November 22, 1950 in Ashe County, North Carolina. His father was Joseph R. [Samuel R. {of Mifflinburg, Union County, Pennsylvania}, Henry M. {of Mifflinburg, Union County, Pennsylvania] Yearick of Kratzerville, Snyder County, Pennsylvania. His mother was Harriet[4] [Phillip[3] {of Northumberland County,

Pennsylvania}, Daniel E.[2], John George[1] {of Girkhausen, Arnsberg, Westfalia, Germany}, Johann "John" George[1a]] Benfer of Kratzerville, Snyder County, Pennsylvania. Elizabeth[9] and Samuel had three children: Virginia Kathaleene, John H. and James R.

g. Maude[9] Sturgill

born on May 30, 1896 in Ashe County, North Carolina. She died on May 25, 1982 in Ashe County, North Carolina. She married Joseph A. D.[9] Goss on June 21, 1914 in Ashe County, North Carolina. He was born on October 11, 1874 in Ashe County, North Carolina. He died on July 21, 1837 in Ashe County, North Carolina. His father was Robert[8] [Jehu[7], John[6] {of Grayson County, Virginia}, Zachariah[5], William[4] {of North Carolina}, William[3] {of Virginia}, John[2], William[1] {born 1606 of England}] Goss of Ashe County, North Carolina. His mother was Catherine Etta[6] [Jacob[5], Peter[4] {of Rural Retreat, Wythe County, Virginia}, John Peter[3] {of York, York County, Pennsylvania}, Peter[2] {of Frederick County, Maryland}, "Old" Peter[1] {Krahbeil of Zaziwil, Cun Berne, Switzerland}] Graybeal of Jefferson, Ashe County, North Carolina. Maude[9] and Joseph[9] had two children: Ruth Mary[10] and one other whose name is not known.

Maude[9] married, second, Lee Huff. The date of their marriage, presumably in Ashe County, North Carolina, is not known. He was born on August [another researcher says September] 13, 1895 in Georgia [possibly Rome, Floyd County]. He died, age 79, of a ruptured abdominal aortic aneurysm on October 13, 1974, probably at Jefferson, Lansing [where he was living at the time], Ashe County, North Carolina and was buried there in the Ashelawn Memorial Gardens at West Jefferson. Lee was a retired policeman at the time of his death. The name of his father and mother is not known. There was no issue.

h. Pearl Irene[9] Sturgill

born on December 13, 1897 in Ashe County, North Carolina. She died in September 1984 at Manheim, Lancaster, Pennsylvania. She married Claude Thomas Roland, probably in Ashe County, North Carolina. The date of their marriage is not known. He was born on December 4, 1896 at Clifton, Ashe County, North Carolina. He died in March 1977 at Peach Bottom, Lancaster, Pennsylvania and was buried there in the Little Britain Presbyterian Cemetery. His father was Amos W. Roland of Sturgills, Ashe County, North Carolina. The name of his mother is not known [the birth index only lists his father's name]. Pearl[9] and Claude had four children: Alean S., Margaret F., John S. and Catherine L.

i. Howard[9] Sturgill

born on December 22, 1899 in Ashe County, North Carolina. He died, age 91, on April 12, 1991 at Oxford, Chester County, Pennsylvania. He married Catherine B.[2] Hayes. The date of their marriage, probably in Philadelphia, Pennsylvania, is not known. She was born on July 22, 1903 at Philadelphia, Pennsylvania. She died, age 91, on August 13, 1994 at Oxford, Chester County, Pennsylvania. Her father was David[1] Hayes of Scotland. Her mother was Rebecca[1] [Thomas[1a]] Birney of Letter Kenny, Ireland. Issue, if any, is not known [no children were listed on the 1930 or 1940 U. S. Census].

2. William Byrum[8] Sturgill

born on April 9, 1869 at Sturgills, Ashe County, North Carolina. He died on October 26, 1886 at Sturgills, Ashe County, North Carolina. He married Elizabeth "Betty" Blevins [Editor's Note: He must have married, age 17, just before he died].

3. Francis Lee[8] "Frank" Sturgill

born on October 30, 1871 at Sturgills, Ashe County, North Carolina. He died on May 13, 1951 in Ashe County, North Carolina. He married Lulu Virginia Stuart in March 1889 at Piney Creek, Ashe County, North Carolina. Lulu was born on September 17, 1872 in Ashe County, North Carolina. She died on March 12, 1950 in Ashe County, North Carolina. Her father was Jackson [Joseph, John Wesley {of Surrey County, North Carolina}] Stuart of Virginia and later of Piney Creek, Ashe County, North Carolina. Her mother was Holey "Hila" [Elijah {of Wilkes County, North Carolina}, Charles {of Montgomery County, Virginia}, Henry] Francis of Piney Creek, Ashe County, North Carolina. Francis[8] and Lulu had three children:

a. Jacob Roscoe[9] Sturgill

born on September 3, 1890 in Ashe County, North Carolina. He died on July 31, 1937 in Grayson County, Virginia. He married Virgie Stella[8] Peacock [Editor's Note: Other researchers call her Virgie Lee Cottrell and give a different ancestral line] on May 29, 1915 in Ashe County, North Carolina. She was born on July 11, 1896 in Grayson County, North Carolina. She died on February 3, 1959 at Greensboro, Guilford County, North Carolina. Her father was John Henry^7 [Silas Henry^6 {of Wayne County, North Carolina}, Simon^5, Simon^4, John^3 {of Surry, Surry County, Virginia}, Samuel^2 {of Chesapeake, Elizabeth County, Virginia}, William^1 {of Killdeale, Yorkshire, England}, William^{1a} {of Abbots, Stanstead, Hertfordshire, England}, John^{2a}, Thomas^{3a}, William^{4a} {born circa 1540}] Peacock of Ashe County, North Carolina. Her mother was Catherine^7 [Nelson^6 {of North Carolina}, Reuben^5, Humphrey^4 {of Culpeper County, Virginia}, William^3 {of Reddies River, Wilkes County, North Carolina}, John^2 {Kilb of Bromfield, Culpeper County, Virginia}, Johann^1 {of Oberjoshback, Germany}, Peter^{1a}, Nikolaus^{2a}] Kilby of Grayson County, Virginia. Jacob^9 and Virgie^8 had eight children: Alda^{10}, Hazel Blanche^{10}, Troy Lee^{10}, Maggie Virginia^{10}, Cora Edith^{10} and three others whose names are not known.

b. Joshua Jackson^9 Sturgill

born on May 18, 1895 in Ashe County, North Carolina. He died on July 12, 1984 at Amador City, Amador County, California. He married Minnie Laura^8 Kilby. Their date and place of marriage is not known. She was born on February 12, 1896 in Kentucky. She died on September 7, 1984 at Auburn, Placer County, California. Her father was James Robey^7

[Thornton[6] {of North Carolina}, Reuben[5], Humphrey[4] {of Culpeper County, Virginia}, William[3] {of Reddies River, Wilkes County, North Carolina}, John[2] {Kilb of Bromfield, Culpeper County, Virginia}, Johann[1] {of Ober-joshback, Germany}, Peter[1a], Nikolaus[2a]] Kilby of Grayson County, Virginia. Her mother was Eva Ruth[7] [Wiley Winston[6] {of Ashe County, North Carolina}, Enoch[5], Zachariah[4] {of Montgomery County, Virginia} Enoch[3] {of Yadkin River, Wilkes County, North Carolina}, (Unknown)[2], James[1] {of Warwick, England}] Osborne of North Carolina. Joshua[9] and Minnie[8] had nine children: Russell T.[10], Ralph Ernest[10], V. Lenora[10], Robert Franklin[10] and five others whose names are not known.

c. Maggie Matilda[9] Sturgill

born on June 27, 1898 in Ashe County, North Carolina. She died on May 19, 1989 in Grayson County, Virginia [another researcher says Ashe County, North Carolina]. She married Isaac Greely[7] Spencer on February 5, 1916 in Ashe County, North Carolina. He was born on March 18, 1893 at Sturgills, Ashe County, North Carolina. He died on March 1, 1957 in Grayson County, Virginia. His father was William Troy[6] [William[5], Isaac[4], Isaac[3], Joseph Charles[2], William D.[1] {of England or Wales}, Alexander[1a] {of England}, Nicholas[2a] {of Cople, Bedford-shire, England}] Spencer of Grayson County, Virginia. His mother was Cynthia Alice[7] [Franklin L.[6] {of Ashe County, North Carolina}, Enoch[5], Zachariah[4] {of Montgomery County, Virginia} Enoch[3] {of Yadkin River, Wilkes County, North Carolina}, (Unknown)[2], James[1] {of Warwickshire, England}] Osborne of Grayson County, Virginia. Maggie[9] and Isaac[7] had eight children: Carl Conley[8], Grace[8], Orba[8], Pearl[8], Lula Belle[8], Carrie, Ann[8], Joseph[8] "Joe" and Clarence[8].

4. Joel Jackson[8] Sturgill

born on August 3, 1874 at Sturgills, Ashe County, North Carolina. He died on June 14, 1900 in Ashe County, North Carolina and is buried there in the Sturgills Cemetery. He married Laura Eunice[7] Spencer on October 31, 1894 in Ashe County, North Carolina. She was born on April 20, 1874 in North Carolina. She died on April 6, 1937 in Ashe County, North Carolina and was buried in the Byrum Hills Baptist Church Cemetery in Helton, Ashe County, North Carolina. Her father was Byron[6] [Isaac[5], Isaac[4] {of Lee County, Virginia}, Joseph Charles[3], William David[2] {of North Carolina}, Alexander[1] {of Devonshire, England}, Nicholas[1a], John[2a], Robert[3a], Robert[4a], Thomas F.[5a] {of Warwickshire, England}, Henry[6a] {of Northamptonshire, England}, Thomas[7a] {de Spencer}, Nicholas[8a], John[9a], William[10a], John[11a], Gallaidus[12a], Thomas[13a] {of Lincolnshire, England}, Thurston[14a] {of Middlesex County, England}, William Talvis Montgomery[15a], Robert D.[16a], Amaury Raoul[17a] {D'Arbilot of LeHarvre, France}, Urso[18a], Amoury A. R.[19a] {of Normandie, France}, Gerold[20a] {De Tancarville, born 976 A.D. at Dellaveville}] Spencer of Grayson County, Virginia and later of Ashe County, North Carolina. Her mother was Cynthia C. [William J.] Walton of Grayson County, Virginia. Joel[8] and Laura[7] had three children:

a. Fitzhue Carl[9] "Carl" [afa Fitcher] Sturgill

born on October 22, 1896 in Ashe County, North Carolina. He died on April 18, 1970 in Ashe County, North Carolina. He married Blannie Emaline[7] Spencer sometime before 1917 [when their first child was born], in Ashe County, North Carolina. She was born on August 29, 1897 at Ashe County, North Carolina. She died on December 30, 1986 in Ashe County, North Carolina. Her father was William Troy[6] "Bud" [William[5], Isaac[4], Isaac[3], Joseph Charles[2], William D.[1] {of England or Wales}, Alexander[1a] {of England}, Nicholas[2a] {of Cople, Bedfordshire, England}] Spencer of Ashe County, North Carolina. Her mother was Alice[7] [Franklin L.[6] {of Ashe County, North Carolina},

Enoch^5, Zachariah^4 {of Montgomery County, Virginia} Enoch^3 {of Yadkin River, Wilkes County, North Carolina}, (Unknown)^2, James^1 {of Warwickshire, England}] Osborne of Grayson County, Virginia. Fitzhue^9 and Blannie^7 had five children: Veva^{10}, John^{10}, Myrtle Ruth^{10}, Bruce^{10} and Joel Worth^{10} [who died an infant].

b. Rebecca E.^{9} Sturgill

born on August 20, 1897 in Ashe County, North Carolina. She died on February 2, 1981 in Ashe County, North Carolina. She married William Clay^9 Kilby, sometime before 1925 [when their son Elmer^{10} was born], in Ash County, North Carolina. He was born on December 27, 1896 in Ashe County, North Carolina. He died on February 10, 1968 in Ashe County, North Carolina. His father was Robert Nelson^8 [Wilborn^7 {of Ashe County, North Carolina}, Nelson^6, Reuben^5, Humphrey^4 {of Culpeper County, Virginia}, William^3 {of Reddies River, Wilkes County, North Carolina}, John^2 {Kilb of Bromfield, Culpeper County, Virginia}, Johann^1 {of Oberjoshback, Germany}, Peter^{1a}, Niko-laus^{2a}] Kilby of Grayson County, Virginia. His mother was Lina E. [Noah, John Wilson {of Ashe County, North Carolina}] Farmer of Grayson County, Virginia. Rebecca^9 and

William[9] had two children: Elmer L.[10] and one other whose name is not known.

c. Cynthia Marilda[9] Sturgill

born on August 26, 1899 in Ashe County, North Carolina. She died on January 13, 1975 at Jefferson, Ashe County, North Carolina. She married Montey [afa Montie] Bryon Owens on January 23, 1923, presumably in Ashe County, North Carolina. He was born on November 29, 1882, probably in Ashe County, North Carolina. He died on February 22, 1983 Grayson County, Virginia. His father was William Alexander [Richard Nash] Owen of Grayson County, Virginia. His mother was Mary Elizabeth[7] [James Harvey[6] {of Bridle Creek, Grayson County, Virginia}, John Calvin[5], Benjamin[4] {of Orange, Sampson County, North Carolina}, Joseph[3] {of Philadelphia, Pennsylvania}, Isaiah[2], Isaiah[1] {of Reading, Berkshire, England, Joseph[1a], John[2a] {of Abingdon, Berkshire, England}, John[3a] {of Worcester, Berkshire, England}, William[4a], Thomas[5a], Robert[6a] {born circa 1470 of Cemely, Somersetshire, England}, Johannes[7a]] Phipps of Ashe County, North Carolina. Cynthia[9] and Montey had a child: Roy Lee.

5. James Estil[8] Sturgill

born on December 22, 1878 at Sturgills, Ashe County, North Carolina. He died on May 30, 1955 at Rugby, Grayson County, Virginia and buried there at Mouth of Wilson in the Haw-Orchard Baptist Cemetery. He married Ella Naomi[10] Ingram on March 6, 1897 at Sturgills, Ashe County, North Carolina. She was born on July 18, 1878 at Rugby, Grayson County, Virginia. She died on August 2, 1915 at Rugby, Grayson County, Virginia and was buried there at Mouth of Wilson in the Haw-Orchard Baptist Cemetery. Her father was John Calvin[9] [William[8], John W.[7], William[6], Abraham[5] III {of Sussex County, Delaware}, Abraham[4], Abraham[3], James[2], Robert[1] {of England and later of Northampton County, Virginia}, Joseph[1a]] Ingram of North Carolina. Her mother was Charity Ann [John Wilson, David] Farmer of Grayson County, Virginia. James[8] and Ella[10] had nine children: Charity Ann[9], Lanta Mae[9] "Lantie", Nancy Emeline[9], William[9] "Bill", Ursa Dell[9] "Ursie", Guida Rose[9], Vesta Blaine[9], Stevenson Conley[9] and Cora[9].

6. Laura Malinda[8] Sturgill

born on January 20, 1884 at Sturgills, Ashe County, North Carolina. She died on October 4, 1935 at Helton, Ashe County, North Carolina. She married

Bowman Byron[10] Pennington on February 7, 1897 in Ashe County, North Carolina. He was born on June 26, 1873 in Grayson County, Virginia. He died on March 10, 1929 in Ashe County, North Carolina. His father was Elisha[9] "Dock" [Levi[8], Levi[7], Micajah[6], Benajah[5], Ephraim[4] {of Morris County, New Jersey}, Ephraim[3], Ephraim[2] {of New Haven, Connecticut}, Ephraim[1] {of Muncaster, England}, William[1a], John[2a]] Pennington of Grayson County, Virginia. His mother was Tabitha Jane [also found as Tobitha Jane and Jane Tabitha] Anderson of Grayson County, Virginia. Laura[8] and Bowman Byron[10] had six children:

a. Lillie Alafair[11] Pennington

born in 1897 in Ashe County, North Carolina. She died an infant in 1898 in Ashe County, North Carolina.

b. Edward[11] Pennington

born in 1900 in Ashe County, North Carolina. He died, approximately age 2, in Ashe County, North Carolina.

c. Chester Harvey[11] Pennington

born on April 22, 1904 in Ashe County, North Carolina. He died, age 3, in 1907 in Ashe

County, North Carolina.

d. Olla Marilda[11] Pennington

born on January 13, 1908 in Ashe County, North Carolina. She died, age 89, of a cardiovascular disease on March 17, 1997 at Jefferson, Ashe County, North Carolina. She married Leslie Alton Jones in Ashe County, North Carolina. He was born on October 15, 1908 at Helton, Ashe County, North Carolina. He died on March 13, 2000 at Jefferson, Ashe County, North Carolina. His father was James Calvin [Robert {of Washington County, Virginia}] Jones of Helton, Ashe County, North Carolina. His mother was Lucinda Toone of Helton, Ashe County, North Carolina. Issue, if any, is not known.

e. Esther Jane[11] Pennington

born on January 17, 1911 in Ashe County, North Carolina. She died on December 10, 1981 in Ashe County, North Carolina. She married Clarence Elmer[5] Griffitts sometime before 1934 [when their child was born], in Ashe County, North Carolina. He was born on May 28, 1905 in Ashe County, North Carolina. He died on November 23, 1971 in Ashe County, North Carolina. His father was Abijah G.[4] [John[3] III {afa Greffetts of Rye Valley, Smyth County, Virginia}, John[2] II, John[1] {of Hundley, Shropshire, England}, Edward[1a] {of Henllon, Cardiganshire, Wales}, John[2a] {born circa 1785 of Parys, Anglesey, Wales}] Griffitts of Ashe County, North Carolina. His mother was Malona [afa Malissia} Brooks of Ashe County, North Carolina. Esther[11] and Clarence[5] had a child: Barbara Ann[6].

f. Walter[11] Pennington

born on January 5, 1919 in Ashe County, North Carolina, He died at birth on Janaury 5, 1919 in Ashe County, North Carolina.

7. Isom[8] Sturgill

born on March 9, 1887 at Sturgills, Ashe County, North Carolina. He died on June 6, 1968 in Grayson County, Virginia and was buried there at Mouth of Wilson in the Haw-Orchard Baptist Cemetery. He married Verney O'Lanta[10] "Lanta" Ingram on February 3, 1903 in Ashe County, North Carolina. She was born on March 9, 1887, probably in Grayson County, Virginia. She died in 1961 in Grayson County, Virginia and was buried there at Mouth of Wilson in the Haw-Orchard Baptist Cemetery. Her father was John Calvin[9] [William[8], John W.[7], William[6], Abraham[5] III {of Sussex

County, Delaware}, Abraham[4], Abraham[3], James[2] {of Somerset County, Maryland}, Robert[1] {of England and later of Northampton County, Virginia}, Joseph[1a]] Ingram of North Carolina. Her mother was Charity Ann[8] [John Wilson[7], David[6], David[5] {of Henrico County, Virginia}, Frederick[4] {of Chesterfield, Chesterfield County, Virginia}, John[3], Henry[2], Thomas[1] (or) Robert[1] {of England}, Thomas[1a]] Farmer of Grayson County, Virginia. Isom[8] and Lanta[10] had eleven children:

a. Jesse Lundy[9] Sturgill

born on November 5, 1903 in Ashe County, North Carolina. He died on October 15, 1977 at Marion, Smyth County, Virginia. He married Pauline Meek[9] Grinstead in 1928 at Chilhowie, Smyth County, Virginia. She was born on January 5, 1909 at Chilhowie, Smyth County, Virginia. She died in May 1984 in Smyth County, Virginia. Her father was Charles Meek[8] [Jasper Newton[7] "Jack," Edward[6], Walton John[5] "Jack" {of Henrico County, Virginia}, John[4] {of Northumberland County, Virginia}, William[3], William[2], William[1] {born circa 1632 in England}] Grinstead of Chilhowie, Smyth County, Virginia. Her mother was Minnie Tarter Williams of Chilhowie, Smyth County, Virginia. Jesse[9] and Pauline[9] had two children: Isom Meek[10] and (Unknown)[10].

b. Grace Phoebe Ann[9] Sturgill

born on November 1, 1905 in Ashe County, North Carolina. She died on January 4, 1992 at Rugby, Grayson County, Virginia and was buried there in the Haw-Orchard Baptist Church Cemetery. She married Edward Columbus[9] "Lum" Farmer on February 21, 1923 at Rugby, Grayson County, Virginia. He was born on March 14, 1902 in Virginia. He died on March 5, 1974 at Mouth of Wilson, Wilson Creek, Grayson County, Virginia. His father was Jessie Allen[8] [John Wilson[7], David[6], David[5] {of Henrico County, Virginia}, Frederick[4] {of Chesterfield, Chesterfield County, Virginia}, John[3], Henry[2], Thomas[1] (or) Robert[1] {of England}, Thomas[1a]] Farmer. His mother was Mary C.[7] "Maggie" [William C.[6], William[5] "Bill," Benjamin[4] "Preacher Ben" {of Guilford County, North Carolina}, Joseph[3] {of Philadelphia, Pennsylvania}, Isaiah[2] {of Chester County, Pennsylvania}, Isaiah[1] {of Reading, Berkshire, England}, Joseph[1a], John[2a] {of Worcester, Worcestershire, England}, John[3a], William[4a]] Phipps. Grace[9] and Edward[9] had four children: Herbert C.[10], Janetta A.[10], Lee Etta[10] and (Unknown)[10].

c. Robert Joel[9] Sturgill

born on June 3, 1907 in Ashe County, North
Carolina. He died on September 21, 1970 at
Elkton, Cecil County, Maryland. He married
Clara Weaver on May 21, 1926 at Elkton, Cecil
County, Maryland. She was born on October 6,
1902 in Ashe County, North Carolina. Her date
and place of death is not known. Her father was
William Granville [Eli Whitney] Weaver of
Ashe County, North Carolina. Her mother was
Lou Money [William Henry {of Rye Valley,
Smyth County, Virginia}, Joseph, Nathaniel]
Medley of Liberty Hill, Tazewell County,
Virginia. Robert[9] and Clara had five children:
Mary C.[10], Lacy H.[10], Gracie[10], Alta[10] and
Robert[10].

d. Cleveland Blaine[9] Sturgill

born on October 23, 1909 at Sturgills, Ashe
County, North Carolina. He died on April 28,
2000 at Kingsport, Sullivan County, Tennessee.
He married, first, Mary Jean[5] Griffitts in 1934.
Her father was Abijah G.[4] [John[3] III {afa
Greffetts of Rye Valley, Smyth County,
Virginia}, John[2] II, John[1] {of Hundley, Shrop-
shire, England}, Edward[1a] {of Henllon, Cardi-
ganshire, Wales}, John[2a] {born circa 1785 of
Parys, Anglesey, Wales}] Griffitts of Ashe

County, North Carolina. Her mother was Elizabeth Malona[5] [afa Malissia} [George Washington[4], David[3], Thomas[2] {of Delaware}, George[1] {of Wales}, Thomas[1a]] Brooks of Ashe County, North Carolina. Cleveland[9] and Mary Jean[5] had at least one child whose name is unknown.

Cleveland[9] married, second, (Unknown) Rowland. Cleveland[9] married, third, Mary Viola Gillespie. Cleveland[9] and Mary Viola had two children: Glendon Blaine[10] and Brandon Avery[10] [Editor's Note: Some researchers also note a Mary Garrett, which may be one in the same as Mary Jean[5] from his first wife].

e. Herbert Franklin[9] Sturgill

born on December 21, 1911 in Ashe County, North Carolina. He died on Sunday, April 4, 2004 in the Frances Marion Manor at Marion, Smyth County, Virginia and was buried there in the South Fork Cemetery. He married Ruby Quillen. The date and place of their marriage is not known. She was born on April 7, 1915. Her place of birth is not known. She died on July 25, 1945 at Chilhowie, Smyth County, Virginia and was buried there in the South Forks Baptist Church Cemetery. The name of her father and mother is not known. Herbert[9] and Ruby had five children: Elda[10], Glenna[10], Lois[10], Dottie[10] and Herbert Dewey[10].

Herbert[9] married, second, Mary Edith Farmer. The date of their marriage in Smyth County, Virginia is not known. She was born on November 1, 1911 in Virginia. She died on October 6, 1976 at Marion, Smyth County, Virginia. Her father was Noah [Wilson {of Ashe County, North Carolina}] Farmer of Grayson County, Virginia. Her mother was Lydia Ellen Thompson of Ashe County, North Carolina, the daughter of Bethany Thompson and Calvin Farmer. There was no issue.

f. Zella May[9] Sturgill

born on July 21, 1914 in Ashe County, North Carolina. She died on March 16, 2002 at Jefferson, Ashe County, North Carolina. She married John Kenneth[6] Eller sometime before 1933 [when their first child was born] in Ashe County, North Carolina. He was born on November 25, 1903 in Ashe County, North Carolina. He died on July 26, 1971 in Ashe County, North Carolina. His father was James Horton[5] "Hort" [Jacob[4], Henry Peter[3] {of Frederick County, Maryland}, George Michael[2] {of Rowan County, North Carolina}, Georg[1] {of Kattenbrunn, Coburg, Bayern, Germany}] Eller of Ashe County, North Carolina. His mother was Elzina [Columbus Franklin "Frank" {of Wilkes County, North Carolina}, William {of Isle of Wight County, Virginia}] Seagraves of Ashe County, North Carolina. Zella[9] and John[6] had a child: Bert Junior[7].

g. Dessie Luella[9] Sturgill

born on March 22,1916 in Ashe County, North Carolina. She died on October 4, 2006 at Marion, Smyth County, Virginia and was buried there in the Thomas Cemetery. She married Marvin Edgar Hubble sometime before 1936 [when their first child was born], probably in Smyth County, Virginia. He was born on July 3, 1909 in Smyth County, Virginia. He died in February 1978 at Marion, Smyth County, Virginia. His father was Ray Edgar [Louis J., Henry R.] Hubble of Virginia. His mother was Hettie Victoria Blankenbeckler of Virginia. Dessie[9] and Marvin had three children: Isom E., Marvin and Monica Dell.

h. Vada Lee[9] Sturgill

born on April 8, 1919 [another researcher says August 27, 1921] in Ashe County, North

Carolina. Her date and place of death is not known [Editor's Note: One researcher sways she married an (Unknown) Jackson].

i. Laura Hattie[9] Sturgill

born on January 19, 1920 in Ashe County, North Carolina [another researcher says January 2, 1917 in Smyth County, Virginia]. Her date and place of death is not known {Editor's Note: One researcher says she married (Unknown) Kelly].

j. Idella Emaline[9] "Della" Sturgill

born on July 20, 1924 in Ashe County, North Carolina. She died of ovarian cancer on May 13, 1972 at Jefferson, Ashe County, North Carolina and was buried in the Haw-Orchard Baptist Cemetery at Rugby, Grayson County, Virginia. She married Guy Calvin[9] Duvall. He was born on May 27, 1922 at Rugby, Grayson County, Virginia. He died, age 90, on August 28, 2012 in Ashe County, North Carolina. His father was Marvin Wayne[8] [John W.[7] {of Ashe County, North Carolina}, James Monroe[6], Samuel B.[5] {of Queen Anne's Parish, Prince George's County, Maryland}, Samuel[4], Samuel[3], Mareen[2], Mareen[1] {of Nantes, Loire-Atlantique, Pays-de-la Loire, France}, Massiott[1a] {of St. Aubin Nieure,

Bouregogne, France}, William[2a], Lawrence[3a] {born circa 1540}] Duvall of Grayson County, Virginia. His mother was Mary Bessie [Hughey Payton Columbus, James M. {of North Carolina}] Walls of Grayson County, Virginia. Idella[9] and Guy[9] had three children: Richard Darell[10], Linda[10] and Rita[10].

Guy[9] married, second, Louise Rye. She had two children from a previous marriage: Brenda and Rex.

k. Flora Alean[9] "Jean" Sturgill

born on August 3, 1926 in Ashe County, North Carolina. Her date and place of death is not known [Editor's Note: She is last found on the 1940 U. S. Census at age 13].

[Editor's Note: Some researchers believe Isom[8] had married, second, Stacey Sheppard, but no further evidence has been found]

8. Isaac Millard[8] "Big Ike" Sturgill

born on September 28, 1890 in Ashe County, North Carolina. He died on June 26, 1970 at Marion, Smyth County, Virginia. He married Cora Clyde[8] Peacock on April 4, 1912 in Grayson County,

Virginia. She was born on April 12, 1889 at Thomas Bridge, Smyth County, Virginia. She died in July 1986 at Marion, Smyth County, Virginia. Her father was John Henry[7] [Silas Henry[6] {of Wayne County, North Carolina}, Simon[5], Simon[4], John[3] {of Surry, Surry County, Virginia}, Samuel[2], William[1] {of Dry Drayton, Cambridgeshire, England}] Peacock of Grayson County, Virginia. Her mother was Catherine {Thornton {of Wilkes County, North Carolina}, Reuben, Humphrey {of Culpeper County, Virginia}, William, John] Kilby of Wilson Creek, Grayson County, Virginia. Isaac[8] and Cora[8] had eight children:

a. Marilda Katherine[9] Sturgill

born on January 18, 1913 in Ashe County, North Carolina. She died on July 10, 2000, probably at West Friendship, Howard County, Maryland. She married Ollie Lee Pipes on September 3, 1930 at West Friendship, Howard County, Maryland. He was born on June 5, 1905 at Holston Valley, Sullivan, Tennessee. He died in July 1986 at West Friendship, Howard County, Maryland. His father was James Hiram [William Riley {of Wilkes County, North Carolina}] Pipes of Wilkes County, North Carolina. His mother was Mary Stuart Johnson of Meadow View, Washington County, Virginia. Katherine[6] and Ollie had three children:

Ollie Lee "Chunky," Barbara Mellin and (Unknown).

b. Elmer Lee[9] Sturgill

born on September 26, 1914 at Sturgills, Ashe County, North Carolina. He died on January 6, 1969 in the Veterans Administration Hospital at Johnson City, Washington County, Tennessee. He married Dorothy Wynne Ward on November 20, 1945, presumably in Shelby County, Tennessee. She was born on January 26, 1921 at Memphis, Shelby County, Tennessee. Her father was William Wynne [John Newton {of Walnut Grove, Washington County, Virginia}, John Wesley] Ward of Shelby County, Tennessee. Her mother was Okie Cleo [George Washington, George, Robert] Gollehon of Smyth County, Virginia. Elmer[9] and Dorothy had one child: Kenneth[10].

c. Laura Levaughn[9] Sturgill

born on September 17, 1916 at Holston, Smyth County, Virginia. She died, age 7 months, 26 days, on May 13, 1917 at Holston, Smyth County, Virginia.

d. Estil Vernon[9] Sturgill

born on March 1, 1918 at Holston Mills, Smyth County, Virginia. He died in January 1988 at Marion, Smyth County, Virginia and was buried there in the South Fork Baptist Church Cemetery.

e. Isaac Millard[9] Sturgill, Jr.

born on January 3, 1921 at Holston Mills, Smyth County, Virginia. He died on May 24, 1970 in Smyth County, Virginia and was buried there at Chilhowie in the South Fork Baptist Church Cemetery. He married Joan Buchanan. The date and place of their marriage is not known. She was born on May 10, 1926 at Clintwood, Dickenson County, Virginia. She died, age 86, on Monday, October 22, 2012 in the Wellmont Hospice House at Bristol, Sullivan County, Tennessee. The name of her father and mother is not known. She married, second, Layton Edward Choate. Isaac[9] and Joan had a child: Rebecca[10].

f. Mabel Nadine[9] Sturgill

born on January 21, 1923 at Holston Mills, Smyth County, Virginia. She died on Sunday, February 13, 2011 at Marion, Smyth County,

Virginia and her remains were interred there in the Rosewood Mauseleum at Rual Retreat. She married James Edward[10] "Riley" Pennington on March 3, 1941 in Smyth County, Virginia. He was born on May 9, 1919 at Brown's Creek, Scott County, Virginia. His father was James Roby[9] [Abraham Asa Eli[8] {of Ashe County, North Carolina}, Andrew[7], Abraham[6] "Abram" {of Surry County, North Carolina}, Ephraim[5] {of Pennsylvania}, Benejah[4], Ephraim[3] {of New Jersey}, Ephraim[2] {of New Haven County, Connecticut}, Ephraim[1] {of Lancashire, England}, William[1a], John[2a], Robert[3a] {of West Chew, London, Middlesex, England}, William[4a] {of Hewhem, Essex, England}, John[5a], John[6a] {of Pennington, Lancashire, England}, John[7a], John[8a], John[9a] {born circa 1393}, Alan[10a]] Pennington of Johnson, Scott County, Virginia. His mother was Clarissa Cordelia[7] "Cordie" [William[6] {of North Carolina}, Elias[5] {of Caroline County, Virginia}, Advid[4] {of Louisa County, Virginia}, Nicholas[3] {of Hanover County, Virginia}, Nicholas[2] {of St. Peter's Parish, New Kent County, Virginia}, Nicholas[1] {of Thaxter, Essex, England}, Samuel[1a], Samuel[2a], Simon[3a], John[4a] {born circa 1510}]] Gentry of Scott County, Virginia [some researchers claim Johnson County, Tennessee]. James[10] and Mabel[9] had two children: Betty[11] and Carol[11].

g. Henry Clay[9] Sturgill

born on February 20, 1924 at Holston Mills, Smyth County, Virginia [his obit says January 30, 1925 at Marion]. He died at home on Wednesday, November 7, 2001 at Culpeper, Culpeper County, Virginia and was buried there in the Hillcrest Memory Gardens. He married Helen Gray Reedy on December 7, 1946 in Smyth County, Virginia. She was born on June 5, 1925 in Smyth County, Virginia. Her father was Harlow W. [Robert J.] Reedy of Grayson County, Virginia. Her mother was Ada B. [Arthur G., Mahlon S.] Cormany of Marion, Smyth County, Virginia. Henry[9] retired in 1988 from the Virginia Department of Transportation, an active member of the Culpeper Baptist Church, Culpeper Ruritan Club, Boy Scout Troop 196 and the Phoenix Lodge 59, Independent Order of Odd Fellows. He had a love of gardening, but was best known as the "Master of the Trout Stream," for his fishing prowess. Henry[9] and Helen had two children: Michael Clay[10] and Philip Reed[10].

h. Mack Howard[9] Sturgill

born on October 10, 1927 at Holston Mills,

Smyth County, Virginia. He died, age 70, on June 13, 1998 in the Bowman Gray Baptist Hospital at Winston-Salem, Forsyth County, North Carolina and was buried at the South Fork Cemetery at Marion, Smyth County, Virginia. He never married.

Known as the "Historical Gossip," Mack[9] was a world traveler, student, author, teacher and avid stamp collector. Before he died, he was named Smyth County's Citizen of the year. He was a veteran of the Korean War and a member of Francis Marion VFW Post 4667. He was interested and worked on various family and local history projects. Before he retired to care for his ailing mother, he taught at Marion High School, Marion College, Wake Forest University, Green Mountain College, Emory & Henry College, Princeton University and North Carolina Wesleyan College.

Francis Sturgill, Jr. Homestead
at Piney Creek, Ashe County, North Carolina

The Life and Times of
Francis[6] Sturgill, Jr.

PATERNAL ANCESTRY: [STURGILL: Francis[5] Sr., James[4], James[3], John Daniel[2], John[1] {of North Petherton Parish, Somersetshire, England}, Richard[1a], George[2a]]

MATERNAL ANCESTRY: [HASH/HACHE: Rebecca[3], John[2] "Old John," John[1] {Hache of England}, Thomas[1a] {born circa 1602}]

FRANCIS[6] was born on September 22, 1782 at Helton Creek, Ashe County, North Carolina. He died on August 13, 1846 at Helton Creek, Ashe County, North Carolina and was buried there in the Sturgill Cemetery. His father was Francis[5] Sturgill, Sr. of Standardsville, Swift Run Creek, Orange County, Virginia. His mother was Rebecca[3] Hash of Montgomery County, Virginia.

FRANCIS[6] married Phoebe[7] Weaver circa 1803 in Ashe County, North Carolina. She was born on October 15, 1783 at Weaver's Ford, Ashe County, North Carolina. She died on June 13, 1855 at Helton Creek, Ashe County, North Carolina. Her father was William[6] [Joshua[5], Samuel[4], Samuel[3], William[2], Samuel[1] {of Shropshire, England}, Thomas[1a], William[2a], Griffith[3a], Jenkin[4a], John[5a], Thomas[6a],

121

Walter[7a], Thomas[8a], Walter[9a], Walter[10a], Walter[11a], Humphrey[12a], Ieuan[13a] {of Wales}, Madoc[14a], Hywel Vychan[15a]] Weaver of Lunenburg County, Virginia. Her mother was Rachel[2] [Moses[1] {of Ireland}] McDaniel of Lunenburg County, Virginia.

FRANCIS[6] bought out all other heirs to his father's estate and lived on this farm until 1838, when he then moved to Helton Creek in Ashe County. The Sturgills Post Office was named after him.

The Children of
Francis[6] Sturgill, Jr.
and Phoebe[6] Weaver

1. Solomon[7] Sturgill
   born on April 4, 1804 at New River, Watauga County, North Carolina. He died on October 13, 1856 at Willard, Carter County, Kentucky. He married Rebecca Thompkins [some researchers call her Rebecca Thompkins Carter, which seems incorrect unless she had a prior marriage] in 1825 in Wilkes County, North Carolina [some researchers say Carter County, Kentucky; others claim Tennessee]. She was born on April 21, 1800 in Wilkes County, North Carolina [another researcher says Tennessee]. She died on July 13, 1877 at Deer Creek, Carter County, Kentucky. Her father was Benjamin [James {of Newark, Essex County,

New Jersey}] Thompkins of Wilkes County, North Carolina. Her mother was Elizabeth [Thomas {of Bedford County, Virginia}] Hampton of Surry County, North Carolina. Solomon[7] and Rebecca had fifteen children: Mary Ann[8], Joel[8], (son)[8], Agnes[8], Sarah[8] "Sally," Didema[8], Benjamin Franklin[8], Elizabeth[8], Nancy[8], John Francis[8], Mathilda[8], Jemima[8], Rebecca[8], Soloman[8] and Amanda Rice[8].

2. Joel[7] Sturgill
born circa 1807/1808 in Ashe County, North Carolina. He died in 1875 in Ashe County, North Carolina. He married Mary Jane[8] Weaver. The date of their marriage, presumably in Ashe County, North Carolina, is not known. Mary Jane[8] was born on October 31, 1813 in North Carolina. She died on September 19, 1895 in North Carolina. Her father was Joshua[7] [Isaac[6], Joshua[5] , Samuel[4] III, Samuel[3] II, William[2], Samuel[1] {of Shropshire, England}, Thomas[1a], William[2a], Griffith[3a], Jenkin[4a], John[5a], Thomas[6a], Walter[7a], Thomas[8a], Walter[9a], Walter[10a], Walter[11a], Humphrey[12a], Ieuan[13a] {of Wales}, Madoc[14a], Hywel Vychan[15a]] Weaver [another source says he was Isaac Weaver, Jr.] of Virginia and later of North Carolina. Her mother was Susannah (Unknown). Joel[7] and Mary Jane[8] had no issue.

2. John[7] Sturgill
   born on November 15, 1813 in Ashe County, North Carolina. He died on August 7, 1882 in Ashe County, North Carolina and was buried there in Zion Hill Cemetery at Helton Creek. He married Obedience[5] "Bidda" Cox in 1832 in Ashe County, North Carolina. She was born on January 10, 1816 in Ashe County, North Carolina. She died on May 6, 1877 in Ashe County, North Carolina. Her father was Willliam[4] [Joshua[3], John[2], Joshua[1] {of Ulster, Ireland}] Cox of Ashe County, North Carolina. Her mother was Elizabeth[7] [Jesse[6], George[5], Thomas[4], Henry[3], Henry[2], George[1] {of England}, John[1a], Richard[2a]] Reeves of Ashe County, North Carolina. John[7] and Obedience[5] had nine children:

   a. Sarah[8] Sturgill
      born in 1832 in Ashe County, North Carolina. She died in 1900 in Scott County, Virginia [another researcher says 1860 at age 28]. She married Elisha Tucker circa 1848/1852 in Ashe County, North Carolina. He was born in 1832 in Ashe County, North Carolina. His date and place of death is not known. The name of his father and mother is not known. Sarah[8] and Elisha had a child: (girl).

   b. Elizabeth[8] Sturgill
      born circa 1834/1835 in Ashe County, North

Carolina. Her date and place of death is not known.

[Editor's Note: Many researchers confuse this Elizabeth[5] with Elizabeth[8], born July 1836, the daughter of David[7] Sturgill and Rosamond Long, who married Alvin M. Richardson and, some say, had also married Floyd Anderson; she is also sometimes confused with Elizabeth[7], born circa 1827/1832, the daughter of Francis[6] Sturgill and Phoebe[7] Weaver who married Elijah Blevins]

c. Phoebe[8] Sturgill
born on September 8, 1835 in Ashe County, North Carolina. She died on March 14, 1898 in Ashe County, North Carolina. She married Lewis Sullivan in 1854 in Ashe County, North Carolina. He was born on December 15, 1835 in Ashe County, North Carolina. His date and place of death is not known. His father was William Sullivan of Ashe County, North Carolina. His mother was Susannah Powers [some researchers show her surname as Bowers] of Ashe County, North Carolina. Phoebe[8] and Lewis had two children: Violinia and Nancy C.

d. William[8] Sturgill
born in 1837 in Ashe County, North Carolina. His date of death in Marion, Smyth County, North Carolina is not known. He married Martha Porter on March 1, 1874 at Helton Creek, Ashe County, North Carolina. She was born in 1837 in Ashe County, North Carolina. Her date of death in Marion, Smyth County, Virginia is not known. The name of her father and mother is not known. Issue, if any, is not known.

e. Martha Jane[8] Sturgill
born on June 12, 1844 in Ashe County, North Carolina. She died on February 8 [another researcher says the 15th], 1922 at Glade Creek, Allegheny County, North Carolina and was buried there in the Crab Tree Primitive Baptist Church Cemetery. She married Hugh[7] Hanks on December 9, 1871, presumably in Ashe [but possibly Allegheny] County, North Carolina. He was born on July 15, 1832 in Allegheny County, North Carolina. He died on August 18, 1913 in Allegheny County, North Carolina. His father was William[6] [James[5] {of Dinwiddie County, Virginia}, Richard[4] {of Richmond County, Virginia}, William[3] II, William[2], Thomas[1] {of England}, John[1a]] Hanks of Lincoln County, North Carolina. His mother was Celia[5]

[Jacob^4, Alexander^3 {of Roanoke, Culpeper County, Virginia}, William^2, John^1 {of Glamus, Angush, Scotland}, Patrick^{1a}, John^{2a}, Patrick^{3a}, John^{4a}, John^{5a}, John^{6a}, John^{7a}, John^{8a}, Patrick^{9a}, John^{10a}, John^{11a}, John^{12a} {De Lyon}, John^{13a} {de Lyons of Warkworth, Northumberland, England}, John^{14a}, Richard^{15a} {of Banbury, Oxfordshire, England}, Roger^{16a}, Roger^{17a}, Richard^{18a}, John^{19a} {born circa 1100}] Lyon of North Carolina [another researcher says his mother was Polly Blackburn of Wilkes County, North Carolina]. Martha^8 and Hugh^7 had four children: Birdie Jane^8, Andrew H.^{8} "Huff," W. Clint^8 and Robert Luther^8.

f. Byrum^8 Sturgill
born on March 15, 1846 in Ashe County, Virginia. He died on March 13, 1921 in Ashe County, Virginia. He married Martha Caroline^9 Pennington on September 30, 1876 in Ashe County, North Carolina. She was born on December 29, 1856 in Ashe County, North Carolina. She died on August 11, 1935 in Ashe County, North Carolina. Her father was Stephen K.^{8} [Samuel^7, Andrew^6, Benajah^5 {of Salisbury, Rowan County, North Carolina}, Ephraim^4 IV {of Morris County, New Jersey}, Ephraim^3 III {of Newark County, Connecticut}, Ephraim^2 II {of New Haven, New Haven

County, Connecticut}, Ephraim[1] {of Muncaster, Cumberland, England}, William[1a] {of Pennington, Lancashire, England}, John[2a] {of Hawkshead, Lancashire, England}, Robert[3a] {of West Cheap, St. Peters, London, Middlesex, England}, William[4a] {of Henham, Essex, England}, "Sir" John V.[5a] {of Muncaster Castle, Cumberland, England}, John[6a] {of Lancashire, England}, John[7a] {of Muncaster, Cumberland, England}, John[8a], John[9a] {of Preston, Richmond, Westmoreland, England}, Alan[10a], William[11a], John[12a], William[13a], John[14a] {born circa 1240}] Pennington of Grayson County, Virginia and later of Ashe County, North Carolina. Her mother was Johanna[6] [Isaac[5] {of Fincastle, Botetort County, Virginia}, Joseph Charles[4] {of Lee County, Virginia}, William David[3] {of North Carolina}, Alexander[2] {of Virginia}, Nicholas[1] {of Cople, Bedfordshire, England}, Nicholas[1a]] Spencer of Virginia and later of Ashe County, North Carolina. Byrum[8] and Martha[9] had seven children: Walter Stephen[9], William Edward[9], James Victor Hugo[9], Myrtie Orlean[9], Lessie Johanna[9], Mamie Artie[9] and Maggie Irene[9].

g. Francis Marion[8] Sturgill
born on December 10, 1848 in Ashe County, North Carolina. He died on December 13, 1937 in Grayson County, Virginia and was returned

for burial in the Sturgill Cemetery at Helton, Ashe County, North Carolina. He married Orpha[3] "Orfey" Testerman on January 3, 1867 in Ashe County, North Carolina, William Sexton, Justice of the Peace presiding. She was born on August 1, 1851 in Ashe County, North Carolina. She died on December 19, 1896 in Grayson County, Virginia and was returned for burial in the Sturgill Cemetery at Helton, Ashe County, North Carolina. Her father was Peter[2] [Thomas[1] {of Hull, England}] Testerman of Grayson County, Virginia. Her mother was Nancy[7] [David[6], David[5] {of Henrico County, Virginia}, Frederick[4] {of Chesterfield, Chesterfield County, Virginia}, John[3] {of Henrico County, Virginia}, Henry I.[2], Thomas[1] {of Easton Neston, Northamptonshire, England}, George[1a] {of Neston, Cheshire, England}, John[2a], Richard[3a], Thomas Ricards[4a] {born circa 1460}] Farmer of Grayson County, Virginia. Francis[8] and Orpha[3] had eleven children: Catherine[9], Luzilla[9], Winfield M.[9], John Wesley[9], Phoebe[9], Birda[9], William Byrum[9], Dorsie[9], Della[9], Charles[9] and Lester H.[9].

h. Melvin[8] Sturgill
born in 1852 in Ashe County, North Carolina. He died in August 1928. He married Celia Emeline[9] Pennington on December 26, 1880 in Ashe County, North Carolina. She was born in

1862 in Ashe County, North Carolina. She died in January 1919 in Ashe County, North Carolina. Her father was Andrew Jackson[8] [Samuel[7] Andrew[6], Benajah[5] {of Salisbury, Rowan County, North Carolina}, Ephraim[4] IV (of Morris County, New Jersey}, Ephraim[3] III {of Newark County, Connecticut}, Ephraim[2] II {of New Haven, New Haven County, Connecticut}, Ephraim[1] {of Muncaster, Cumberland, England}, William[1a] {of Pennington, Lancashire, England}, John[2a] {of Hawkshead, Lancashire, England}, Robert[3a] {of West Cheap, St. Peters, London, Middlesex, England}, William[4a] {of Henham, Essex, England}, "Sir" John V.[5a] {of Muncaster Castle, Cumberland, England}, John[6a] {of Lancashire, England}, John[7a] {of Muncaster, Cumberland, England}, John[8a], John[9a] {of Preston, Richmond, Westmoreland, England}, Alan[10a], William[11a], John[12a], William[13a], John[14a] {born circa 1240}] Pennington of Grayson County, Virginia. Her mother was Elizabeth[6] "Betsey" [Reuben[5] {of Wilkes County, North Carolina}, Humphrey[4] {of Culpeper County, Virginia}, William[3] {of Wilkes County, North Carolina}, John[2] {of Bromfield, Culpeper County, Virginia}, Johann[1] {of Ober-josbach, Rheingau-Taunis-Kreis, Hessen, Germany}]] Kilby of Grayson County, Virginia. Melvin[8] and Celia[9] had eight children: Drucilla Alafair[9],

Claude Winford[9], Bonnie[9], Festus Euclee[9], Ocran Chesil[9], "Owen Burris[9], Ulla Vinton[9] and Waldon[9].

i. Estil[8] Sturgill
    born on February 2, 1856 in Ashe County, North Carolina. He died, age 58, on December 17, 1915 [Editor's Note: Most researchers claim he died in California; if so he was returned to Virginia for burial]. He was buried in the Azen Missionary Baptist Church Cemetery at Konnarock, Washington County, Virginia. He married Laura Ball sometime before 1880 [when their child was born], presumably in Ashe County, North Carolina. She was born in 1850. She died in 1896. Her place of death is not known. The name of her father and mother is not known. Estil[8] and Laura had one child: William Luther[9].

    Estil[8] married, second, Emaline[8] Osborne in Grayson County, Virginia. She was born on September 27, 1858 in Grayson County, Virginia. She died on April 4, 1930 at Rugby, Grayson County, Virginia and was buried there at Mouth of Wilson in the Haw-Orchard Baptist Cemetery. Her father was Franklin Leander[7] [Enoch[6], Zachariah[5] {of Montgomery County, Virginia}, Enoch[4] {of Yadkin River, Rowan

County, North Carolina}, Ephraim[3] {of Williamsburg, James City County, Virginia}, (Unknown)[2], James[1] {of Warwickshire, England}] Osborne of Ashe County, North Carolina. Her mother was Melissa Melvina[4] [John[3], Mathias[2] {of Bethlehem, Northampton County, Pennsylvania}, Mathias[1] {of Mulhausan, Moravia, Germany}] Weiss of Grayson County, Virginia. Issue, if any, is not known.

Emaline[8] had married, first, John Melvin Reedy on February 14, 1893 in Grayson County, Virginia. He was born on March 9, 1850 in Grayson County, Virginia. He died on January 4, 1947 in Grayson County, Virginia. His father was Jackson [John, Christopher Columbus {of Montgomery County, Pennsylvania}, George Peter] Reedy of Grayson County, Virginia. Her mother was Rebecca N. Henderson of Grayson County, Virginia. Emaline[8] and John had two children: Carl and Jessie Lee.

John had married, first, Susanne Anderson sometime before 1874 [when their first child was born] in Grayson County, Virginia. She was born on November 21, 1854 in Grayson County, Virginia. She died on April 4, 1930 [another researcher claims 1888] in Grayson County, Virginia. Her father was Isaac D.

[William] Anderson of Grayson County, Virginia. Her mother was Matilda Prichard of Grayson County, Virginia. John and Susanne had four children: Lovie, Laura, Beaulah and Ella.

4. Mary Jane[7] "Polly" Sturgill
born in 1813 [another researcher says 1810] at New River, Ashe County, North Carolina. She died on August 22, 1880 [another record says 1879] in Smyth County, Virginia. She married Luther David Mink in 1834 in Smyth County, Virginia. He was born circa 1807/1809 in Smyth County [but possibly in Washington County, where his parents were then living], Virginia. He died on July 21, 1892, in Smyth County, Virginia. His father was Peter Mink of Somerset County, Pennsylvania and later of Newton County, Missouri. His mother was Lavina [David {Wadkins}] Watkins of Pennsylvania [who had married, first, John Minton]. Mary[7] and Luther had four children:

a. Elizabeth Mink
born in 1843 in Smyth County, Virginia. Her date and place of death is not known. She married Marshall Mabe on March 21, 1862. He was born circa 1840.

b. Member Ann Mink

born in 1854 in Smyth County, Virginia. She died in 1928. She married Samuel[5] Rosenbaum on March 7, 1882 in Smyth County, Virginia. He was born on October 3, 1832 at Marion, Smyth County, Virginia. He died on September 16, 1901 at Marion, Smyth County, Virginia. His father was Adam Andrew[4] [John[3] {of Lancaster County, Pennsylvania}, Alexander[2], Antonius Conradus[1] {of Orlen, Kur-Pfalz, Germany}, Hans Bernard[1a] {of Katholisch Duelman, Muenster, Westfalen, Prussen}] Rosenbaum of South Fork of Holston River, Washington County, Virginia. His mother was Christiana[4] [Frederick[3] {of Lancaster County, Pennsylvania}, Thomas[2], Johann Thomas[1] {of Germany}, Johann Wolfgang[1a] {Koppenhoffer}, Jacob[2a]] Copenhaver of Shenandoah County, Virginia. Member and Samuel[5] had six children: Melissa[6], William[6], Mary[6], Luther[6], Charles[6] and Emery[6].

Samuel[5] had married, first, Elizabeth Miller O'Bryant [afa O'Brian and O'Bryan] on June 1, 1859 in Smyth County, Virginia. She was born on March 18, 1831 in Smyth County, Virginia. She died on January 12, 1877 in Smyth County, Virginia. The name of her father and mother is not known. Issue, if any, is not known.

c. Caroline Mink

born in 1850 in Smyth County, Virginia. Her date and place of death is not known. She married James C. Bogle/s in 1869. He was born circa 1845 in North Carolina. The name of his father and mother is not known. Issue, if any, is not known.

d. Lavina Jane Mink

born on May 29, 1852 in Smyth County, Virginia. She died on March 29, 1886 in Ashe County, North Carolina. She married Wiley Winton[6] Osborne on February 9, 1871, presumably in Ashe County, North Carolina. He was born on April 14, 1850 in Ashe County, North Carolina. He died on July 9, 1939 in Lancaster County, Pennsylvania. His father was Enoch[5] [Zachariah[4] {of Montgomery County, Virginia}, "Captain" Enoch[3] {of Yadkin River, Yadkin County, North Carolina}, Ephraim Washington[2] {of Grayson County, Virginia}, Jonathan[1] {of Warwickshire, England}, James[1a], John[2a] {of Ashford, Kent, England}, Thomas[3a]] Osborne of Ashe County, North Carolina. His mother was Ruth[7] [William[6] {of Grayson County, Virginia}, Timothy[5] {of Wallingford, New Haven County, Connecticut}, Joseph[4], Stephen[3], John[2], Edward[1] {of Hillmorton, Warwickshire, England}] Perkins of Ashe County,

North Carolina. Lavina and Wiley[6] had six children: Cordelia A.[7], Eva Ruth[7], Mary Denora[7], Muncie Mink[7], Alevia Levina[7] and Ada Ellen[7].

4. Nancy[7] Sturgill
born in 1815 in Ashe County, North Carolina. She died about 1890 in Ashe County, North Carolina. She married Solomon[6] Blevins circa 1840 in Ashe County, North Carolina. He was born circa 1819 in Ashe County, North Carolina. He died circa 1897 in Ashe County, North Carolina. His father was Jesse Lynch [who did not marry his mother] of Ashe County, North Carolina. His mother was Elizabeth[5] [Elisha[4], James[3], James[2], William[1] {of Liverpool, England}, William[1a] {of Wales}, Henry[2a] (Bleddyn), James[3a], William[4a], William[5a] {Blethen}, Gruffydd[6a] {Beleddyn}, John[7a] {Bleddyn}] Blevins of Ashe County, North Carolina. Nancy[7] and Solomon[6] had six children:

a. Mary[7] Blevins
born in 1841 in Ashe County, North Carolina. Her date and place of death is not known. She married Benjamin Franklin[7] Ball He was born on December 24, 1837 in North Carolina. He died on January 6, 1926 in North Carolina. His father was Joseph[6] [Nathan[5], John[4], William[3], Samuel[2], William[1] {of Wiltshire, England},

William[1a] {of London, England}, William[2a], John Paris[3a] {of Barkham Manor, Berkshire County, England}, John Paris[4a], William[5a], Robert[6a], William[7a] {born before 1446}] Ball of North Carolina. His mother was Hannah Pancoast [James, Basil, James] Brooke of North Carolina. Mary and Benjamin[7] had five children: Virginia[8], Ethel[8], Etta[8], Eliza[8] and William J.[8].

Benjamin[7] married, first, America Teague. Benjamin[7] and America had two children: Roby Lee[8] and John Franklin[8] [Editor's Note: No other information on this marriage has been found].

b. Francis Marion[7] Blevins
born on February 23, 1843 in Ashe County, North Carolina. He died on December 14, 1933 at Konnarock, Washington County, Virginia. He married Mary Ann[6] Blevins on July 19, 1862 in Ashe County, North Carolina. She was born on June 10, 1838 in Ashe County, North Carolina. She died on September 7, 1907 in Ashe County, North Carolina. Her father was Andrew Zachariah[5] [Joseph[4] {of Ashe County, North Carolina}, James[3] {of Montgomery County, Virginia}, James[2] {of Prince George County, Virginia}, William[1] {of Formby, Merseyside, England}, William[1a], Henry[2a] {of

North Meons, Lancashire, England}, James[3a] {Bleddyn of Llanasa, Flints North, Wales}, William[4a] {Blethyn of Mathern, Cymru, Gwent, Wales}, William[5a], Gruffyd[6a] {Bleddyn}, John[7a] {born circa 1450}] Blevins of Grayson County, Virginia. Her mother was Charity[7] [Aaron[6] {of Elkins Circle, Wilkes County, North Carolina}, William[5] {of Kent County, Delaware and later of Rowan County, North Carolina}, John[4] {of Bute County, which was later divided into Warren and Franklin Counties, North Carolina}, John[3] {of Perquimans County, North Carolina, William[2], John[1] {of England}, Haute[1a] {of Allington Castle, Maidstone, Kent, England}, George[2a], "Sir" Thomas[3a] "The Younger" {Wiat}, "Sir" Thomas[4a] "The Elder," "Sir" Henry[5a], Richard[6a], Robert[7a] {of Southange, Yorkshire, England}, William[8a], Adam Southange[9a], "Admiral" (Unknown)[10a] {born circa 1285} of Kent, England}] Wyatt of Grayson County, Virginia. Francis[7] and Mary Ann[6] had a child: Chloe Martha[8].

c. Jesse F. Lynch[7] Blevins
born on February 17, 1846 in Ashe County, North Carolina. He died on April 18, 1934 at Helton, Ashe County, North Carolina and was buried there in the Jesse Blevins Family Cemetery. He married Margaret[7] Stringer on

December 25, 1869 in Ashe County, North Carolina. She was born on January 2, 1852 in Grayson County, Virginia. She died on November 27, 1918 at Helton, Ashe County, North Carolina. Her father was Jefferson[6] [John[5], Reuben E.[4] {of Louisa County, Virginia}, Edward[3] {of Saluda Christ Church Parish, Middlesex County, Virginia}, Daniel[2], Josiah[1] {of Liverpoole, Lancashire, England and later of Norfolk County, Virginia}, Samuel[1a] {of Yorkshire, England}, William[2a] {of Rudgwick, Sussex, England}] Stringer of Ashe County, North Carolina. Her mother was Catherine Johnson of Ashe County, North Carolina. Issue, if any, is not known.

d. William Johnson[7] Blevins
    born on January 19, 1850 in Ashe County, North Carolina. He died on December 15, 1915 in Ashe County, North Carolina. He married Margaret Stuart on February 9, 1875 in Ashe County, North Carolina. She was born on August 24, 1835 in Ashe County, North Carolina. She died on April 29, 1937 in Ashe County, North Carolina. Her father was Jackson Stuart of Surry County, North Carolina. Her mother was Hiley [afa Ayla] Francis of Ash, Brunswick County, North Carolina. William[7] and Margaret had eight children: Casper C.[8],

Mary Ann[8], Soloman Jackson[8], Lula[8], Hiley Columbia[8], Frances[8] "Franky," Eliazer[8] "Eli" and Bettie[8].

e. Wilborn[7] "Bucky" Blevins
born on March 15, 1853 at Hilton, Ashe County, North Carolina. He died on August 13, 1928 at Sturgills, Ashe County, North Carolina and was buried there in the Blevins Cemetery.

f. Wesley[7] Blevins
born in 1855 at Hilton, Ashe County, North Carolina. His date and place of death is not known.

Soloman[6] Blevins married, second, Tobitha[8] [also found as Bertha] Ham on November 20, 1893 in Ashe County, North Carolina. She was born on June 6, 1848 in Ashe County, North Carolina. She died on April 9, 1933 in Ashe County, North Carolina and was buried there in the Jonathan Perry Cemetery. Her father was Levi[7] [Thomas[6] {of Virginia}, William[5] {of Elk Creek, Grayson County, Virginia}, Thomas[4], Thomas[3] {of Caroline County, Virginia}, Jerome[2] {of York County, Virginia}, Jerome[1] {of Bristol, Somersetshire, England}] Ham of Ashe County, North Carolina. Her mother was Milly Taylor of Rutherford County, North Carolina. Solomon[6] Blevins and Tobitha[8] Ham had no issue.

Tobitha[8] had married, first, Solomon[3] Perry on December 23, 1863 in Ashe County, North Carolina. Solomon[3] was born on April 5, 1805 in Ashe County, North Carolina. He died on November 23, 1890 at Horse Creek, Ashe County, North Carolina. His father was Richard[2] [Solomon[1] {of England] Perry of Wilkes County, North Carolina. His mother was Catherine[6] [Cornelius[5] {of Ashe County, North Carolina}, Cornelius[4] {of Raritan, Somerset County, New Jersey}, Cornelius[3], Cornelius[2], Cornelius[1] {of Flanders, Holland}, Cornelius[1a]] Vanover of Virginia. Tobitha[8] and Solomon[3] had seven children:

i. Emanuel Huffman[4] Perry
    born on December 26, 1866 in Ashe County, North Carolina. He died on December 9, 1903 in McDowell County, West Virginia. He married Effie Candis[5] Sheets [the sister of Ellis[5] Sheets who married Emanuel[4]'s sister Mildred[4]] on January 28, 1887 in Grayson County, Virginia. She was born on January 4, 1870 at Mouth of Wilson, Grayson County, Virginia. She died on January 29, 1949 in Smyth County, Virginia. Her father was Jordan[4] [Catherine[3] {Sheets who had a son Jordan[4] by Absolom C. Bower, the son of John Bower of Ashe County, North

141

Carolina}, Andrew[2] {of Rowan County, North Carolina, Martin[1] {of Germany}] Sheets of Peak Creek, Ashe County, North Carolina. Her mother was Easter[5] [George Washington[4], Christian[3], George[2], Michael George[1] {of Germany}] Miller of Ashe County, North Carolina. Emanuel[4] and Effie[5] had four children: Mary Easter[5], Lester[5], Baxter[5] and Ellis L.[5].

j. James Gentry[4] Perry
born on December 6, 1869 in Ashe County, North Carolina. He died on May 14, 1950 in Washington County, Virginia. He married Elzina Senatta[5] Miller on February 5, 1886 in Ashe County, North Carolina. She was born on February 5, 1869 in Ashe County, North Carolina. She died on December 25, 1940 in Smyth County, Virginia. Her father was Harrison Baker[4] [George Washington[3], Christian[2], Carmichael[1] {afa Carmikle Mueller of Germany}] Miller of Ashe County, North Carolina. Her mother was Phoebe Jane [Jason, Isaac {of Weaver's Ford, Ashe County, North Carolina}] Weaver of Ashe County, North Carolina. James[4] and Elzina[5] had ten children: Ada Imogene[5], Albert H.[5], Alonzo L.[5], Lee Bryan[5], Edith Minerva[5] "Minnie," Minerva Eldora[5], Nelia Rosetta[5], (Infant)[5], Sally A.[5] "Lelia," and

Howard L.[5].

k. Mildred E.[4] "Millie" Perry
born in 1871 in Ashe County, North Carolina.
She died in 1945, possibly in Smyth County,
Virginia. She married Ellis[5] Sheets [the brother
of Effie[5] Sheets who married Mildred[4]'s brother
Emanuel[4]] on January 22, 1888 in Ashe County,
North Carolina. He was born on July 25, 1863 in
Ashe County, North Carolina. He died on June
14, 1948 in Smyth County, Virginia. His father
was Jordan[4] [Catherine[3] {Sheets who had a son
Jordan[4] by Absolom C. Bower, the son of John
Bower of Ashe County, North Carolina},
Andrew[2] {of Rowan County, North Carolina,
Martin[1] {of Germany}] Sheets of Peak Creek,
Ashe County, North Carolina. His mother was
Easter[5] [George Washington[4], Christian[3],
George[2], Michael George[1] {of Germany}] Miller
of Ashe County, North Carolina. Mildred[4] and
Ellis[5] had two children: Ettie[6] and Horten P.[6].

l. Luvenie M.[4] [afa Lavenia] Perry
born on January 23, 1873 in Ashe County,
North Carolina. She died on November 23, 1904
in Ashe County, North Carolina. She married
[as his second wife] Nelson[4] Ham on December
31, 1888 in Ashe County, North Carolina. He
was born on February 20, 1856 in Ashe County,

North Carolina. He died on December 15, 1934 in Casey County, Kentucky. His father was Larkin[3] [Thomas[2] {of Ashe County, North Carolina}, William[1] {Hamm of Hamm, Norderheim-Westfalen, Germany and later of Newberry, Newberry County, South Carolina}] Ham of Virginia. His mother was Rebecca[5] [Richard[4] {of Sussex County, New Jersey}, Cornelius[3], Cornelius[2], Cornelius[1] {of Flanders, Holland}, Cornelius[1a]}] Vanover of Ashe County, North Carolina. Luvenie[4] and Nelson[4] had two children: Lillard[5] and Nettie Elizabeth[5].

Nelson[4] married, first, Amanda Roark in 1873 in Ashe County, North Carolina. She was born on September 15, 1856, presumably in Ashe County, North Carolina. She died on January 22, 1876 in Ashe County, North Carolina. The name of her father is not known. Her mother was Sarah [Jesse, Charles {of Augusta County, Virginia}] Roark of Ashe County, North Carolina. Nelson[4] and Amanda had two children: Dorothy Canzadia[5] and Edward[5].

Nelson[4] married, third, Rhoda J. Calhoun, presumably in Ashe County, North Carolina. She was born in May 1882, presumably in Ashe County, North Carolina. She died in 1919 in Ashe County, North Carolina. Her father was

James Porter [Felix Anderson, James {of Surry County, North Carolina}, William {of Duck Creek, Kent County, Delaware}, William] Calhoun of Ashe County, North Carolina. Her mother was Mary J. [Ransom, Bennett] Phillips of North Carolina. Nelson[4] and Rhoda had five children: Ira[5], Wiley E.[5] and three whose names are not known.

m. Abigail Bertha[4] Perry
born circa 1875 in Ashe County, North Carolina. Her date and place of death is not known.

n. Nancy Elizabeth[4] Perry
born on May 6, 1878 in Ashe County, North Carolina. She died on May 20, 1960 in Carter County, Tennessee. She married Roby Ross Roark. The date of their marriage in Ashe County, North Carolina is not known. He was born on May 11, 1874 in Ashe County, North Carolina. He died on December 13, 1928 in Carter County, Tennessee. His father was Nathaniel Wiley [Charles B. {of Virginia}, Charles] Roark of Ashe County, North Carolina. His mother was Martha L. [Nathaniel Perry {of Rowan County, North Carolina}] Canter of Ashe County, North Carolina. Nancy[4] and Roby had at least one child: Bertha Mae.

o. Eve Elizabeth[4] Perry
born on March 30, 1886 in Ashe County, North Carolina. She died on May 18, 1953 in Ashe County, North Carolina. She married Robert Johnson Blevins on September 30, 1901 in Ashe County, North Carolina. He was born on September 25, 1881 in Ashe County, North Carolina. He died on January 30, 1967. His place of death is not known. His father was Francis Marion [Solomon, Jesse Lynch {father who did not marry the mother}] Blevins of Ashe County, North Carolina. His mother was Mary Ann[6] [Andrew Z.[5] {of Ashe County, North Carolina}, Joseph[4], James Dilton[3] {of England and later of Bridal Creek, Grayson County, Virginia}, Jack[2] {of Prince George County, Maryland}, William[1] {of Fromby, Wales}, William[1a], Henry[2a] {Bleddyn of North Meons, Lancashire, England}, James[3a] {of Uansa, Flints North, Wales}, William[4a] {Blethyn of Mathern, Cymru, Gwent, Wales}, William[5a] {of Llandoff, Morgannwg, Cymru, Wales}, Gruffydd[6a], John[7a] {born circa 1450}] Blevins of Virginia. Issue, if any, is not known.

Solomon[3] Perry had married, first, Elizabeth Ham sometime before 1826 [when their first child was born] in Ashe County, North Carolina. Elizabeth was born circa 1805 in North Carolina. Her date and place of death is not known. The name of her father and mother is not known. Solomon[3] and Elizabeth had eight children:

a. Levi[4] Perry
born circa 1826 in Ashe County, North Carolina. His date and place of death is not known. He married Catherine (Unknown) in 1849 in Ashe County, North Carolina. She was born in 1821 in Ashe County, North Carolina. Her date and place of death is not known. The name of her father and mother is not known. Levi[4] and Catherine had four children: Elizabeth[5], Soloman[5], Jane[5] and Stephen[5].

b. Richard[4] Perry
born on July 7, 1828 in Ashe County, North Carolina. He died on August 21, 1913 in Ashe County, North Carolina. He married Evaline[3] Ham on August 24, 1852 in Ashe County, North Carolina. She was born in 1832 in Ashe County, North Carolina. She died on March 5, 1916 in Ashe County, North Carolina. Her father was Thomas[2] [William[1] {Hamm of Hamm, Norderheim-Westfalen, Germany and later of Newberry, Newberry County, South Carolina}] Ham of Ashe County, North Carolina. Her mother was Ann[7] [Zachariah[6] {of Overton County, Tennessee}, John[5] {of Knoxville, Knox County,

Tennessee}, Thomas[4] {of Prince Georges County, Maryland}, John[3] {of Talbott County, Maryland}, John[2] {Aldridge of Northumberland County, Virginia}, George[1] {of Worstead, Norfolk, England}] Eldridge of Grayson County, Virginia. Richard[4] and Evaline[3] had five children: Edith[5], Elizabeth[5], Wiley[5], Rhoda Sara[5] and Jonathan[5].

c. William[4] Perry
born circa 1830 in Ashe County, North Carolina. His date and place of death is not known. He married Jane Taylor on June 6, 1860 in Whitley County, Kentucky. She was born circa 1841 in Ashe County, North Carolina. Her date and place of death is not known. Her father was William "Hootie Bill" [John {of Virginia}] Taylor {born 1821} of Ashe County, North Carolina. Her mother was Mary[3] "Polly" [Richard[2] {of Wilkes County, North Carolina}, Solomon[1] {of England}] Perry of Ashe County, North Carolina. Issue, if any, is not known.

d. Jane[4] Perry
born circa 1833 in Ashe County, North Carolina. Her date and place of death is not known. She had a child out of wedlock: Jefferson D. {Perry}.

e. Catherine[4] Perry
born circa 1838 in Ashe County, North Carolina. Her date and place of death is not known. She married (Unknown) Ham.

f. Edith[4] "Eda" Perry
born on January 9, 1843 in Ashe County, North Carolina. She died on September 29, 1919 in Ashe County, North Carolina. She married James A.[6] Greer on November 17, 1865 in Ashe County, North Carolina. He was born on October 29, 1839 in Ashe County, North Carolina. He died on April 1, 1925 in Ashe County, North Carolina. His father was Alexander[5] [James[4] {of Wilkes County, North Carolina}, Benjamin[3] {of Albemarle County, Virginia}, John[2] {of Gunpowder River, Baltimore County, Maryland}, James[1] {of Capenoch, Dumfrieshire, Scotland}, James[1a], William[2a] {Grierson, born circa 1550}] Greer of Tennessee. His mother was Lydia ""Diddy" [Ezekiel {of Stokes County, North Carolina}, James {of Northam, Goochland County, Virginia}, John {of Charles Parish, York County, Virginia}, Edward {of Curdsville, Buckingham County, Virginia}, William, John] Curd of Carter County, Tennesee and later of Grayson County, Virginia. Edith[4] and James[6] had nine children: Nancy B.[7], William Andrew[7], Alexander F.[7],

James Madison[7], Wiley[7], Lydia J.[7], Rhoda[7], Rosa[7] and Cora E.[7].

g. Jonathan[4] Perry
born circa 1840/1841 in Ashe County, North Carolina. His date and place of death is not known.

h. Mary[4] Perry
date of birth in Ashe County, North Carolina is not known. Her date and place of death is not known [she may have died young].

6. **Joshua[7] Sturgill**
born on December 9, 1816 in Ashe County, North Carolina. He died on August 30, 1894 in Ashe County, North Carolina. He married Phoebe Marilda[9] Weaver on November 30, 1865 in Ashe County, North Carolina. She was born on July 14, 1849 at Weaver's Ford, Ashe County, North Carolina. She died on March 15, 1936 in Ashe County, North Carolina. Her father was Andrew[8] [Isaac Vance[7], William[6], Joshua[5], Samuel[4], Samuel[3], William[2], Samuel[1] {of Shropshire, England}, Thomas[1a], William[2a], Griffith[3a], Jenkin[4a], John[5a], Thomas[6a], Walter[7a], Thomas[8a], Walter[9a], Walter[10a], Walter[11a], Humphrey[12a], Ieuan[13a] {of Wales}, Madoc[14a], Hywel Vychan[15a]] Weaver of Weaver's Ford, Ashe County, North Carolina. Her mother

was Malinda^8 [Isaac^7, Isaac^6, Joshua^5, Samuel^4, Samuel^3, William^2, Samuel^1 {of Shropshire, England}, Thomas^{1a}, William^{2a}, Griffith^{3a}, Jenkin^{4a}, John^{5a}, Thomas^{6a}, Walter^{7a}, Thomas^{8a}, Walter^{9a}, Walter^{10a}, Walter^{11a}, Humphrey^{12a}, Ieuan^{13a} {of Wales}, Madoc^{14a}, Hywel Vychan^{15a}] Weaver of Ashe County, North Carolina. Joshua^7 and Phoebe^9 had eight children: John Andrew^8, William Byrum^8, Francis Lee^8, Joel Johnson^8, James Estil^8, Laura Malinda^8, Isom^8, Isaac Millard^8.

7. Jane^7 Sturgill

born in 1824 in Ashe County, North Carolina. Her date and place of death is not known. She married Andrew Jackson^7 Porter circa 1853 in Ashe County, North Carolina. He was born circa 1825 in Ashe County, North Carolina. His date and place of death is not known [some researchers say 1862 in Mississippi, but has not been verified]. His father was Landlot Lott^6 "Lotty" [Jedithah^5 {of Lancaster County, Virginia}, Edward Sanders^4, John^3, Thomas^2 {of Westmoreland County, Virginia}, Edward^1 {of England}] Porter of Brown's Creek, Union County, South Carolina. His mother was Rachel Nelson of Union County, South Carolina. Jane^7 and Andrew^7 had seven children:

a. William^8 Porter

date of birth in Ashe County, North Carolina is

not known. His date and place of death is not known.

b. Joshua Franklin[8] Porter
born on January 23, 1845 in Ashe County, North Carolina. He died on April 9, 1904 in Ashe County, North Carolina. He married Catherine[4] Blevins circa 1871 in Ashe County, North Carolina. She was born on February 25, 1839 in Ashe County, North Carolina. She died in 1875. Her father was George[3] [James B.[2] {of Montgomery County, Virginia}, James Dilton[1] {of England}] Blevins of Ashe County, North Carolina. Her mother was Lydia [James, John {of Granville County, North Carolina}] Duncan of Ashe County, North Carolina. Joshua[8] and Catherine[4] had two children: George Washington[9] and Louettra[9] "Ettie."

Joshua[8] married, second, Phoebe Caroline West circa 1876 in Ashe County, North Carolina. She was born on August 13, 1855 in Smyth County, Virginia. She died in 1887, presumably in Ashe County, North Carolina. Her father was William H. [George Henry {of Pennsylvania}, Christopher {of Washington County, Virginia}] West of Smyth County, Virginia. Her mother was Martha Ann[7] [Reason[6], Joseph[5] {of Frederick County, Maryland}, Samuel[4], Thomas[3] {of

Prince George's County, Maryland}, Thomas[2] {of Anne Arundel County, Maryland}, Thomas[1] {of Ringmer, Sussex County, England}] Plummer of Smyth County, Virginia. Joshua[8] and Phoebe had two children: Jane[9] [afa Jennie] and Martha Ida[9].

Joshua[8] married, third, Melissa[8] Spencer on April 1, 1889 in Ashe County, North Carolina. She was born on February 9, 1860 in Virginia. She died on December 29, 1934. Her father was William[7] [Isaac[6], Isaac[5] {of Fincastle County, Virginia}, Joseph Charles[4] {of Lee County, Virginia}, William D.[3] {of North Carolina}, Alexander[2], Nicholas[1] {of Cople, Bedfordshire, England}, Nicholas[1a], Nicholas[2a], Robert[3a], Thomas[4a], John[5a], Robert[6a], John[7a], Robert[8a], Thomas[9a], Henry[10a], Thomas[11a] {of Badby, Northamptonshire, England}, Nicholas[12a] {le DeSpencer of Difford, Worcestershire, England}, John[13a], William[14a], John[15a] {of Swolelfield, Bedfordshire, England}, Gafridus[16a] "Geoffrey," Gafridus[17a], Thurston[18a] {of London, Middlesex, England}, William Talvas[19a] {of Elington, Lincolnshire, England}, Robert[20a], Amaury Raoul[21a] {D'Albetot, born 1066}] Spencer of Virginia. Her mother was Mahala[8] "Aley" [Isaac Vance[7] {of Weaver's Ford, Ashe County, North Carolina}, William[6] {of Halifax, Halifax County,

Virginia}, Joshua[5] {of New Kent County, Virginia}, Samuel[4], William[3] {of Charles River County, which later became York County, Virginia}, William[2], Samuel[1] {of Shropshire, England}, Thomas[1a], William[2a]] Weaver of Virginia. Joshua[8] and Melissa[8] had two children: Laura[9] and Franklin[9].

c. Wesley[8] Porter
   date of birth in Ashe County, North Carolina is not known. His date and place of death is not known.

d. Troy[8] Porter
   date of birth in Ashe County, North Carolina is not known. His date and place of death is not known.

e. Phebe[8] Porter
   date of birth in Ashe County, North Carolina is not known. Her date and place of death is not known.

f. Cicero[8] Porter
   born in 1857 in Ashe County, North Carolina. His date and place of death is not known. He married Phoebe Sarah[6] Jones sometime before 1884 [when their first child was born] in Ashe County, North Carolina. She was born in 1859

in Ashe County, North Carolina. Her date and place of death is not known. Her father was William[5] Jonathan[4], Joseph Walker[3] {of St. John's Parish, Prince Georges County, Maryland}, Ellis[2] {of Chester County, Pennsylvania}, Ellis[1] {of Carnavon, Carnavonshire, Wales}, Richard[1a] {of Holyhead, Anglesey, Wales}] Jones of Helton, Ashe County, North Carolina. Her mother was Rebecca[7] [Francis[6] Jr., Francis[5] Sr., James[4], James[3], John Daniel[2], John[1] {of North Petherton Parish, Somersetshire, England}, Richard[1a], George[2a]] Sturgill of Ashe County, North Carolina. Cicero[8] and Phoebe[6] had three children: Robert[9], Barnett Oscar[9] and Fannie Victoria[9].

g. Wiley[8] Porter
date of birth in Ashe County, North Carolina is not known. His date and place of death is not known.

8. Rebecca[7] Sturgill
born on May 13, 1825 in Ashe County, North Carolina. She died on May 20, 1896 at Helton Creek, Sturgills, Ashe County, North Carolina. She married William[3] Jones circa 1852/1853 [before their first child was born] in Ashe County, North Carolina. He was born in 1824 at Helton, Ashe County, North Carolina. He died sometime before

1880 in Ashe County, North Carolina. His father was Jonathan[2] [Joseph[1] {of Wales and later of Maryland}] Jones of Ashe County, North Carolina. His mother was Nancy[2] [Johann Thomas[1] {of Lichtenberg, Brandenburg, Prussia}, Johann Jacob[1a], Harvey[2a], Lewis[3a], Robert E.[4a]] Testerman of Ashe County, North Carolina. Rebecca[7] and William[3] had six children:

a. Polly[4] Jones
   born circa 1853 in Ashe County, North Carolina. Her date and place of death is not known.

b. Laurinda Laura[4] Jones
   born circa 1854 at Helton, Ashe County, North Carolina. She died in 1925 at Little Britain, Lancaster County, Pennsylvania. She married Ambrose[4] Weaver on October 1, 1874 in Ashe County, North Carolina. He was born on November 17, 1849 at Horse Creek, Ashe County, North Carolina. He died on August 12, 1910. His place of death is not known. His father was Elihu[3] [Joshua[2] {of Lee County, Virginia}, William[1] {of England}] Weaver of Ashe County, North Carolina. His mother was Jane Jennie Miller of Ashe County, North Carolina. Laurinda[4] and Ambrose[4] had six children: William Wiley[5], James Bethal[5], Victoria Alic[5], Flora Jane[5], Arthur[5] and Rosa Belle[5].

156

c. Jarvis[4] Jones

born circa 1856 in Ashe County, North Carolina. He died sometime after 1930 at Linn, Cedar County, Missouri. He married Zilpha Bethany Phipps on February 4, 1875 at Helton, Ashe County, North Carolina. She was born on September 4, 1856 in Ashe County, North Carolina. She died on August 30, 1937 in Ashe County, North Carolina. Her father was James [John] Harvey Phipps of Bridle Creek, Grayson County, Virginia. Her mother was Evaline[8] [Joshua[7] {of Weaver's Ford, Wilkes County, North Carolina}, William[6] {of Halifax, Halifax County, Virginia, Joshua[5] {of New Kent County, Virginia}, Samuel[4], William[3] {of Charles River County, which later became York County, Virginia}, William[2], Samuel[1] {of Shropshire, England}, Thomas[1a], William[2a]] Weaver of Whitetop, Grayson County, Virginia. Jarvis[4] and Zilpha had five children: Minnie[5], William Harvey[5], Boydon[5], Lola Belle[5] and Byman[5].

Zilpha married, second, Daniel Miller in 1902 in Ashe County, North Carolina. He was born circa 1855/1857 in Ashe County, North Carolina. He died on December 24, 1935 in Ashe County, North Carolina. The name of his father and mother is not known. There was no issue.

d. Bethel[4] Jones
born on December 23, 1855 in Ashe County, North Carolina. He died on February 26, 1940 at Duhring, Mercer County, West Virginia. He married Lelar (Unknown) in 1889 in Ashe County, North Carolina. She was born in May 1869 in North Carolina. She apparently died before 1902 [when Bethel[4] remarried], presumably in Ashe County, North Carolina. Bethel[4] and Lelar had two children: Ambrose[5] and Frank[5].

Bethel[4] married, second, Mary Katherine Powers on November 27, 1902 in Ashe County, North Carolina. She was born in May 1868 in Ashe County, North Carolina. She died on September 2, 1936 at Goodwill, Mercer County, West Virginia. Her father was James [Searl] Powers of Ashe County, North Carolina. Her mother was Susan Burkett of Ashe County, North Carolina. Bethel[4] and Mary had four children: Oscar[5], Anna Laura[5], Carrie E.[5] and Walter Cecil[5].

e. Phebe Sarah[4] Jones
born circa 1860 in Ashe County, North Carolina. Her date and place of death is not known. She married Cicero Porter sometime before 1884 [when their first child was born] in Ashe

County, North Carolina. He was born in 1857 in Ashe County, North Carolina. His date and place of death is not known. His father was Andrew Jackson[7] [Landlot Lott[6] "Lotty" {of Brown's Creek, Union County, South Carolina}, Jedithah[5] {of Lancaster County, Virginia}, Edward Sanders[4], John[3], Thomas[2] {of Westmoreland County, Virginia}, Edward[1] {of England}] Porter of Ashe County, North Carolina. His mother was Rachel Nelson of Union County, North Carolina. His mother was Jane[7] [Francis[6] Jr., Francis[5] Sr., James[4], James[3], John Daniel[2], John[1] {North Petherton Parish, Somersetshire, England}, Richard[1a], George[2a]] Sturgill of Ashe County, North Carolina. Phoebe[6] and Cicero[8] had three children: Robert[9], Barnett Oscar[9] and Fannie Victoria[9].

f. William Huffman[4] Jones
    born on October 26, 1863 in Ashe County, North Carolina. He died on February 5, 1942 at Rock, Mercer County, West Virginia. He married Zelda [afa Zilah] Elizabeth Pennington sometime before 1887 [when their first child was born] in Ashe County, North Carolina. She was born in 1868 in Ashe County, North Carolina. She died in 1900 in Ashe County, North Carolina. Her father was Elisha "Doc" [Samuel {although some researchers call him Levi}]

Pennington of either Wilkes County, North Carolina or Grayson County, Virginia. Her mother was Tabitha Jane [Jesse] Anderson of Grayson County, Virginia. William[4] and Zelda had eight children: Whitlow R.[5] and Dora Alice[5], Dalla Jane[5], Oscar[5], Hasque[5], Smith[5], Hattie[5] and Maggie L.[5].

William[4] married, second, as her fourth husband, Julia Anne "Julie" Burton on November 11, 1914 in Mercer County, West Virginia. She was born on April 29, 1856 at Goodwill, Mercer County, West Virginia. She died of heart disease on July 9, 1942 at Goodwill, Mercer County, West Virginia. Her father was Elias [Travis {of Giles County, Virginia}, Elias {of Tazewell, Tazewell County, Virginia}] Burton of Bland County, Virginia. Her mother was Elvira Sarah [Andrew M.] Stowers of Clear Fork, Bland County, Virginia. William[4] and Julia had no issue.

Julia had married, first, John S.[5] Bailey circa 1872 in Mercer County, West Virginia. He was born circa 1848 in Botetourt County, Virginia. He died on May 18, 1883 in Mercer County, West Virginia. His father was Floyd Richard[4] [Samuel L.[3] {Montcalm, Tazewell County, Virginia}, Richard Peyton[2], Jr. {of the Blackwater Section, Bedford, now Franklin, County, Virginia}, Richard Peyton[1] {of Wigan, Lancashire, England}] Bailey of Mercer County, West Virginia. His mother was Zelphia Sulfrany Adeline "Zylphia" [John S. {of Grayson, Cabell County, West Virginia}, John {of Botetourt County, Virginia} Mooney of Rock, Mercer County, West Virginia. John[5] and Julia had a child: Alexander L.[6].

Julia had married, second, John Harrison[5] Bailey on March 11, 1875 in Mercer County, West Virginia. He was born circa 1858 in Mercer, Loudoun County, Virginia. He died on May 7 1883 in Mercer County, West Virginia. His father was James Madison[4] [William[3] {of Tazewell, Tazewell County, Virginia}, Reuben[2], Richard Peyton[1] {of Wigan, Lancashire, England}, James[1a], Samuel L.[2a], Edward[3a] {Bayley}]] Bailey of Mercer County, West Virginia. His mother was Sarah "Sally" Strong of Virginia. Julia and John[5] had eight children: E. S.[6], Bell Zora[6] "Belzora," Josephine S.[6], George Kelley[6], William P.[6], Sarah J.[6], Blackburn B.[6] and Emma Zella[6].

Julia had married, third, (Unknown) Tilley in 1897 in Mercer County, West Virginia. Julia and (Unknown) Tilley had no issue.

9. Elizabeth[7] "Betsey" Sturgill
   born in 1827 in Ashe County, North Carolina. She
   died sometime between 1866 [when her last child
   was born] and 1871 [when Eli[6] remarried] in
   Grayson County, Virginia. She married Eli[6] Blevins
   in 1849, either in Ashe County, North Carolina or
   in Grayson County, Virginia. He was born on
   March 15, 1832 in Ashe County, Virginia. He died
   in 1901 in Washington County, Virginia. His father
   was Wells[5] [James B.[4] {of Grayson County,
   Virginia}, James Dilton[3] {of Montgomery County,
   Virginia}, James D.[2] {of Prince George County,
   Virginia}, William[1] {of Fromby, Wales}, William[1a],
   Henry[2a] {Bleddyn of North Meons, Lancashire,
   England}, James[3a] {of North Wales}, William[4a]
   {Blethyn of Mathern, Monouthshire, Wales},
   William[5a] {Blethin, born circa 1546, of Llandaff,
   Morgannwyg, Cymru, Wales}] Blevins of Ashe
   County, North Carolina. His mother was
   Elizabeth[5] [Abraham[4] {of Rowan County, North
   Carolina}, Ephraim[3] {of Morris, Morris County,
   New Jersey}, Ephraim[2] {of New Haven County,
   Connecticut}, Ephraim[1] {of England}] Pennington
   of Ashe County, North Carolina. Elizabeth[7] and
   Eli[6] had eight children: Sarah Ann[7], Melvina[7],
   Granville[7], Wiley Haywood[7], Lydia[7], Susan[7], John
   W.[7] and Martha J.[7].

   Eli[6] married, second, Susan Rouse on June 1, 1871

in Washington County, Virginia. She was born circa 1829/1833 in Washington County, Virginia. She died on January 5, 1917 in Washington County, Virginia. Her father was Phillip Issac [Philip] Rouse of Lee County, Virginia. Her mother was Margaret Rowe of Washington County, Virginia. There was no issue.

The Life and Times of
Francis[5] Sturgill, Sr.

PATERNAL ANCESTRY: [STURGILL/STODGILL: James[4], James[3], John Daniel[2], John[1] {of North Petherton Parish, Somersetshire, England}, Richard[1a], George[2a]]

MATERNAL ANCESTRY: [CALLOWAY: Susannah Ann, Joseph, Joseph]

FRANCIS[5] was born circa 1755 at Standardsville, Swift Run Creek, Orange County, Virginia. He died in December 1807 at Piney Creek, Ashe County, North Carolina. His father was James[4] Stodgill of Orange County, Virginia and later of Ashe County, North Carolina. His mother was Susannah Ann Calloway of Orange County, Virginia.

FRANCIS[5] married Rebecca[3] Hash in 1776 in Virginia. She was born circa 1758 in Montgomery County, Virginia. She died in 1841 at Piney Creek, Ashe County, North Carolina. Her father was John[2] [John[1] {Hache of England and later of Montgomery County, Virginia}, Thomas[1a] {born circa 1602 of Tenterden, Kent, England}] Hash of Grayson County and later of Montgomery County, Virginia. Her mother was Rebecca [Jacob] Anderson of Fincastle, Grayson County, Virginia.

FRANCIS[5] served with the Virginia Militia during the Revolutionary War.

FRANCIS[5] was living on the New River farm in 1807 when he died. The farm was known as the "Wells Place" in Ashe County, North Carolina. The farm was in five tracts, two of which he'd purchased from Zacharia Wells. The other three tracts were granted to Francis[5] by the State on grants #3, #4 and #5 — Ashe County, North Carolina. Later the farm became known locally as the McMillan farm.

The Children of
Francis[5] Sturgill, Sr.
and Rebecca[3] Hash

1. Lydia[6] Sturgill
born on February 25, 1778 in Grayson County, Virginia. She died on June 15, 1861 in Allegheny County, North Carolina. She married Solomon Columbus[7] Parsons in 1796 in Rutherford County, North Carolina. He was born on June 5, 1772 at Turkey Knob, Allegheny County, North Carolina. He died on January 18, 1860 in Allegheny County, North Carolina and is buried there near Turkey Knob in the Parsons Cemetery. His father was William Robert[6] [Robert[5], Jonathan[4], Jonathan[3], Jeffery[2], Jephery[1] {of Loddiswell, Devonshire, England}, Jephery[1a]] Parsons of Albemarle Parish,

Surry County, Virginia. His mother was Mary[2] "Polly" [William[1] {of Dent, Yorkshire, England and later of Sussex, Surrey County, Virginia}, William[1a] {of Edinbourgh, Midlothian, Scotland}]] Craig of Turkey Knob, Allegheny County, North Carolina. Lydia[6] and Solomon[7] had fifteen children:

a. John[8] Parsons
born on January 19, 1805 in Ashe County, North Carolina. He died on January 24, 1794 at Turkey Knob, Allegheny County, North Carolina. He married Margaret Gambill in 1825. She was born circa 1802/1805 in Ashe County, North Carolina. She died in 1838 in Allegheny County, North Carolina. Her father was William [Martin Cleveland {of Culpeper County, Virginia}] Gambill of Wilkes County, North Carolina. Her mother was Cynthia Cox of Wilkes County, North Carolina. John[8] and Margaret had six children: Lydia[9], Cynthia[9], William[9], Solomon Columbus[9] II, Sarah[9] and John Stokes[9].

John[8] married, second, Phebe[4] Laxton in 1846, presumably in Allegheny County, North Carolina. She was born in 1822 in Virginia. She died in 1904 in Allegheny County, North Carolina. Her father was Thomas[3] [Thomas[2], Thomas[1] {of Scotland and later of Anne Arundel County,

Maryland}] Laxton of Wilkes County, North Carolina. Her mother was Ruth Green of Wilkes County, North Carolina. John[8] and Phebe[4] had nine children: Phebe Ella[9], David Freedland[9], Thomas Floyd[9], Joseph Melvin[9], Ruth Manderville[9], Robert Cleveland[9], George Douglas[9], Levi Gordon[9] and Mary Jane[9].

b. Rebecca[8] Parsons
born circa 1806 in Ashe [or Allegheny] County, North Carolina. She died on August 5, 1868 in Grayson County, Virginia. She married Alvin Dixon in 1827 in Ashe County, North Carolina. He was born in 1804 in Ashe County, North Carolina. He died sometime after 1843 in Grayson County, Virginia. His father was Moses Dixon of Grayson County, Virginia and later of Allegheny County, North Carolina. His mother was Sarah ["Captain" Enoch {of Rowan County, North Carolina}, Ephraim {of Williamsburg, James City, County, Virginia} Osborne of Montgomery County, Virginia. Rebecca[8] and Alvin had seven children: Solomon, Levi Preston, Drucilla, Lydia J., Mazie Dell, Emeline and Matilda.

c. Robert S.[8] Parsons
born in 1807 in Ashe County, North Carolina. He died on December 2, 1870 in Wise County,

Virginia. He married, first, Elizabeth Wells on May 7, 1832 in Harlan County, Kentucky. She was born in 1807 in Virginia. She died in 1845, probably in Harlan County, Kentucky. The name of her father and mother is not known. Robert[8] and Elizabeth had six children: Rebecca[9], Abigail[9], Ira Clay[9], Nancy[9], Margaret[9] and Robert C.[9].

Robert[8] married, second, Anna L. Blanton in 1846, presumably in Harlan County, Kentucky. She was born circa 1830 in Virginia. She died in 1859, probably in Harlan County, Kentucky. Her father was William Blanton. Her mother was Elizabeth (Unknown). Robert[8] and Anna had seven children: Caldonia[9], Joseph Franklin[9], Craig[9], Lavina[9], Elizabeth[9], John Liburn[9] and Mary Ann[9] "Polly."

d. Marion[8] Parsons
   born circa 1810 in Ashe County, North Carolina. His date and place of death is not known [he may have died young].

e. Caleb[8] Parsons
   born on November 22, 1812 in Ashe County, North Carolina. He died on April 12, 1909 in Ashe County, North Carolina. He married Katherine[5] Landreth on October 27, 1836 in

Ashe County, North Carolina. She was born on October 26, 1812 in Ashe County, North Carolina. She died on August 29, 1900 in Allegheny County, North Carolina. Her father was Benjamin[4] [Stephen[3], William[2] {of Augusta County, Virginia}, Thomas[1] {of Hume, Borders, Scotland}, James[1a] {of Coldstream, Borders, Scotland}, George[2a], Patrick[3a] {born circa 1583 of Berwick, Scotland] Landreth of Ashe County, North Carolina. Her mother was Temperence "Tempa" Lawrence of North Carolina. Caleb[8] and Katherine[5] had nine children: Franklin B.[9], Alexandra D.[9], Charles Monroe[9], Joseph Conrad[9], Volney Carson[9], Lucy Matilda[9], Lydia E.[9], Justin[9] and Sarah[9].

f. William B.[8] Parsons

born on September 22, 1815 in Ashe County, North Carolina. He died on August 8, 1853 in Allegheny County, North Carolina. He married Lucinda[7] Halsey on March 26, 1846 in Ashe County, North Carolina. She was born on October 21, 1827 at Piney Creek, Allegheny County, North Carolina. She died on July 3, 1887 in Yancy County, North Carolina. Her father was William[6] "Bucky" [William[5] {of Columbia, Warren County, New Jersey}, William[4] {of Morris County, New Jersey}, Recompense[3], Nathaniel[2] {of Southhampton,

Suffok County, New York}, Thomas[1] {of Kempston, Bedfordshire, England}, Thomas[1a] {of Golden Parsonage, Great Gaddesden, Hertfordshire, England}, Robert[2a] {known as Robert Halsey Chambers}, Thomas[3a] {Halsey Chambers}, John[4a] {Halsey Chambers, born circa 1498}] Halsey of Grayson County, Virginia. His mother was Judah Peak/e of Grayson County, Virginia. William[8] and Lucinda[7] had four children: Lafeyette[9], Mastin[9], Caldona[9] and John C.[9]

g. Joseph B.[8] Parsons
born on November 9, 1820 in Wise County, Virginia. He died on November 9, 1868 in Allegheny County, North Carolina. He married Mary S. "Polly" Draughan on July 24, 1856 in Ashe County, North Carolina. She was born circa 1840 in North Carolina. She died sometime after 1900 in Ashe County, North Carolina. Her father was Elias Draughan of Ashe County, North Carolina. Her mother was Catherine[6] [Aquilla[5] {of Franklin County, Virginia}, William[4] {of Baltimore, Baltimore County, Maryland}, William[3], John[2] {of Gunpowder River, Baltimore County, Maryland}, James[1] {of Capenoch, Dumfries, Scotland}] Greer of Grayson County, Virginia. Joseph[8] and Mary had six children: Preston Draughan[9],

Solomon Greer[9], Sarah Katherine[9], Crumpler[9], William David Craig[9] and Lydia Virginia[9].

h. David[8] Parsons
born on February 7, 1822 in Ashe County, North Carolina. He died on April 30, 1864 in Wise County, North Carolina [Another record says April 30, 1862 at Letcher, Letcher County, Kentucky]. He married Derinda [afa Dorinda and Derilda] Emeline Privette on March 24, 1848. She was born on November 7, 1822 in Wake County, North Carolina. She died on August 19, 1904 at Letcher, Letcher County, Kentucky. Her father was Willis [Jacob {of Chowan County, North Carolina}, William {of Wake County, North Carolina}] Privette of Wake County, North Carolina. Her mother was Elizabeth [Housand {of Bedford County, Virginia}, Housen {of Northumberland County, Virginia}] Harrell of North Carolina. David[8] and Derinda had ten children: Mariah Amazia[9] "Mazie," Matilda Jane[9], Altamira[9] [afa Alta Myra], Maryan Elizabeth[9] "Polly," Margaret E.[9], Joseph Lilburn[9], Lydia Angelina[9] "Liddy," John William[9], Willis Melvin[9] and Martha Emeline[9].

i. Nancy[8] Parsons
born circa 1826 in Ashe County, North Carolina. She died circa 1890 in Lawrence County,

Kentucky. She married Chrisly^6 "Christopher" Estep on November 18, 1852 in Harlan County, Kentucky. He was born circa 1818 in Ashe County, North Carolina. He died on January 19, 1875 in Lawrence County, Kentucky. Her father was Isaac^5 [John^4 {of Frederick County, Maryland}, Shadrach^3 {of Ann Arundel County, Maryland}, Thomas^2, Richard^1 {of Middlesex County, England}] Estep of Ashe County, North Carolina. Her mother was Charlotte^7 [Elisha^6 {of Wilkes County, North Carolina}, "Yankee" John^5 {of Sheffield, Berkshire County, Massachusetts}, John^4 {of Hadley, Hampshire County, Massachusetts}, Josiah^3, Samuel^2, Richard^1 {of Braintree, Essex County, England}, Richard^{1a}, John^{2a} {of London, Middlesex, England}, John^{3a}, Robert^{4a}, Reynold^{5a}, John^{6a} {of Leicester, England}, John^{7a}, John^{8a}, John^{9a} {Chyrch}, John^{10a} {born circa 1365 at Geround Manor, Great Parnden, Essex, England}] Church of Ashe County, North Carolina and later of Carter County, Tennessee. Nancy^8 and Chrisly^6 had six children: Lydia R.^{7}, Chrisly C.^{7}, Mary E. P.^{7}, Alzinia^7, Nancy Louisa^7 and Stella L.^{7}.

Chrisly^6 married, first, Mary Swift circa 1839 in Russell County, Virginia. She was born circa 1808 in North Carolina. She died in 1851 in Russell County, Virginia. The name of her father and mother is not known. Chrisly[6] and Mary had one child: George[7].

j. Mary[8] Parsons
born on June 12, 1827 in Ashe County, North Carolina. She died on February 8, 1913 at Piney Creek, Allegheny County, North Carolina. She married Ira Josiah[7] Halsey on August 10, 1850 at Piney Creek, Allegheny County, North Carolina. He was born on April 22, 1815 at Piney Creek, Allegheny County, North Carolina. He died on December 18, 1861 at Piney Creek, Allegheny County, North Carolina. His father was William[6] "Bucky" [William[5] {of Columbia County, New Jersey}, William[4] {of Morris County, New Jersey}, Recompense[3], Nathaniel[2] {of Southampton, Suffok County, New York}, Thomas[1] {of Kempston, Bedfordshire, England}, Thomas[1a] {of Golden Parsonage, Great Gaddesden, Hertfordshire, England}, Robert[2a] {known as Robert Halsey Chambers}, Thomas[3a] {Halsey Chambers}, John[4a] {Halsey Chambers, born circa 1498}] Halsey. His mother was Judah Peake of Piney Creek, Allegheny County, North Carolina. Ira[7] and Mary[8] had five children: J. E.[8], Sarah Adeline[8], Newton C.[8], Victoria Ellen[8] and John Monroe[8].

Ira[7] had married, first, Fannie[3] McMillan on August 21, 1834 at Piney Creek, Allegheny County, North Carolina. She was born on August 18, 1815. She died on September 6, 1849 at Piney Creek, Allegheny County, North Carolina. Her father was James[2] [John[1] {of Edinburgh, Scotland}] McMillan. Her mother was Thursa "Thursey" ["Captain" Martin Cleveland {of Culpeper County, Virginia}, Henry {of Hanover County, Virginia}, Thomas {believed to be of Rhode Island}] Gambill. Ira[7] and Fannie[3] had a child: Franklin Benjamin[8].

k. Alvin Dixon[8] Parsons [a twin]
    born on June 3, 1829 in Ashe (or Allegheny) County, North Carolina. He died on July 3, 1918 in Wise County, Virginia. He married Phoebe Loretta Tolliver on April 2, 1854 in Ashe County, North Carolina. She was born on April 30, 1836 in Ashe County, North Carolina. She died on April 29, 1913 in Wise County, Virginia. Her father was Charles H. [John {of Fauquier County, Virginia}, John] Tolliver of Ashe County, North Carolina. Her mother was Patience [Daniel {of Allegheny County, North Carolina}, John {of Morris County, New Jersey}] Jones of Ashe County, North Carolina. Alvin[8] and Phoebe had twelve children: Charles M.[9], Solomon Columbus[9], Mary E.[9], Rufus F.[9],

Missouri E.[9], Alexander U. S. Grant[9], Drucy C.[9], Cora G.[9], Joseph M.[9], Rosa B.[9], Elizabeth[9] "Eliza" and Sarah I.[9] "Sally."

l. Alexander D.[8] Parsons [a twin]
    born on June 3, 1829 in Ashe County, North Carolina. He died on January 30, 1868 in Allegheny County, North Carolina.

m. James[8] Parsons
    born in 1830 in Ashe County, North Carolina. He died in 1906 in Allegheny County, North Carolina. He married Mary[5] "Polly" Landreth on August 22, 1863 in Allegheny County, North Carolina. She was born circa 1833, presumably in Ashe County, North Carolina. Her date and place of death is not known. Her father was Benjamin[4] [Stephen[3], William[2] {Augusta County, Virginia}, Thomas[1] {of Hume, Borders, Scotland}, James[1a] {Coldstream, Borders, Scotland}, George[2a], Patrick[3a] {born circa 1583 of Berwick, Scotland}] Landreth of Ashe County, North Carolina. Her mother was Temperence "Tempa" Lawrence of Ashe County, North Carolina. James[8] and Mary[5] had three children: Rebecca[9], William[9] and Craig[9].

n. Craig S.[8] Parsons
    born 1833 in Ashe County, North Carolina. His

date and place of death is not known. He married Alfia "Allie" Williams, probably in Allegheny County, North Carolina [their date of marriage is not known]. She was born circa 1842 in North Carolina. She died in 1860 in Allegheny County, North Carolina. The name of her father and mother is not known. Craig[8] and Alfia had a child: Martha D.[9].

2. John[6] Sturgill

born circa 1779 in Grayson County, Virginia. He died circa 1865 in Allegheny County, North Carolina and was buried at Crackers Neck near Big Stone Gap, Virginia. He married, first, Jemima[4] Wells circa 1799 in Grayson County, Virginia. She was born in 1782 in Virginia. She died on March 15, 1856 in Grayson County, Virginia. Her father was Zacharia[3] [Richard[2] {of Baltimore County, Maryland}, "General" James[1] II {of Somersetshire, England}, James[1a]] Wells, Jr. of Grayson County, Virginia. Her mother was Abigail Elizabeth[3] [Caleb[2] {of Williamsburg, James City County, Virginia}, Jonathan[1] {of Warwickshire, England and later of Williamsburg, James City County, Virginia}, James[1a], John[2a] {of Ashland, Kent County, England}, Thomas[3a]] Osborne of Lebanon, Russell County, Virginia and later of McMinn, Athens County, Tennessee. John[6] and Jemima[4] had fourteen children:

a. Rebecca[7] Sturgill
   born in 1799 in Grayson County, Virginia. She
   was later baptized on June 3, 1826 in Harlan
   County, Kentucky. She died, age 81, in 1880 in
   Osborne County, Kansas. She married Jordan
   Neithercutt on February 2, 1815 in Lee County,
   Virginia. He was born in 1790 in North
   Carolina. He died on April 25, 1878 in Osborne
   County, Kansas and was buried there in the
   Bristow Cemetery. His father was William
   [Moses, George, John {of Farnham, Richmond,
   Virginia] Neithercutt [one researcher says he
   was adopted] of Cartaret County, North Caro-
   lina. The name of his mother is not known.
   Rebecca[7] and Jordan had ten children: (son),
   Jemima, (son), (daughter), David, Abigail,
   George Washington, Solomon Jordan, Sarah J.
   and Rebecca.

b. David[7] Sturgill
   born circa 1800 in Grayson County, Virginia.
   He died in 1862 in Wise County, Virginia
   [where in 1860 he was living with his family].
   He married Rachel[3] Boggs circa 1821/1823 in
   Virginia. She was born on January 26, 1804 in
   Lee County, Virginia. She died circa 1862 [in
   1860, she, age 56] in Wise County, Virginia. Her
   father was Hugh[2] [James Lee[1] {of Ireland},
   John[1a]] Boggs of Wilkes County, North Caro-

lina. Her mother was Elizabeth[2] [John[1] {of Germany}] Blubaugh of Lee County, North Carolina. David[7] and Rachel[3] had thirteen children: Hugh[8], Joel[8], Elizabeth Minerva[8], Francis[8], Jordan[8], James[8], McGuire[8], Jemima[8], Nancy[8], Mathias[8], Samuel[8], Anny[8] and Sarah[8].

c. Abigail[7] Sturgill

born on November 30, 1801 Allegheny County, North Carolina. She died on October 16, 1894 in Wise County, North Carolina. She married Mathias Kelly on January 13, 1820 in Grayson County, Virginia. He was born on December 28, 1797 [another researcher says 1799] in Virginia. He died on December 15, 1872 in Wise County, Virginia. His father was John J. Kelly of Lee County, Virginia. His mother was Henrietta Jackson [although another researcher says it was Hanna Ritter]. Abigail[7] and Mathias had three children: William Henry, John Jackson and Mathias.

d. Solomon D.[7] Sturgill

born circa 1804 in Virginia. He died on October 13, 1856 in Kentucky. He married Rebecca[6] Tompkins circa 1826, presumably in Tennessee. She was born on April 21, 1809 in Tennessee. She died on July 13, 1887 at Willard, Carter County, Kentucky. Her father was John

Benjamin[5] [James Edwin[4] {of Newark, Essex County, New Jersey}, Eleazar[3], Jonathan[2] {Milford, New Haven County, Connecticut}, Micah[1] {of Edlesborough, Buckinghamshire, England}, Ralph[1a] {of Movington, Hertfordshire, England}, John[2a] {Tomkyns}, James[3a], William[4a], Thomas[5a], William[6a] {of London, Middlesex County, England}, Roger[7a] {of Lostwithiel, Cornwall, England}, Thomas[8a], Thomas[9a] {of Charton, Hertfordshire, England}, Robert[10a], William[11a] {de Cantilope, born circa 1176}] Thompkins of Wilkes County, North Carolina. Her mother was Elizabeth[8] [Thomas[7] {of Albemarle County, Virginia}, Jacob[6], John[5] {of New Kent County, Virginia}, John[4] {of Hampfield, Gloucester County, Virginia}, John[3] {of James City, York County, Virginia}, Thomas[2] {of Kecoughtan Parish, Elizabeth City County, Virginia}, William[1] {of England}, Laurence[1a] {of Twickenham, Middlesex, England}, John[2a], Thomas[3a] {de Hampton}, John[4a] {born circa 1460}] Hampton of Wilkes County, North Carolina. Solomon[7] and Rebecca[6] had a child: Matilda[8].

e. (daughter)[7] Sturgill
   born circa 1805 in Virginia. Her date and place of death is not known. She married (Unknown) Massey.

f. John[7] Sturgill

   date of birth, presumably in Virginia, is not known. His date and place of death is not known.

g. Francis[7] "Frank" Sturgill

   born in 1808 in Virginia. He died in 1883 in Letcher County, Kentucky. He married Ruth Bishop in 1828. She was born on November 26, 1808 in Virginia. She died on May 26, 1883 of fever in Wise County, Virginia [another researcher believes she died in Letcher County, Kentucky]. Her father was Franklin Bishop of Virginia. Her mother was Lavina (Unknown) of Virginia. Francis[7] and Ruth had nine children: John G.[8], Ora[8], Anna[8], Clarinda[8], Isaac[8], Andrew[8], Jemima[8], Mahala[8] and Francis[8].

h. Andrew[7] Sturgill

   born on July 12, 1810 in Grayson County, Virginia [another researcher says Allegheny County, North Carolina]. He died on November 16, 1890 in Wise County, Virginia. He married Nancy[7] Booth in 1830 in Russell County, Virginia. She was born on August 24, 1815 in Russell County, Virginia. She died on December 16, 1893 in Wise County, Virginia. Her father was "Reverend" William[6] [Stephen[5] {of Bridgeport, Fairfield County, Connecticut}, Stephen[4] {of Stratford, Fairfield County, Connecticut}, Joseph[3], Joseph[2], Richard[1] {of Great Budnarth, Cheshire, England}, Richard[1a], George[2a] {of Dunham, Massey, Cheshire, England}, George[3a], William[4a] {born circa 1473}] Booth of Grayson County, Virginia. Her mother was Sarah [James {of Montgomery County, Virginia}] Taylor. Andrew[7] and Nancy[7] had four children: William[8], Joel[8], James[8] and Drucilla[8].

i. Sarah[7] Sturgill
born circa 1798 in Lee County, Virginia. She died in 1886 at Slant, Scott County, Virginia. She married William[4] "Billy" Davidson on July 27, 1819 in Virginia. He was born circa 1799 in Virginia. He died in 1891 at Slant, Scott County, Virginia. His father was William[3] [James[2], Samuel[1] {of Ireland}] Davidson of Russell County, Virginia. His mother was Elizabeth Clark of Washington County, Virginia. Sarah[7] and William[4] had two children: Hiram[5] and William Reeves[5].

Sarah[7] married, second, the "Reverend" William[6] Booth on August 4, 1830 in Grayson County, Kentucky. He was born on October 3, 1786 at Winchester, Montgomery County, New York. He died sometime between 1860 and 1870 in Wolfe County, Kentucky. His father was Stephen[5] [Stephen[4] {of Stratford, Fairfield County, Connecticut}, Joseph[3], Joseph[2], Richard[1] {of Great Budnarth, Cheshire, England}, Richard[1a], George[2a] {of Dunham, Massey, Cheshire, England}, George[3a], William[4a] {born circa 1473}] Booth of Bridgeport, Fairfield County, Kentucky. His mother was Nancy Ann Cosby of Westchester County, New York. Sarah[7] and William[6] had a child: Sarah Ann[7]

William[6] Booth married, second, Sarah Taylor on March 11, 1813 in Kentucky [another record says Virginia]. She was born on March 2, 1794 in Virginia. She died between 1825 and 1830 in Russell County, Virginia. Her father was James Taylor of Montgomery County, Virginia. Her mother was Sally Smith of Virginia. William[6] and Sarah had two children: Nancy[7] and Virginia Jane[7].

j. Rachel[7] Sturgill
    born circa 1816 in Virginia. She died in 1906 at Quicksand, Breathitt County, Kentucky. She married Samuel[5] Maggard circa 1834, probably in Kentucky. He was born on July 25, 1814 in Knox County, Kentucky. He died on October 12, 1879 at Quicksand, Breathitt County, Kentucky. His father was Samuel[4] [John[3], Samuel[2] {of Lancaster County, Pennsylvania},

Hans[1] "John" {of Rekhenbach, Kendertal, Bern Kanton, Switzerland}, Malchior[1a] {Maegert}] Maggard of Rockingham County, Virginia. His mother was Rebecca[7] [Benjamin[6] {of Scott County, Virginia}, Nathaniel[5] {of Bristol Parish, Prince George, Virginia}, John[4] {of Henrico County, Virginia}, Nicholas[3] {of Charles City, Accomack County, Virginia}, Edward[2] {of Charles City, Charles County, Virginia}, Christopher[1] {of County Durham, England}, Geoffrey Mason[1a] {of Worcester, Worcestershire, England}] Robertson of Shenandoah County, Virginia. Rachel[7] and Samuel[5] had ten children: John David[6], Moses[6] "Branch Mose," Mary[6] "Polly," William[6] "Billy," Jemima[6] "Mima," Sarah[6] "Sally," Samuel[6], Jane[6] "Winnie," Nancy[6] and Roseanna[6].

k. Nancy[7] Sturgill
   born 1818 in Grayson County, Kentucky. She died in 1912 at Webbville, Lawrence County, Kentucky. He married Elisha[6] Pennington on November 27, 1835 in Lawrence County, Kentucky. He was born on October 20, 1814 in Knox County, Kentucky. He died sometime after January 26, 1851 [the date of his will] in Lawrence County, Kentucky. His father was William[5] [Ephraim[4], Ephraim[3] {of New Jersey}, Ephraim[2] {of New Haven County, New Jersey},

Ephraim[1] {of Lancashire, England}, William[1a]] Pennington of North Carolina. His mother was Abigail Susan[4] "Abbie" [James[3] {of Lunenberg County, Virginia}, James[2] {of Old Surry County, Virginia}, Stephen[1] {of Scotland}] Caudill of Wilkes County, North Carolina. Nancy[7] and Elisha[6] had a child: Sarah Jane[7].

Nancy[7] married, second, Lindsey Oliver[5] Lester on December 12, 1852 in Lawrence County, Kentucky. He was born on January 1, 1811 at Paint Lick, Tazewell County, Virginia. He died in 1882 in Kentucky. His father was Jesse[4] [Thomas[3] {of Fairfax County, Virginia}, Thomas[2] {of Amelia County, Virginia}, John[1] {of Coventry Meath, Ireland}] Lester of Tazewell County, Virginia. His mother was Nancy[1] Collins of Saint Clement, Cornwall, England. Nancy[7] and Lindsey[5] had four children: James Harvey[6], Lindsey O.[6], Lafayette[6] and George W.[6].

Lindsey[5] had married, first, Margaret Gillespie on December 25, 1840 in Tazewell County, Virginia. She was born circa 1811 in Virginia. She died circa 1852, presumably in Lawrence County, Kentucky. The name of her father and mother is not known. Issue, if any, is not known.

Nancy[7] married, third, William Riley[4] Webb on October 14, 1883 in Lawrence County, Kentucky. He was born on May 13, 1815 in Lawrence County, Kentucky. He died on August 29, 1885 in Lawrence County, Kentucky. His father was James B.[3] [James[2] {of Berks County, Pennsylvania}, John Harrod[1] {of Tetbury, Gloucestershire, England}], John[1a], Robert[2a]] Webb of Lee County, Virginia. His mother was Elizabeth[6] [William[5], Ephraim[4], Ephraim[3] {of New Jersey}, Ephraim[2] {of New Haven County, New Jersey}, Ephraim[1] {of Lancashire, England}, William[1a]] Pennington of Lee County, Virginia. There was no issue.

William[4] had married, first, Martha "Patsy" Jordon on September 11, 1836 in Lawrence County, Kentucky. She was born on June 1, 1817. Her place of birth is not known. She died on February 14, 1864, presumably in Kentucky. Her father was James C. Jordon of Guilford County, North Carolina. Her mother was Martha Ballard of North Carolina. William[4] and Martha had three children: Lindsey D.[5], "Doctor" Franklin[5] and James Buchannan[5].

William[4] had married, second, Rachel Harmon sometime after 1864 in Kentucky. She was born in 1826 in Kentucky. She died sometime before

1883 [when he remarried] in Kentucky. The name of her father and mother is not known. William[4] and Rachel had one child: Anderson[5].

l. Elizabeth[7] Sturgill
born on March 5, 1823 in Virginia. She died on December 7, 1922 in Carter County, Kentucky. She married John Martin[4] Webb on August 13, 1839 in Harlan County, Kentucky. He was born on October 19, 1817 in Harlan County, Kentucky. He died on June 12, 1911 in Lawrence County, Kentucky. His father was James Buchanen[3] [James[2] {of Berks County, Pennsylvania}, John Harrod[1] {of Tetbury, Gloucestershire, England}, John[1a], Robert[2a]] Webb of Lee County, Virginia. His mother was Mary Lou Ella [George {of Greenup County, Kentucky}] Meenach of Carter County, Kentucky. Elizabeth[7] and John[4] had a child: Rachel[5].

m. Agnes[7] Sturgill
born on April 8, 1825 in Wise County, Virginia. She died on October 24, 1917 at Dry Fork, Lawrence County, Kentucky. She married Levi J.[4] Webb at Lawrence County, Kentucky. He was born on June 16, 1821 in Lawrence County, Kentucky. He died on September 15, 1848 in Lawrnece County, Kentucky and was buried there in the Webbville Cemetery at Webbville.

His father was James Franklin[3] [James Franklin[2] {of Berks County, Pennsylvania}, John Harrod[1] {of Tetbury, England}] Webb of Lee County, Virginia. His mother was Elizabeth "Betsey" [William {of Lawrence County, Kentucky}, Ephraim {of Wilkes County, North Carolina}, Ephraim, Ephraim, Ephraim {born 1645}] Pennington of Lee County, Virginia. Agnes[7] and Levi had two children: Elizabeth M. and Martha.

Agnes[7] married, second, John Washington Pennington on November 11, 1849 in Lawrence County, Kentucky. He was born on January 27, 1827 in Lawrence County, Kentucky. He died on October 30, 1904 in Lawrence County, Kentucky. His father was John W. [William {of Lawrence County, Kentucky}] Ephraim {of Wilkes County, North Carolina}, Ephraim, Ephraim, Ephraim {born in 1645}] Pennington of Lee County, Virginia. His mother was Rachel [Zachariah {of North Carolina}] Morgan of South Carolina. Agnes[7] and John had eight children: Jemima, Rachel, Andrew, Nancy, Verna, Louisiana, America and Abby.

n. (daughter)[7] Sturgill
   date of birth, presumably in Wise County, Virginia, is not known. She may have died young.

[Editor's Note: Some researchers say there was a child, James, born in 1844 who married a Catherine Stidham and had a child Orbin; however, this is unlikely, as Jemima[4] Wells would have been age 62 at his birth]

John[6] lived with but didn't marry Jane Abbott about 1855 in Harlan County, Kentucky and moved back to Wise County. Jane was born in 1807 in Kentucky. Her date and place of death is not known. The name of her father and mother is not known. In the 1860 U. S. Census for Letcher County, Kentucky, John[6] was living with Jane and child Araminda, age 6, [Editor's Note: The family story is that John[6] had hired Jane to help take care of Jemima during her illness and after her death, John[6] and Jane continued living together]. John[6] and Jane had two children:

o. Aramenta[7] [afa Araminda] Sturgill
   born circa 1854/1856 in Letcher County, Kentucky. Her date and place of death is not known.

p. Liddy/Lidy[7] Sturgill
date and place of birth and death is not known.

3. James[6] Sturgill
born on October 11, 1781 in Allegheny County, North Carolina [another researcher says Grayson County, Virginia]. He died on July 9, 1855 at King's Creek, Allegheny County, North Carolina and was buried there in the South Fork Cemetery. He married Mary Herrin [afa Herring] in 1802 in Allegheny County, North Carolina. She was born on August 25, 1781 [another source says October 15, 1783] in Allegheny County [another researcher says Wilkes County], North Carolina. She died on September 4, 1864 at South Fork, Ashe County, North Carolina and was buried there in the South Fork Cemetery. Her father was Henry Herrin of Ashe County, North Carolina [another source says her father was William Herron/Herring]. The name of her mother is not known. James[6] and Mary had eleven children:

a. Francis[7] Sturgill
he was born in 1804 in Ashe County, North Carolina. He died in 1845 in Ashe County, North Carolina. He married Rebecca Hall in 1832 in Ashe County, North Carolina. She was born in 1813 in Ashe County, North Carolina. Her date and place of death is not known. The

name of her father and mother is not known. Francis[7] and Rebecca had six children: Andrew[8], James[8], John Anderson[8], Nancy[8], Sarah[8] and William[8].

Rebecca married, second, Alexander Hall in Letcher County, Kentucky. [Editor's Note: Church records show that Rebecca, widow of Francis[7], was excluded from the church in 1847 for having an illegitimate child {presumably Dicey Hall, born 1834}. Rebecca then left Ashe County and moved to Letcher County, Kentucky, where she married a widower, Alexander Hall].

b. Daniel[7] Sturgill
born circa 1805/1806 in Ashe County, North Carolina. He died in 1865 in Ashe County, North Carolina. He married Jane Hewlin in 1830 in Wilkes County [another researcher says Allegheny County], North Carolina. She was born in 1816 in Allegheny County, North Carolina. She died on June 15, 1871 in Ashe County, North Carolina. Her father was John Hewlin of Allegheny County, North Carolina. Her mother was Mary (Unknown) of Allegheny County, North Carolina. Daniel[7] and Jane had three children: Mary[8], James William[8] and Noah[8].

c. Joshua[7] Sturgill
born on August 1, 1808 in Ashe County, North Carolina. He died on April 2, 1892 in Ashe County, North Carolina. He married Susan Long in 1830 in Ashe County, North Carolina. She was born on January 8, 1813 in Ashe County, North Carolina. She died on December 29, 1894 in Ashe County, North Carolina. Her father was Tobias Long of North Carolina. The name of her mother is not known. Joshua[7] and Susan had ten children: Levi B.[8], David Andrew[8], James Daniel[8], George W.[8], Zilpha[8], Tobias Street[8], Phebe Jane[8], Joel Robert[8], Drewry[8] and Elizabeth[8].

d. David[7] Sturgill
born on July 10, 1810 in Ashe County, North Carolina. He died on September 15, 1891 in Allegheny County, North Carolina. He married Ellender "Nellie" Jones in 1828 in North Carolina. She was born on February 28, 1808, probably in Allegheny County, North Carolina. She died on June 21, 1833 in North Carolina. Her father was John [John of Allegheny County, North Carolina}] Jones of Henry County, Virginia. Her mother was Leah [John {of Cecil County, Maryland}] Long of Wilkes County, North Carolina. David[7] and Ellender had two children: William[8] and (daughter)[8].

David[7] married, second, Rosamond Long in 1835 in North Carolina. She was born in 1816 in North Carolina. She died on December 24, 1876 in Ashe County, North Carolina. Her father was Isaiah Long of Wilkes County, North Carolina. The name of her mother is not known. David[7] and Rosamond had ten children: Elizabeth[8], Mary[8], Mazie[8], Jestine[8], James[8], Emeline[8], Lowry[8], Nancy Caroline[8], Phoebe Ann[8] and Isaiah Francis[8].

David[7] married, third, Elzina Hamby on November 17, 1883. She was born in 1830 in Ashe [another record says Allegheny] County, North Carolina. Her date and place of death is not known. The name of her father and mother is not known. There was no issue.

e. Elijah[7] Sturgill
   born in 1812 in Ashe County, North Carolina. His date and place of death is not known. He married Lutitia Ann (Unknown) in Harlan County, Kentucky. She was born in 1824. Her date and place of death is not known. The name of her father and mother is not known. Issue, if any, is not known.

f. John[7] Sturgill
   born on November 15, 1813 in Ashe County,

North Carolina. He died on August 17, 1882 at Piney Creek, Ashe County, North Carolina and was buried there in the Old South Fork Baptist Church Cemetery. He married Jane[6] DeBord on April 17, 1839 in Ashe County, North Carolina. She was born on November 25 [another source says the 11th], 1815 in Ashe County, North Carolina. She died on April 13, 1854 at Piney Creek, Ashe County, North Carolina and was buried there in the Old South Fork Baptist Church Cemetery. Her father was Benjamin[5] [Reuben[4], George[3] {of Richmond County, Virginia}, John[2], James[1] {Deborde of Berwick upon Tweed, Northumberland, England}, James[1a], Evereaud Percell[2a] {deBordeaux of Grenoble, Isere, Rhone-Alpes, France and later of Canterbury, Kent, England}, Piere[3a], Francis[4a], Bernard[5a] {de Rostegui, of de Lanage}] DeBord of Washington County, Virginia. Her mother was Mary "Polly" [Robert Drury {Smith}] Stitt of Grayson County, Virginia. John[7] and Jane[6] had five children: John Burke[8], William[8], Mary[8], James Weaver[8] and John Burke[8].

John[7] married, second, Mary[6] DeBord [believed to be Jane's sister], on December 19, 1854 in Ashe County, North Carolina. She was born on November 15, 1813. She died on March 13, 1904 in Ashe County, North Carolina and was buried there in the Crab Creek Cemetery. If, in fact, she was Jane[6]'s sister, her father was [See Jane[6] Debord's lineage above]. If so, her mother was [See Jane[6] Debord's lineage above]. John[7] and Mary[6] had four children: Sheffy[8], Wilson[8], Rachel[8] and Richard[8].

g. Sarah[7] Sturgill

born in September 1820 in Ashe County, North Carolina. Her date and place of death is not known. She married Jefferson[6] Pierce [afa Pearce] of North Carolina circa 1857. He was born on December 9, 1817 in Smyth County, Virginia. He died on January 12, 1906 at Grassy Creek, Ashe County, North Carolina. His father was Moses Arthur[5] [Thomas[4] {of Chester County, Pennsylvania}, George[3] {of Winscome, Somerset, England}, Joshua[2] {of Thornbury, Chester County, Pennsylvania}, George[1] {of Winscom, Somerset, England}, Richard George[1a], George[2a], George[3a] "The Elder" {born circa 1580}] Pierce of North Carolina. His mother was Ellender "Ellen" Bird of the Cherokee Nation of North Carolina. Sarah[7] and Jefferson[6] had a child: Ephraim[7].

Jefferson[6] had married, first, Sally Bourn on March 7, 1839 in Grayson County, Virginia. Her date and place of birth and death is not known. The name of her father and mother is not known. Jefferson[6] and Sally had six children: Mary Ann[7], Caroline[7], Malinda[7], Alexander[7], James F.[7] and Nancy[7].

h. James[7] Sturgill
born on May 28, 1816 in Ashe County, North Carolina. He died on July 22, 1901 Allegheny County, North Carolina. He married Susan Hewlin in 1839 in North Carolina. She was born on July 24, 1814 in North Carolina. She died on December 19, 1869 in Allegheny County, North Carolina and was buried in the South Fork Baptist Church Cemetery in Ashe County, North Carolina. Her father was John Hewlin of North Carolina. Her mother was Mary (Unknown). James[7] and Susan had nine children: Jane[8], Rebecca[8], Elizabeth[8], Mary Jane[8], Sarah[8], Martha[8], William Danield[8], James David[8] and Susan Malinda[8].

James[7] married, second, Elizabeth Richardson Baldwin on July 27, 1879 in North Carolina. She was born in 1832 in North Carolina. She died on May 10, 1919 in Allegheny County, North Carolina and was buried there in the Cranberry Primitive Baptist Church Cemetery. The name of her father and mother is not known. There was no issue.

i. Rebecca[7] Sturgill
    born on July 11, 1830 in Ashe County, North
    Carolina. She died on February 15, 1892 in
    Grayson County, Virginia. She married Lewis
    Hamilton[7] Halsey on May 2, 1841 at Grayson
    County, Virginia. He was born in December 27,
    1819 at Wilson, Grayson County, Virginia. He
    died on September 17, 1888 at Wilson Grayson
    County, Virginia. His father was Robert[6]
    "Bobby" [Moses[5] {of Scuttle, Hale County,
    Wyoming}, Nathanial[4] {of Hampton County,
    New York}, Nathan[3], Jeremiah[2] {of South-
    ampton, Suffolk County, Long Island, New
    York}, Thomas[1] {of England}, Thomas[1a] {of
    Flamstead, Hertfordshire, England}, Robert[2a]
    {Halsey aka Chambers}, Thomas[3a], John[4a] {born
    circa 1498}] Halsey of Wilson, Grayson County,
    Virginia. His mother was Polly Allen of
    Hillsville, Carroll County, Virginia. Rebecca[7]
    and Lewis[7] had six children: Mary Jane[8], Robert
    Franklin[8] "Francis," James William[8], Rosa-
    mond[8], Martha Ann[8] and Rebecca[8].

j. Nancy[7] Sturgill
    born in 1825 in Ashe County, North Carolina.
    Her date and place of death is not known. She
    married Jacob DeBord in 1849 in Allegheny
    County, North Carolina. He was born circa
    1820/1822 in Allegheny County, North Caro-

lina. His date and place of death is not known. His father was Elijah DeBord of Ashe County, North Carolina. His mother was Mary [Reuben {of Washington County, Virginia}, George {of North Farnham Parish, Richmond County, Virginia}] Groseclose of Ashe County, North Carolina. Nancy[7] and Jacob had five children: Benjamin, Joshua, Malinda, Mary C. and Jacob R. "Bud."

k. Joseph King [7] "Joel" Sturgill
    born in 1829 in Ashe County, North Carolina. He died on October 27, 1864 near Richmond [city of], Virginia and was buried there in a Confederate Cemetery. He married Matilda[4] Jones on April 20, 1857 in Ashe County, North Carolina. She was born in 1831 in Ashe County, North Carolina. She died on July 23, 1903 in Ashe County, North Carolina. Her father was Hudson[3] [John[2] {of Morris County, New Jersey}, Isaac[1] {of Wales, United Kingdom}] Jones of North Carolina. Her mother was Barsheba[3] [John B.[2] {of Allegheny, Madison County, North Carolina}, John[1] {of England}] Williams of North Carolina. Joseph[7] and Matilda[4] had one child: Rebecca[8].

"Joel" and Matilda[4] made their house on a farm at King's Creek. During the U. S. Civil War,

198

"Joel" was called for duty with the Confederate Army. None of his family ever heard from him again. Then, in 1953, his grave was discovered in a Confederate Cemetery near Richmond where he had been killed in the battle of Richmond. Matilda[4] never remarried.

4. **Francis[6] Sturgill, Jr.**

was born on September 22, 1782 at Helton Creek, Ashe County, North Carolina. He died on August 13, 1846 at Helton Creek, Ashe County, North Carolina and was buried there in the Sturgill Cemetery. He married Phoebe[7] Weaver circa 1803 in North Carolina. She was born on October 15, 1783 at Weaver's Ford, Ashe County, North Carolina. She died on June 13, 1855 at Helton Creek, Ashe County, North Carolina. Her father was William[6] [Joshua[5], Samuel[4], Samuel[3], William[2], Samuel[1] {of Shropshire, England}, Thomas[1a], William[2a], Griffith[3a], Jenkin[4a], John[5a], Thomas[6a], Walter[7a], Thomas[8a], Walter[9a], Walter[10a], Walter[11a], Humphrey[12a], Ieuan[13a] {of Wales}, Madoc[14a], Hywel Vychan[15a]] Weaver of Lunenburg County, Virginia. The name of her mother was Rachel[2] [Moses[1] of Ireland] McDaniel of Lunenburg County, Virginia. Francis[6] and Phoebe[7] had eight children: Joel[7], John[7], Mary[7], Nancy[7], Joshua[7], Jane[7], Rebecca[7] and Elizabeth[7].

5. William[6] Sturgill
born circa 1784 in Grayson County, Virginia [another source thinks North Carolina]. He was killed in a sawmill accident circa 1838 in the Arkansas Territory and was buried at the foot of Black Mountain. He married, first, Sophia King circa 1806/1808 in Wise County, Virginia. They met on a horse trading trip and they eloped. She was disinherited by her family, but they later reconciled. She was born circa 1793/1794 at Newport, Newport County, Rhode Island [another record says she was born in Virginia]. She died of yellow fever in 1824 at Big Stone Mountain, Wise County, Virginia. Her father was "Doctor" David[6] [Job[5], David[4], John[3], Phillip[2] {of Weymouth, Norfolk County, Massachusetts}, John[1] {of Sherborne, Dorsetshire, England}, John[1a]] King, MD of Taunton, Bristol County, Massachusetts and later of Newport, Newport County, Rhode Island [another record says, incorrectly, that her father was Edward King of Rhode Island]. Her mother was Ann Gordon of Newport County, Rhode Island. William[6] and Sophia had nine children:

a. Mary[7] "Polly" Sturgill
born in 1807 in North Carolina. She died in October 1879 in North Carolina. She married David[6] Greer in 1833 in Ashe County, North Carolina. He was born in 1807 in Wilkes

200

County, North Carolina. His date of death in Ashe County, North Carolina is not known. He was buried there in the William Greer Family Cemetery at Lansing. His father was John[5] [Benjamin[4] {of Albemarle County, Virginia}, John[3] {of Gunpowder River, Baltimore, Maryland}, John[2], James[1] {of Capenoch, Dumfrieshire, Scotland}, "Sir" James[1a] {Grier}, William[2a] {Grierson}, Roger[3a], John[4a], Roger[5a], Roger[6a], Vedast[7a] {born circa 1419 of Lag, Dumfrieshire, Scotland}] Greer of Wilkes County, North Carolina. His mother was Nancy Elizabeth Owens of Tyrell County, North Carolina. Mary[7] and David[6] had at least six children: Elihu[7], Elizabeth[7], Alexander[7], Rebecca[7], George[7], William[7] and possibly others.

b. Phoebe[7] Sturgill
born in 1809 in Ashe County, North Carolina. Her date of death in Gallia County, Ohio is not known. She married Fielding[6] Sturgill on December 2, 1829, probably in North Carolina. He was born in 1789 in Grayson County, Virginia. He died in 1864 in Lawrence, Lawrence County, Ohio. His father was Lewis[5] [James[4], James[3], John Daniel[2], John[1] {of North Petherton Parish, Somersetshire, England}, Richard[1a], George[2a]] Sturgill of Grayson County, Virginia. Phoebe[7] and Fielding[6] had seven

children: William[7], Susan A.[7], Armand[7], James W.[7], Mary[7], Malinda[7] and Elvery[7].

c. Sabra[7] Sturgill

born on December 1, 1811 in Ashe County, North Carolina. She died sometime after 1880 in Galia County, Ohio. She married John C. Sanders on July 1, 1832 in Ashe County, North Carolina. He was born in 1794 in Fluvanna County, Virginia. He died in 1870 in Galia County, Ohio. His father was John [John, William {of Westmoreland County, Virginia}] Saunders of St. James Northam Parish, Goochland County, Virginia. His mother was Ann[6] [John[5] {of Warren County, North Carolina}, Thomas[4] {Cauthen of Essex County, Virginia}, James[3] {Cauthorn}, Richard[2], Richard[1] {Cawthorne of London, England}, Richard[1a] {of Yorkshire, England}] Cothen of Goochland, Goochland County, Virginia. Sabra[7] and John had ten children: Mary Martha, Rebecca, William, John H., Gordon, Ira Wayne, William, Samuel Herman, Patterson and George Riley.

d. Rebecca[7] Sturgill

born on December 1, 1813 in Ashe County, North Carolina. She died on August 9, 1870 in Letcher County, Kentucky.

e. Alvin[7] Sturgill
born on April 9, 1815 in Ashe County, North Carolina. He died on June 18, 1904 in Pickering, Nodaway County, Missouri. He married Rachel C. Wray on January 15, 1841, probably in Ashe County, North Carolina [but possibly in Monroe County, Virginia]. She was born on December 3, 1815 in Monroe County, Virginia. She died in 1903 at Pickering, Nodaway County, Missouri. Her father was Thomas Wray of Rockingham County, Virginia. Her mother was Rachel [Walter, Daniel {Neale of Charles County, Maryland}, John] Neal of Bedford County, Virginia. Alvin[7] and Rachel had nine children: Julia Melissa[8], Sarah[8], William Thomas[8], Mary Elizabeth[8], Carolyn Rachel[8], Josephine[8], Jane[8], Jennie[8] and Alvin J.[8].

f. Joseph[7] Sturgill
born in 1818 in Ashe County, North Carolina. He died in 1876 at Shawneetown, Gallitan County, Illinois. He married Susan[7] Clark. She was born circa 1830 in Kentucky. She died in July 1876, possibly in Hamilton County, Illinois. Her father was Henry W.[6] [Jeremiah[5], Jeremiah[4], John[3] {of Gloucester, Essex County, Massachusetts}, Joseph[2], Edmund[1] {of England}] Clark of Windham, Windham County, Connecticut. Her mother was Sarah E. "Sally" (Unknown) of

Kentucky. Joseph[7] and Susan[7] had six children: Sarah[8], William Riley[8], Malissa[8], Joseph Grant[8], Agnes[8] and Willis[8].

Joseph[7] married, first, Rosalina Wiseman circa 1843/1844 in Ohio. She was born circa 1830, possibly in Ohio but maybe in Kentucky. She died sometime before 1857 [when Joseph[7] had his first child with his second wife, Susan[7] Clark]. The name of her father and mother is not known. Joseph[7] and Rosalina had one child: (child)[8].

g. William King[7] Sturgill
born on March 4, 1820 in Ashe County, North Carolina. He died in April 1882 in Gallia County, Ohio. He married Rhoda Farrell on September 19, 1839 in Gallia County, Ohio. She was born on October 27, 1819 in Virginia. She died on September 4, 1882 at Etna Furnace, Lawrence County, Ohio. The name of her father and mother is not known. William[7] and Rhoda had ten children: Henry Harrison[8], Edward[8], Nancy Sophia[8], America[8], Mary Ellen[8], Rebecca[8], Melvina[8], William Francis[8], Matilda A.[8] "Tillie," and Belle[8].

h. Nancy Sophia[7] Sturgill
born on February 18, in 1824 in Grayson

County, Virginia. She died on January 21, 1888 at Crawford, Dent County, Missouri and was buried in the Hutson Walker Cemetery at Sligo, Dent County, Missouri. She married George[1] Hutson in Ohio. He was born circa 1821/1823 in Scotland. He died at Crawford, Dent County [another researcher says Washington County], Missouri. His father was John[1a] of Scotland. His mother was believed to be Isabella[1a] Brotherton of Scotland. Nancy[7] and George[1] had eight children: Elizabeth[2] "Eliza," John[2], Elihu[2], Eli[2], Adam[2], Lucinda[2], Hiram[2] and George Sherman[2].

i. John David[7] Sturgill
born in 1825 in Grayson County, Virginia. His date of death, either at Shawneetown, Gallitan County, Illinois or Wise County, Virginia, is not known. He married Isabell Morgan. John[7] and Isabell had six children: Edward[8], Charles[8], Isabell[8], Caroline[8], Alice[8] and Francis[8].

John[7] married, second, Mary Gillenwater.

William[6] married, second, Katherine E. Brown on March 12, 1839 in Lawrence County, Ohio. Her date and place of birth and death is not known. The name of her father and mother is not known. Issue for William[6] and Katherine, if any, is not known.

6. Joel Cass[6] Sturgill
born on March 20, 1786 in a log cabin about three miles below the forks of the New River in Allegheny County, North Carolina. He died in 1878 in Scott County, Virginia [where in 1836 he and his family had moved]. He married Rachel Waters circa 1810 in Ashe County, North Carolina. She was born on February 18, 1790 in Wilkes County, North Carolina. She died on May 10, 1862 near Milan, Sullivan County, Missouri. Her father was John Philip[1] Waters of Scotland [Editor's Note: Family lore calls him a "Frenchman" who settled among the Cherokee Indians of western North Carolina and who married a half-breed Indian, Elizabeth Cullum. After her death, he remarried, abandoned his children and left the area for parts unknown]. Her mother was Elizabeth Cullum {also found as Collum and Cullon} [Editor's Note: Her father was a Cherokee Indian] of western North Carolina. Joel[6] and Rachel had fourteen children:

a. Lydia[7] Sturgill
born on September 8, 1808 in Ashe County, North Carolina. She died on December 22, 1863 in Lee County, Kentucky. She married Braxton J.[7] Cox in 1830 in Ashe County, Virginia. He

was born on March 15, 1810 in Wilkes County, North Carolina. He died on January 30, 1902 in Wolfe County, Kentucky. His father was Braxton Dickerson[6], Matthew[5] {of Essex County, Virginia}, Matthew[4], William C.[3] {of Shepherdswell Parish, Kent, England}, Henry Richardson[2], William Robert[1] {of Steeple, Ashton, Wiltshire, England who in 1598 arrived in America on the ship *Goodspeed*}, John Richmond[1a] {of Penbrook Hall, Cambridgeshire, England}, Richard[2a] {of Whaddan, Buckinghamshire, England}, John[3a] {born circa 1493}] Cox of Botetort County, Virginia. His mother was Nancy [William] Allison of Yancy County, North Carolina. Lydia[7] and Braxton[7] had seven children: Nancy Carolyn[8], Joel Sturgus[8], Polly[8], Temperance[8], Braxton S.[8], Lydia Jane[8] and Ambrose[8].

Braxton[7] married, second, Marian[4] [afa Mary A.] Caudill circa 1860 in Yancy County, North Carolina. She was born in 1815 in Letcher County, Kentucky. Her date and place of death is not known. Her father was James[3] [James[2] {of Lunenburg County, Virginia}, James[1] {of Scotland}] Caudell/Caudill of Wilkes County, North Carolina. Her mother was Sarah Elizabeth (Unknown). There was no issue. Marian[4] had married, first, Harrison Banks.

b. Catherine Ann[7] Sturgill
born on May 5, 1813 in Ashe County, North Carolina. She died on December 19, 1890, probably at Indian Creek, which was about four miles from Elgin, Union County, Oregon. She married Joshua[8] Weaver on July 4, 1833 in Ashe County, North Carolina. He was born on May 23, 1811 in Ashe County, North Carolina. He died on October 21, 1906 near Elgin, Union County, Oregon. His father was "Captain" Isaac[7] [Isaac[6], Joshua[5] {of New Kent County, Virginia}, Samuel[4], Samuel[3], William[2] {of Charles River County, Virginia}, Samuel[1] {of England}, Thomas[1a], William[2a]] Weaver, Jr. of Wilkes County, North Carolina. His mother was Jane[3] ["Colonel" Gideon[2] {of Hanover County, Virginia}, Nathaniel[1] {of Wales and later of Surrey County, North Carolina}, Gideon[1a], Abraham[2a] {of Boldre, Hampshire, England}, Ralph[3a] {of Egliwysilan, Glamorganshire, Wales}, Ralph[4a], Daniel[5a], Edward[6a], Edward[7a] {of Pen Coed, Llanfarthin, Monmoulthshire, England}, Richard Gwyn[8a] {of Grey, Wales}, "Sir" Richard[9a], "Sir" Llewellyn[10a] {of Castlemarch, Cardhill, Glenmorganshire, Wales}, "Sir" Rees Vychan[11a], "Sir" Llewellyn Vychan[12a], Llewellyn Madock[13a] {born circa 1350 in Wales}] Lewis

of Ashe County, North Carolina. Catherine[7] and Joshua[8] had six children: Joel[9], Isaac Franklin[9], Carolina Rachel[9], Charity Ann[9], Mary Ellen[9] and Nancy Evaline[9].

c. William M.[7] "Big Bill" Sturgill
born on February 16, 1813 in Ashe County, North Carolina. He died on August 13, 1883 in Ashe County, North Carolina. He married Sarah[6] Osborne on August 21, 1834 in Ashe County, North Carolina. She was born on May 10, 1818 in Ashe County, North Carolina. She died on October 21, 1906 in Ashe County, Virginia. Her father was Robert James[5] [Ephraim[4] {of Shenandoah County, Virginia}, Robert[3] {of Grayson County, Virginia}, Ephraim[2] {Williamsburg, James City County, Virginia}, Jonathan[1] {of Warrick, England), James[1a]] Osborne of Botetourt County, Virginia. Her mother was Lydia Cornett of Virginia. William[7] and Sarah[6] had twelve children: Wilborn Waters[8], Jonathan F.[8], Robert P.[8], Mary Elizabeth Jane[8], John Tyler[8], William Francis[8], Lewis Jackson[8], Sarah Caroline[8], Joel[8], Francis David[8], George Henry[8] and Stephen Lewis[8].

d. (daughter)[7] Sturgill
born in 1815 in Ashe County, North Carolina. She died an infant in 1815 in Ashe County, North Carolina [Editor's Note: This daughter may be one in the same as Malinda[7] or Sarah Jane[7] Sturgill].

e. Malinda[7] Sturgill
date of birth in Ashe County, North Carolina is not known. Her date and place of death is not known.

f. Sarah Jane[7] Sturgill
date of birth in Ashe County, North Carolina is not known. Her date and place of death is not known.

g. Francis Harvey[7] Sturgill
born on January 13, 1816 in Ashe County, North Carolina. He died on August 1, 1877 at Powder River, Baker County, Oregon. He married Jemima Caroline Richmond circa 1840 in Scott County, Virginia. She was born in 1819 in Alabama [another record says Tennessee]. She died on August 28, 1865 at Powder Ridge, Baker County, Oregon. Her father was Isaac Richardson. Her mother was Ester Louise Osborne of Franklin County, Virginia. Francis[7] and Jemima had fourteen children: George

Benton[8], William Richmond[8], Benjamin Franklin[8], Joel Madison[8], Lewis Cass[8], Ester Caroline[8], John Isaac[8], Lydia[8], Rebecca[8], Rachael[8], Mary Elizabeth[8], Stephen Douglas[8], Henry[8] and Robert B.[8].

h. Rebecca[7] Sturgill
born on October 8, 1817 in Ashe County, North Carolina. She died on November 30, 1873 in Jasper County, Missouri. She married Jacob John[7] Spencer in 1840. He was born in 1815. He died in 1874, probably in Jasper County, Missouri. His father was Aaron[6] Joseph Charles[5], William D.[4], Alexander[3], Nicholas[2], Nicholas[1] {of Worcestershire, England}]] Spencer of Lee County, Virginia. Her mother was Rachel [Joseph, William] Dougherty of Montgomery County, Virginia. Rebecca[7] and Jacob[7] had nine children: Richard Waters[8], Louisa A.[8], Jonathan B.[8], Willard P. M.[8] [or P.H.], Robert M.[8], Mary A.[8], David A.[8], Nancy Dora Jane[8] and Rachel[8].

i. Mary Ann[7] Sturgill
born on May 26, 1819 in Ashe County, North Carolina. She died on December 27, 1888, probably in Sullivan County, Missouri. She married Joseph Harris circa 1840. He was born on March 19, 1821. He died on June 4, 1912, probably in Sullivan County, Missouri. His father was

Charles [Matthew] Harris of Stokes County, North County. His mother was Pricilla [Elijah] Collins of Stokes County, North Carolina. Mary Ann[7] and Joseph had seven children: Pricilla, Rachel Catherine, James Know Polk, Rebecca Jane, Martha Ellen, John and Sarah Elizabeth.

j. Ester Caroline[7] Sturgill
    born in 1821 in Ashe County, North Carolina. She died circa 1888 at Walla Walla, Walla Walla County, Washington. She married Felix C.[3] Knifong on February 17, 1847 in Sullivan County, Missouri. Apparently they were divorced, because during the 1891 Chicago World's Fair he is recorded as driving a stage coach in a "Wild West" show. He was born in 1814 in Russell County, Virginia. He died in 1850 at Milan, Sullivan County, Missouri. His father was Martin Jesse[2] [Martin Jesse[1] {Newfang of Steinbach, near Saarbrucken, Saarland, Austria}, Georg Balthasar[1a]] Knifong of Rowan County, North Carolina. His mother was Eve [Michael] Wolfe of Lebanon County, Pennsylvania. Ester[7] and Felix[3] had three children: John W.[4], Luciana[4] "Lucy," and Felix[4].

Felix[3] married, first, Lucy Hamilton in 1833 in Russell County, Virginia. She was born in 1818 in Russell County, Virginia. She died on March

19, 1835 [during childbirth] in Virginia. Her father was Nathan Hamilton of Russell County, Virginia. Her mother was Nancy Stone of Russell County, Virginia. Felix[3] and Lucy had a child: Harriett E.[4].

Ester[7] married, second, Hugh G. Warren on October 7, 1851 in Ashe County, North Carolina. He was born circa 1820 in Ashe County, North Carolina. His date of death, probably in Sullivan County, Missouri, is not known. The name of his father and mother is not known. Ester[7] and Hugh had six children: Mary Catherine, Felix, Robert Schuyler, Susan Inez, Solomon and Joel F.

Hugh married, first, Mary Ann Carr on May 6, 1837 in Monroe County, Indiana. She was born circa 1821 in Kentucky. She died circa 1850 in Sullivan County, Missouri. The name of her father and mother is not known. Hugh and Mary Ann had five children: Amanda E., Elizabeth Ellen, Henry E., Nancy and Sarah Jane.

k. Jacob Peck[7] Sturgill
born in 1830 in Ashe County, North Carolina. His date of death in Baker County, Oregon is not known. He married Elizabeth Jane "Eliza"

Hill circa 1852 in Sullivan County, Missouri. She was born circa 1834 in Alabama. Her date of death, probably in Baker, Union County, Oregon, is not known. Her father was Jacob B. Hill of Tennessee. Her mother was Eliza Bragg of Alabama. Jacob[7] and Elizabeth had nine children: Mary Ester[8], Nancy Ellen[8], John B.[8], Rachel Caroline[8], Sarah Jane[8], Martha Ann[8], Lucinda M.[8], Francis[8] and Susan[8].

l. John Carter[7] [afa Center] Sturgill
   born in 1823 Ashe County, North Carolina. He died on June 13, 1856 at West Point, Lincoln County, Missouri. He married Sarah Ann Donoho on March 30, 1848 in Sullivan County, Missouri. She was born in 1827 at Milan, Sullivan County, Missouri. She died in 1855 at West Point, Lincoln County, Kansas. Her father was Thomas Sanders [Robert {of Virginia}] Donaho of Madison County, Kentucky. Her mother was Dianna Dicey Ann Weathers of Madison County, Kentucky. John[7] and Sarah had three children: James William[8], Mary Ellen[8] and Sarah Ann[8] "Sally."

m. Lewis James[7] Sturgill
   born in 1826 in Ashe County, North Carolina. He died on May 19, 1896 at Pattonsville, Scott County, Virginia and was buried there in the

Sturgill and Speers Cemetery at Stickleyville. He married Lucinda Merinda[8] Ward circa 1848/1850 at Rocky Station, Lee County, Virginia. She was born circa 1825/1830 in Carter County, Tennessee. Her date and place of death is not known. Her father was Samuel[7] [Daniel[6], Benjamin[5] {of Cumberland and Pittsylvania Counties, Virginia}, Benjamin[4] {of Henrico County, Virginia}, Richard[3] {of Sheffield Varina, Henrico County, Virginia}, "Captain" Seth[2], Richard[1] {of England}, Seth[1a] {born circa 1595/1596 of Abbington, Cambridgeshire, England}, John[2a] {of Warde of Ratcliffe, London, Middlesex, England}, Seth[3a]] Ward of Ashe County, North Carolina. Her mother was Orpha Julie Bradley[3] [James[2] {of Augusta County, Virginia}, Andrew James[1] {of County Cork, Ireland}, Hugh[1a]] Lloyd of Carter County, Indiana. Lewis[7] and Lucinda[8] had nine children: Huston[8], Samuel P.[8], Joel Francis[8], John K.[8], James Lewis[8], William N.[8], Orpha[8], Andrew Felix[8] and I.N.[8].

n. James George[7] Sturgill
born on May 23, 1828 in Ashe County, North Carolina. He died on November 29, 1909 at Suisun, Solano County, California. He married Mary Ann Donoho on August 13, 1848 in Sullivan County, Missouri. She was born on

March 19, 1829 at Milan, Sullivan County, Missouri. She died on August 14, 1902 at Oakland, Alameda County, California. Her father was Thomas Sanders [Robert {of Virginia}] Donaho of Madison County, Kentucky. Her mother was Dianna Dicey Ann Weathers of Madison County, Kentucky. James[7] and Mary had seven children: John William[8], Sarah Ellen[8], George Washington[8], Lewis Edgar[8], Katherine Jane[8], Jacob Lee[8] and Henry Height[8].

o. Solomon Waters[7] Sturgill
born in 1831 in Ashe County, North Carolina. His date of death, probably at Baker, Union County, Oregon, is not known. He married Mary Ann Huffman Cummings in 1875 in Sullivan County, Missouri. She was born on September 17, 1843 in Sullivan County, Missouri. She died on Marcy 21, 1921, presumably at Baker, Union County, Oregon. The name of her father and mother is not known. Issue, if any, is not known.

7. David[6] Sturgill
born circa 1788 in Grayson County, Virginia. He died sometime between 1847 and 1850 [he didn't appear on the 1850 U. S. Census] in Ashe County, North Carolina and was buried there in one of the

unmarked graves in the old church cemetery. He married Rebecca Richardson in 1810, presumably in North Carolina. She was born circa 1788 in North Carolina. She died in 1838 in Sullivan County, Missouri. Her father was Canady {afa Canada} [Jonathan {of Bedford County, Virginia}] Richardson of Virginia [another researcher says Ashe County, North Carolina]. Her mother was Jane[3] [John[2] {of Lancaster County, Pennsylvania}, John Joshua[1] {of Northern Ireland, United Kingdom} Cox of Ashe County, North Carolina [another researcher says her mother was Margaret Lee of Virginia]. David[6] and Rebecca had five children:

a. John W.[7] Sturgill [afa Sturgeon]
   born in 1812 in Ashe County, North Carolina. He died on June 13, 1852 in Johnson County, Kentucky.

b. Patsy[7] Sturgill
   born in 1815 in Ashe County, North Carolina. Her date of death in Floyd County, Kentucky is not known.

c. Elijah[7] "Eli" Sturgill
   born circa 1831 in Ashe County, North Carolina. He died on October 26, 1885 at Wise, Wise County, Virginia. He married Emiline Louvina

Creech on September 11, 1851 at Harlan, Harlan County, Kentucky. She was born on December 27, 1831 at Harlan, Harlan County, Kentucky. She died on November 28, 1918 at Wise, Wise County, Virginia. Her father was Elijah Lee [Jonathan {of Forsyth County, North Carolina}, John {of Johnston County, North Carolina}] Creech of Lee County, Virginia. Her mother was Sarah "Sally" [John Nathan {of Philadelphia, Delaware County, Pennsylvania}] Day of Harlan, Harlan County, Kentucky. Elijah[7] and Emiline had twelve children: Elijah Oliver[8], Catherine[8], Sarah[8], Daniel[8], Elize[8], James David[8], William[8], Mary Jane[8], Ira[8], Iva[8], Emeline[8] and John Calvin[8].

d. James[7] Sturgill
born in 1836 in Ashe County, North Carolina. He died on August 8, 1864 as a prisoner of war in the Union Prison at Elmira, Chemung County, New York. He enlisted, age 23, as a Private on June 8, 1861 in Company A, 1st Cavalry Regiment, C.S.A., North Carolina.

e. Eleanor[7] "Nellie" Sturgill
born in July 1831 in North Carolina. Her date and place of death is not known. She married Richard A. Richardson on May 5, 1850 at Jefferson, Ashe County, North Carolina. He was

born in July 1831 at Peak Creek District, Ashe County, North Carolina. He died on March 10, 1862 at Goldsboro, Wayne County, North Carolina. His father was James Stit Richardson of Ashe County, North Carolina. His mother was Mary Elizabeth[5] [Nicholas[4] {of Sussex County, North Carolina}, Richard[3] {of Hanover County, Virginia}, Samuel B.[2] {of St. Peter's Parish, New Kent County, Virginia}, Nicholas[1] {of Taxted, Essex, England}, Samuel[1a], Samuel[2a], Simon[3a], John[4a] {born circa 1510 of Lindsell, Essex, England}] Gentry of Wilkes County, North Carolina. Eleanor[7] and Richard had three children: John Campbell, Andrew J. and Richard A.

8. Rebecca[6] Sturgill
   born on March 1, 1791 in Grayson County, Virginia. He died on January 1, 1829 in Allegheny County, North Carolina and was buried there in the Old Sturgill Cemetery at Piney Creek on the Big Rock farm. She married William[7] Weaver on December 20, 1811 in Allegheny County, North Carolina. He was born on February 22, 1789 in Culpeper, Culpeper County, Virginia. William[7] died on September 9, 1876 in Allegheny County, North Carolina. He was buried with his second wife in the Weaver Cemetery near the mouth of Prathers Creek on the South Fork of the New

River. He married, second, Sarah Griffith Johnson sometime after 1829 in Allegheny County, North Carolina. William[7] and Sarah had one child: Andrew Jackson[8]. His father was John[6] [Joshua[5], Samuel[4] III, Samuel[3], William[2], Samuel[1] {of Shropshire, England}, Thomas[1a], William[2a], Griffith[3a], Jenkin[4a], John[5a], Thomas[6a], Walter[7a], Thomas[8a], Walter[9a], Walter[10a], Walter[11a], Humphrey[12a], Ieuan[13a] {of Wales}, Madoc[14a], Hywel Vychan[15a]] Weaver of Virginia. His mother was Mary Ashley of Ashe County, North Carolina. Rebecca[6] and William[7] had six children:

a. Nancy[8] Weaver
born in October 1812 in Ashe County, North Carolina. She died young in 1817 in Ashe County, North Carolina.

b. James Littleberry[8] "Little Jimmy" Weaver
born on September 20, 1815 in Ashe County, North Carolina. He died on July 29, 1901 at Piney Creek, Allegheny County, North Carolina. He married Anne "Annie" Johnson circa 1840 in Ashe County, North Carolina. She was born on April 4, 1822 in Allegheny County, North Carolina. She died on December 11, 1867, presumably in Allegheny County, North Carolina. The name of her father and mother is not known. James[8] and Annie had nine children:

Nancy Jane[9], Lutitia[9], William Johnson[9], Felix C.[9], John F.[9], Mary Jane[9], James Andrew[9], Annie Caroline[9] and Alexander Pinkney[9].

c. Nathan[8] Weaver
born on April 14, 1818 at Prather's Creek, Ashe [section that later became Allegheny] County, North Carolina. He died on January 11, 1910 in Allegheny County, North Carolina and was buried there in the family cemetery on Road 1302 West of Peden. He married Lucinda[5] Shephard on April 21, 1847 in Ashe County, North Carolina. She was born on November 19, 1821 at Reddies River, Wilkes County, North Carolina. She died on December 17, 1857 in Allegheny County, North Carolina. Her father was Larkin[4] [John[3] {of St. George Parish, Spotsylvania County, Virginia}, John J.[2], George[1] {of Banff, Banffshire, Scotland}, Edward Thomas[1a], Walter[2a] {born circa 1665 of Leathen, Scotland}] Shephard of Readies River, Wilkes County, North Carolina. Her mother was Alice "Alley" [Thomas] Eavin of Readies River, Wilkes County, North Carolina. Nathan[8] and Lucinda[5] had three children: Martha[9], Mary Ann[9] and William Henry[9].

Nathan[8] married, second, Eleanor[6] Ward on April 117, 1859 in Grayson County, Virginia. She was born on April 9, 1832 in Grayson County, Virginia. She died on September 16, 1879 at Prather's Creek, Allegheny County, North Carolina and was buried there in the Nathan Weaver Cemetery. Her father was Benjamin[5] [Nathan[4] II {of Coal Creek, Grayson County, Virginia}, Wells[3] {of Henrico County, Virginia}, Nathan[2] {of Queen Anne's Parish, Prince Georges County, Maryland}, James[1] {of Inishowen Peninsula, County Donegal, Ireland and later of Grayson County, Virginia}] Ward of Grayson County, Virginia. Her mother was Jane[4] [Joshua McGowan[3] {of Bridle Creek, Grayson County, Virginia}, David[2] {of Lancaster County, Pennsylvania}, Joshua I.[1] {of Ulster, Northern Ireland, United Kingdom}, Richard[1a]] Cox of Grayson County, Virginia. Nathan[8] and Eleanor[6] had seven children: Sarah Elizabeth[9], Joshua[9], (infant)[9], James Mastin[9], Rebecca Jane[9], Isaac[9] and Laura Ella[9].

Nathan[8] married, third, America[6] Eller circa 1883, presumably in Allegheny County, North Carolina. She was born on July 27, 1841 in Wilkes County, North Carolina. She died on February 18, 1903 at Prather's Creek, Allegheny County, North Carolina and was buried there in the Nathan Weaver Cemetery. Her father was Simeon[5] [John[4] {of Frederick County, Maryland}, Peter[3], George Michael[2] {of Rowan County, North Carolina}, Peter Casper[1] {of Baveria, Germany}, Johann Adam Valatin[1a] {of East Prussia, Germany}, Johann[2a], Matthes[3a] {born 1585 of Kenigsberg, Prussia}] Eller of Wilkesboro, Wilkes County, North Carolina. Her mother was Fanny[3] [James[2], George[1] {of Glasgow, Scotland}] McNiell of Reddies River, Wilkes County, North Carolina. There was no issue.

America[6], age 18, married, first, William R. Whittington on March 9, 1859, presumably in Wilkes County, North Carolina. By 1880 she was divorced. He was born circa 1829/1830 in Wilkes County, North Carolina. His date and place of death is not known. His father was Allen [John Leonard] Whittington of Wilkes County, North Carolina. His mother was Elizabeth Lenderman of Wilkes County, North Carolina. America[6] and William had three children: Gaither, Nora Caroline and Thomas A.

d. Mary[7] Weaver
born on May 8, 1820 in Ashe County, North Carolina. She died on January 30, 1897 in

Allegheny County, North Carolina. She married Henry John Williams on January 1, 1843 in Allegheny County, North Carolina. He was born on August 20, 1822 at Ashville, Buncomb County, North Carolina. He died on August 7, 1904 in Allegheny County, North Carolina and was buried there in the Mt. Zion Cemetery at Piney Creek. His father was John B. Williams of Buncomb County, North Carolina. His mother was Jane Baker of North Carolina. Mary[7] and John had eight children: Hugh Lowery, Polly A., Felix J. William Hardin, Rebecca, John H., Nathan and Mary.

Henry married, second, Jane Wyatt.

e. Nancy Clarinda[7] Weaver
born on January 13, 1823 in Ashe County, North Carolina. She died on March 2, 1900 at Armour, Douglas County, South Dakota. She married Tobias Jones on February 17, 1842 in Allegheny County, North Carolina. He was born on March 12, 1821 in North Carolina. His date and place of death is not known. His father was Daniel Jones of North Carolina. His mother was Eleanor Long of North Carolina. Nancy[7] and Tobias had four children: Noah, Leander, Aaron and William.

There is a family story that this Nancy[7] opened an old trunk in the attic where there were some dolls belonging to the first Nancy[7], who had died as a child, had been packed away. She carried the dolls down stairs and told her mother she had found "her" dolls, she knew the names of each of them, supposedly the names the first Nancy[7] had given them.

f. Alpha[7] Weaver
   born on January 16, 1827 in Ashe County, North Carolina. She died on July 9, 1904 in Allegheny County, North Carolina and was buried there in the Mt. Zion Methodist Church Cemetery at Piney Creek. She married, first, John Reed Jones circa 1843 in Allegheny County, North Carolina. He was born on October 8, 1823 in Ashe County, North Carolina. He died, age 89, on March 18, 1913 in Allegheny County, North Carolina. His father was Levi [John {of Henry County, Virginia}, John {of Allegheny County, North Carolina}] Jones of Ashe County, North Carolina. His mother was Nancy Dickey of Virginia. Alpha[7] and John had a child: Rebecca.

   Alpha[7] married, second, Thomas Nathan[5] Blevins in 1853 in Miami County, Ohio. He was born on October 16, 1823 in Ashe County,

North Carolina. He died circa 1861, possibly in Indiana. His father was Nathan Matthew[4] [James[3] II {of "old" Lunenburg County, Virginia}, James[2] {of Montgomery County, Virginia}, William[1] {of England and later of Westerly County, Rhode Island}] Blevins of Haw River, Alamance County, North Carolina. His mother was Rachel[3] [Charles {of Fincastle, Botetort County, Virginia}, James[2] {of Tazwell County, Virginia}, Richard[1] {of Ireland}, Thomas[1a] {of Londondary, Ulster, Northern Ireland, United Kingdom}, William[2a], Ire[3a]] Skaggs of Virginia [another researcher says Lydia Vaughn of Virginia]. Alpha[7] and Thomas[5] had three children: Nathan Weaver[6] [born in Ohio], Samuel Madison[6] [born in Ohio] and Thomas H.[6] [born in Indiana].

Nathant[5] had married, first, Catherine Younce on October 9, 1842 in Miami County, Ohio. She was born on January 7, 1825 in Ashe County, North Carolina. She died on August 6, 1852 in Miami County, Ohio. Her father was Joseph Younce of Ashe County, North Carolina. Her mother was Elizabeth Sheets of Ashe County, North Caro-lina. Nathan[5] and Catherine had four children: William Henry Harrison[6], Lydia[6], Martha[6] and Elizabeth[6].

Alpha[7] married, third, William Hardin[6] Treadway on March 4, 1861 in Monroe County, Indiana. He was born on October 16, 1831 in Ashe County, North Carolina. He died on October 16, 1901 in Harrodsburg, Monroe County, Indiana. His father was William Hardin[5] [Richard[4] {of Anson County, North Carolina}, Daniel[3] {of Baltimore, Baltimore County, Maryland}, Richard[2], Richard[1] {of St. Peter, Buckinghamshire, England}, William[1a], "Sir" Robert[2a] {of Easton, Northamptonshire, England}, John[3a] {of Rutlandshire, England}, Robert[4a], Thomas[5a] {of Amersham, England}] Treadway of Ashe County, North Carolina. His mother was Susan[3] [Christian[2] {of Elizabeth, Lancaster County, Pennsylvania}, Jehu[1] {of Basel, Basel Town, Switzerland}] Burkett of Jefferson, Ashe County, North Carolina. Issue, if any, is not known.

William H.[6] had married, first, Sarah Johnson in 1853 in Monroe County, Indiana. Her date and place of birth and death is not known. The name of her father and mother is not known. William[6] and Sarah had six children: John H.[7], Nancy Anne[7], Josephine[7], Horace Norval[7], James Franklin[7] and Sarah Alice[7].

William H.[6] married, third, Lucy Margaretta Baxton in 1874 in Monroe County, Indiana. She was born in June 1849 in Monroe County, Indiana. Her date and place of death is not known. The name of her father and mother is not known. William[6] and Lucy had six children: John H.[7], Nancy Ann[7], Josephine[7], Horrace Norval[7], James F.[7] and Sarah A.[7].

Alpha[7] married, fourth, Cabell Wilson cicrca 1865 in Monroe County, Indiana. He was born in 1825 in Allegheny County, North Carolina. The name of his father and mother is not known. Alpha[7] and Cabell had a child: W. L. [Wilson].

Alpha[7] married, fifth, Daniel[4] Hoppers on October 28, 1895 in Allegheny County, North Carolina. He was born on July 24, 1824 in Allegheny County, North Carolina. He died, age 75, in 1899 in Allegheny County, North Carolina. His father was Jacob[3] [Daniel[2] {of New Jersey}, Georg[1] {Happes of Schoenau, Baden, Germany}, Johann Michael[1a]] Hoppers of Wilkes County, North Carolina. His mother was Susannah Spurlin of Whitehead, Allegheny County, North Carolina. There was no issue.

Daniel[4] had married, first, Matilda Taliaferro [Tolliver] on April 1, 1847 in Ashe County, North Carolina. She was born on October 10, 1823 in Ashe County, North Carolina. She died on February 2, 1895 in Allegheny County, North Carolina and was buried there on Doughton Mountain. Her father was William "Billy" [John {of Fauquier County, Virginia}, Charles {Talaferro of Essex County, Virginia}, Richard Johnathan] Tolliver of Wilkes County, North Carolina. Her mother was Elizabeth "Betsey" Long of Grayson County, Virginia. Issue, if any, is not known.

9. Jane[6] Sturgill
born circa 1793 in Grayson County, Virginia. Her date and place of death is not known. She married William D. Jones circa 1815 in Grayson County, Virginia. He was born on March 26, 1789 in Brunswick County, Virginia. His date and place of death is not known. His father was John Jones of Morris County, New Jersey and later of Rowan [later known as Allegheny] County, North Carolina. His mother was Annie Norman of Rowan [later known as Allegheny] County, North Carolina [another source says his parents were Henry Jones and Sallie Lightfoot]. Jane[6] and William may have moved to western Virginia or Eastern Kentucky, but no further record has been found. Jane[6]

and William had at least one child and possibly others:

a. Reed Jones
   his date and place of birth and death is not known.

William married, second, Jane Gambill. The date of their marriage, presumably in Ashe County, North Carolina, is not known. She was born circa 1830 in Ashe County, North Carolina. She died circa 1901, presumably in Ashe County, North Carolina. Her father was John [William Martin {of Wilkes County, North Carolina}, Martin {of Culpeper County, Virginia}, Martin Henry {of Hanover County, Virginia}, Thomas] Gambill of Ashe County, North Carolina. Her mother was Ann Williams of Ashe County, North Carolina. Issue, if any, is not known.

10. Frances[6] "Ann" Sturgill
    born circa 1795 in Grayson County, Virginia. She died during childbirth circa 1813 in Allegheny County, North Carolina. She married Timothy[6] Perkins circa 1812 in Allegheny County, North Carolina. He was born circa 1779 in Wilkes County, North Carolina. He died in 1834 in Allegheny County, North Carolina. The family were loyalists [to the English King] and some feel

that he was killed because of his loyalty during a skirmish in Ashe County, North Carolina. He was buried in the Sturgill Cemetery with his first wife "Ann" Sturgill [another source says he was buried in the Zion Hill Cemetery near Sturgills, North Carolina]. His father was Joseph[5] [Stephen[4], John[3], Edward[2], Thomas[1] {of Hillmorton Parish, Warwickshire, England}, Thomas[1a], Henry[2a], Thomas[3a], William[4a]] Perkins of North Carolina. His mother was Phebe Maulthrop of North Carolina. Frances[6] and Timothy[6] had a child:

j. Lydia[7] Perkins
born in 1813 in Allegheny County, North Carolina. Her date and place of death is not known. She married (Unknown) Price.

[EDITOR'S NOTE: Some researchers claim Timothy[6] was born much earlier {in 1736} and had married a first wife, Miriam[4] Sperry, with whom he had ten children. More research is needed.]

Timothy[6] may have married, first, Miriam[4] Sperry in 1764 in Connecticut. She was born on February 19, 1740/1741 at Wallingford, New Haven County, Connecticut. She died circa 1777 at Old Fields, Ashe County, North Carolina. Her father was Abel[3] [Daniel[2], Richard[1] {of Scotland}, John[1a], John[2a]}] Sperry of New Haven County, Connecticut. Her mother was Miriam [John] Hotchkiss of New Haven County, Connecticut. Timothy[6] and Miriam had ten children:

a. Luther/Lighteral[7] Perkins
born circa 1765 in New Haven, New Haven County, Connecticut. His date and place of death is not known.

b. Jared[7] Perkins
born on January 26, 1766 at New Haven, New Haven County, Connecticut. He died on January 30, 1951 at Grant, Grayson County, Virginia. He married Phebe Russell circa 1792 in Grayson County. She was born circa 1777 in Virginia. She died in 1845 in Grayson County, Virginia and was buried there in Volney. The name of her father and mother is not known. Jared[7] and Phebe had nine children: Parzade[8] [afa Parzaid] Joannah[8], Trepheny[8] "Phenia," Joseph[8], William[8] Temperence[8] "Tempie," Philip[8], Hezekiah[8] and Aarod[8].

c. Jabez[7] Perkins
born on November 6, 1766 at New Haven, New Haven County, Connecticut. He died on December 27, 1835 in Whitley County, Kentucky. He married Nancy Ann Creekmore in Grayson County, Virginia. She was born in 1760

in Grayson County, Virginia. She died in 1836 in Whitley County, Kentucky. Her father was David L. Creekmore of Norfolk County, Virginia. Her mother was Frances Ballentine of Norfolk County, Virginia. Jabez[7] and Nancy had nine children: Solomon[8], Jesse Alvin[8], Timothy[8], Lucy[8], Patty[8], Jabez[8], Amy[8], William[8] and Nancy[8].

d. Aaron[7] [afa Aarod] Perkins
born in 1769 at New Haven, New Haven County, Connecticut. He died circa 1827/1828 in Grayson County, Virginia. He married Mary "Polly" Pennington circa 1794 in Grayson County, Virginia. She was born circa 1773, possibly in New Haven County, Connecticut. She died in 1817 in Grayson County, Virginia. The name of her father and mother is not known. Aaron[7] and Mary had nine children: Lewis[8], Matilda[8], Lighteral[8], Pamelia[8], David Levi[8], William Morrison[8], Linnian[8], Daniel[8] and Christopher[8].

e. Timothy[7] Perkins, Jr.
born on June 25, 1771 at New Haven, New Haven County, Connecticut. He died on March 8, 1851 in Ashe County, North Carolina. He married Tabitha Anderson on May 15, 1795 in Grayson County, Virginia. She was born on

March 20, 1775 in Wythe County, Virginia. She died on March 4, 1838 in Ashe County, North Carolina. The name of her father and mother is not known. Timothy[7] and Tabitha had fourteen children: Rebecca[8], Stephen[8], Elizabeth[8], Susan[8], Allen L.[8], Mattie[8], Lucy[8], Celia[8], Johnson T.[8], Mary Ann[8], Stralia[8], Jennie[8], Phoebe[8] and Calvin[8].

f. Levi[7] Perkins
born on May 26, 1772 in Grayson County, Virginia. He died on March 4, 1838. He married Minnie Hale. She was born circa 1772. She died circa 1842. The name of her father and mother is not known. Issue, if any, is not known.

g. Stephen[7] Perkins
born on January 3, 1773 in Grayson County, Virginia. He died in August 1844 in Grayson County, Virginia. He married Ruth[5] Hitchcock circa 1802, presumably in Grayson County, Virginia. She was born circa 1782 in Wilkes County, North Carolina. She died in 1844 in Grayson County, Virginia. Her father was Jushua[4] [William[3] III, William[2] II, William[1] {of England}] Hitchcock of Baltimore, Baltimore County, Maryland. Her mother was Caroline Typhene[5] "Tana" [Joshua[4], Stephen[3], John[2], Edward[1] {of Hillmorton, Warwickshire, Eng-

land}] Perkins of New Haven, New Haven County, Connecticut. Stephen[7] and Ruth[5] had ten children: John[8], Samuel[8], Isaac[8], Timothy[8], Stephen[8], Amy[8], Lucy[8], Matilda[8], Rebecca[8] and Linton[8].

h. Gordon[7] Perkins
born on November 13, 1773 in Grayson County, Virginia. He died on January 22, 1851 in Grayson County, Virginia. He married Joannah[5] Stamper in 1801. She was born on May 11, 1781 in Ashe County, North Carolina. She died in July 1861 in Grayson County, Virginia. Her father was James[4] [Jonathan Brooks[3] {of Middlesex County, Virginia}, Powell[2], John[1] {of Crosthwaite Church, Keswick, Cumberland County, England}, Philip[1a] {born circa 1625}]] Stamper of Amherst County, Virginia. Her mother was Sarah Moore. Gordon[7] and Joannah[5] had nine children: Sarah[8] "Sally," Alexander[8], Phebe[8], Elijah[8], Eli W.[8], Lucinda[8], Adah[8], Mariam[8] and Timothy Fletcher[8].

i. Lucy[7] Perkins
born on February 1, 1776 in Grayson County, Virginia. She died on November 28, 1948 in Grayson County, Virginia. She married Joseph Young on October 20, 1796 in Grayson County, Virginia. He was born on September 21, 1771 in

Grayson County, Virginia. He died on January 22, 1857, presumably in Grayson County, Virginia. His father was Ezekial Young of Grayson County, Virginia. His mother was Ruth Whitehead of Grayson County, Virginia. Lucy[7] and Joseph had five children: Joseph, Robert, William, Thomas and Ezekial.

[Editor's Note: Some researchers list a son, William[7] Perkins, born in 1783, but this was after Miriam Sperry Perkins died]

11. Nancy Elizabeth[6] Sturgill
born on October 24, 1799 in Grayson County, Virginia. She died on July 11, 1881 in Allegheny County, North Carolina and was buried there in the Jones family cemetery near Laurel Springs. She married, first, Nathan[7] Weaver in 1816 in Allegheny County, North Carolina. He was born circa 1791/1795 in North Carolina. He died in 1824 in North Carolina. His father was William[6] [Joshua[5], Samuel[4], Samuel[3], William[2], Samuel[1] {of Cardington Parish, Shropshire, England}, Thomas[1a], William[2a], Griffith[3a], Jenkin[4a], John[5a], Thomas[6a], Walter[7a], Thomas[8a], Walter[9a], Walter[10a], Walter[11a], Humphrey[12a], Ieuan[13a] {of Wales}, Madoc[14a], Hywel Vychan[15a]] Weaver of Lunenburg, Ashe County, North Carolina. His mother was Mary[4] [John[3], Thomas[2] II, Thomas[1] I, John[1a] {of England}] Ashley

of North Carolina. Nancy Elizabeth[6] and Nathan[7] had three children:

a. Ira[8] Weaver
born in 1818 in Ashe County, North Carolina. His date of death in New Mexico is not known.

b. Nathan[8] Weaver
born on November 19, 1821 in Ashe County, North Carolina. He died on December 17, 1857 in Ashe County, North Carolina. He married Lucinda Shepherd on April 21, 1847 in Ashe County, North Carolina. She was born on November 19, 1821 at Reddies River, Wilkes County, North Carolina. She died on December 17, 1857 in Allegheny County, North Carolina. Her father was Larkin Shepherd of Reddies River, Wilkes County, North Carolina. Her mother was Aley Erwin of Ashe County, North Carolina. Nathan[7] and Lucinda had three children: Martha[8], Mary Ann[8] and William Henry[8].

[Editor's Note: Some researchers believe he also had married a Nellie Ward {with seven children listed — no dates — but there hardly seems time if he died in 1857]

c. Nancy[8] Weaver
born circa in 1822 in Grassy Creek, Ashe County, North Carolina. She died on April 9, 1897 at Keoke, Lee County, Virginia. She married Thomas Clarkston sometime before 1856 [when their child was born] in Virginia. He was born on April 15, 1821 at Crab Orchard, Lee County, Virginia. He died on May 22, 1894 at Wise, Wise County, Virginia. His father was Thomas Clarkston of Jonesboro, Washington County, Tennessee. His mother was Ellender Nellie Feathers of Drip Rock, Leslie County, Tennessee. Nancy[8] and Thomas had a child: Mary Ellen.

Nancy Elizabeth[7] married, second, Allen Bartlett[6] Stedham [another researcher says Daniel Stidham] circa 1826, presumably in North Carolina. He was born circa 1790 in Wilkes County, North Carolina. He died sometime after 1859, presumably in Kentucky. His father was Samuel[5] [Adam[4] {of New Castle County, Delaware}, Christoper[3], Adam[2], Timen[1] {Stiddem of Sweden}] Stedham of Anson County, North Carolina. The name of his mother is not known. Nancy Elizabeth[7] and Daniel[6] Stedham had seven children:

d. Harvey R.[7] Stedham
born on April 1, 1826 in Ashe County, North

Carolina. His date and place of death is not known. He married Emaline "Emily" Taylor; their marriage bonds were recorded on June 4, 1850 in Ashe County, North Carolina. Her date and place of birth and death is not known. Her father and mother may have been Charles Taylor and Mahon (Unknown) [who in 1860 lived next door]. Harvey[7] and Emaline had seven children: Catherine[8], Calvin Preston[8], Singleton[8], Madison[8], Mary[8], John[8] and William[8].

e. Calvin W.[7] Stedham
born on January 13, 1830 in Ashe County, North Carolina, but possibly in Ashland County, Kentucky [another researcher says Virginia]. He died, age 56, on November 6, 1884 at Pound, Wise County, Virginia. He married Susan (Unknown).

f. Sarah[7] "Sallie" Stedham
born on April 1, 1830 in Ashe County, North Carolina. She died sometime after 1900 and was buried in the Burleson Cemetery in Avery County, North Carolina. She married George A.[6] Grimsley on July 28, 1847 in Ashe County, North Carolina. He was born on June 10, 1828, presumably in Culpeper County, Virginia, but possibly in Avery County, North Carolina. He

died sometime after 1900 {when, age 73, he last appears on the U. S. Census] in Avery County, North Carolina and was buried there in the Burleson Cemetery. His father was James[5] Thomas[4], James[3] {of North Farnham, Rappahannock County, Virginia}, Thomas[2], John[1] {of London, England}, Thomas[1a] {of Leicestershire. England}, Francis T.[2a] {born circa 1585 at Clayboad Parish, Leicestershire, England}] Grimsley of Culpeper County, Virginia. His mother was Catherine [John] Bower of Wilkes County, North Carolina. Sarah[7] and George[6] had five children: William Allen[7], Salina[7], Catherine[7], Eli[7] and Chainy Louise[7] "Chana."

g. William[7] Stedham
born circa 1832 in Ashe County, North Carolina. He died in 1863 in Ashe County, North Carolina. He married an unknown person on May 24, 1853 in North Carolina. Issue, if any, is not known.

h. Beneter[7] Stedham
born circa 1837 in Ashe County, North Carolina. His date and place of death is not known.

i. Allen Bartlett[7] Stedham
born circa 1840 in Ashe County, North Carolina. He died in 1939 in Allegheny County,

North Carolina and was buried there in the Twin Oaks Cemetery. He married an unknown person on September 20, 1869 in North Carolina. Issue, if any, is not known.

Allen[7] married, second, an unknown person on August 4, 1881 in Allegheny Township, Davidson County, North Carolina. Issue, if any, is not known.

j. Lewis Samuel[7] Stedham
born on May 22, 1842 in Ashe County, North Carolina. He died on March 17, 1939 at Westwood, Boyd County, Kentucky. He married Martha Nancy Taylor sometime before 1864 [when their first child was born] in North Carolina. She was born on June 10, 1846 on the Cherokee Indian Reservation in North Carolina. She died on January 1, 1914 in Ashland County, Kentucky. Her father was John Taylor of North Carolina. Her mother was Nancy (Unknown) of North Carolina. Lewis[7] and Martha had at least one child: Sarah[8].

Nancy Elizabeth[7] married, third, Daniel Jones, as his second wife, circa 1837 in Allegheny County, North Carolina. He was born on December 26, 1775 in Henry County, Virginia. He died on October 13, 1857 in Allegheny County, North

Carolina and was buried in the Jones Cemetery near Scottville, Allegheny County, North Carolina. His father was John Jones of Morris County, New Jersey and later of Rowan [later known as Allegheny] County, North Carolina. His mother was Annie Norman of Rowan [later known as Allegheny] County, North Carolina [another source says his parents were Henry Jones and Sallie Lightfoot]. Nancy Elizabeth[7] and Daniel Jones had two children:

a. Rebecca Jane Jones
born on June 17, 1838 in Allegheny County, North Carolina. She died on May 3, 1934 at Laurel Springs, Allegheny County, North Carolina. She, age 15, married Jonathan Horton Doughton on March 5, 1854, presumably in Allegheny County, North Carolina. He was born on February 12, 1832 at Laurel Springs, Allegheny County, North Carolina. He died on October 20, 1906 at Laurel Springs, Allegheny County, North Carolina and was buried there in the Laurel Springs Baptist Church Cemetery. The name of his father and mother is not known. Rebecca and Jonathan had seven children: Rufus Alexander, Robert L., George, Bettie J., Cora E., Franklin and Emory J.

b. Caroline Jones
born on June 27, 1840 in Allegheny County, North Carolina. She died on October 11, 1905, presumably in Allegheny County, North Carolina. She married Francis Marion[6] "Frank" Hash on August 27, 1867 in Allegheny County, North Carolina. He was born on January 28, 1843, presumably in Grayson County, Virginia. He died on December 27, 1893, presumably in Allegheny County, North Carolina. His father was James Phipps[5] [William Horton[4] {Hashe of Montgomery, later Grayson, County, Virginia}, William Horton Lewis[3], John[2] "Old John," John[1] {of England}] Hash of Grayson County, Virginia. His mother was Margaret Adeline [Joshua, Jonathan] Stamper of Grayson County, Virginia. Caroline and Frank[6] had four children: Reece Clinton[7], Laura Ann[7], William Edwin[7] and John Horton[7].

Daniel had married, first, Ellender "Nellie" Long. The date and place of their marriage is not known. She was born on January 11, 1781 in Ashe County, North Carolina She died on March 12, 1801 in Allegheny County, North Carolina. Her father was John [Gabriel Tobias, Edward {Longue}] Long of Cecil County, Maryland. Her mother was Susannah[4] [John[3] {of Hopewell, Hunterdon, New Jersey}, Francis[2] {of Staten Island, Richmond

County, New York}, John[1] {of England}, Govert[1a] {Van of The Netherlands}] Vannay of Potts Creek, Rowan County, North Carolina. Daniel and Ellender had nine children: Tobias, Martha Caroline "Patsy," Elizabeth, Patience, Mary, Phoebe, John R., Rochel and Cynthia.

12. Nancy[6] Sturgill
born on January 15, 1803 in Allegheny County, North Carolina. She died on November 3, 1894 in Allegheny County, North Carolina and was buried there in Fielden Ward Farm near Turkey Knob. She married Andrew[5] Osborne in 1829 in Allegheny County, North Carolina. He was born on November 15, 1799 in Grayson County, Virginia. He died in January 1877 in Allegheny County, North Carolina and was buried there at Fielden Ward Farm near Turkey Knob. His father was Enoch[4] [Enoch[3], Ephraim[2], Jonathan[1] {of Warwickshire, England}] Osborne of Grayson County, Virginia. His mother was Mary[2] [Thomas[1] {of Pleasington, Blackthorn, Lancashire, England and later of Pittsylvania County, Virginia}, Thomas[1a], John[2a], John[3a], Thomas[4a], John[5a], Thomas[6a]] Livesay of Franklin County, Virginia. Nancy[6] and Andrew[5] had three children:

a. Rebecca[6] Osborne
born in 1831 in Allegheny County, North

Carolina. She died in March 8, 1880 in Grayson County, Virginia. She married Riley[8] Ward sometime before 1854 [when their first child was born] in Grayson County, Virginia. He was born in 1820 in Grayson County, Virginia. His date and place of death is not known. His father was Zachariah[7] [Nathan[6], Wells[5] {of Queen Anne's Parish, Prince Georges County, Maryland}, Nathan[4], James[3] {of Charles County, Maryland}, John[2], George[1] {of London, England}] Ward of Buck Mountain, Grayson County, Virginia. His mother was Tabitha[4] [John[3], John[2], John[1] {of England and later of Montgomery County, Virginia}, Thomas[1a] {born circa 1602 of Tenterden, Kent, England} Hash of Grayson County, Virginia. Riley[8] and Rebecca[6] had three children: Tamsey Tabitha[9], Andrew Jackson[9] and Zacharaiah Fielden[9].

b. Mary Jane[6] "Polly" Osborne
born on November 2, 1833 in Grayson County, Virginia. She died on April 7, 1874 at Elk Creek, Grayson County, Virginia. She married Alexander Dixon[8] Osborne sometime before 1860 [when their first child was born] in Grayson County, Virginia. He was born in July 1834 in Grayson County, Virginia. His date and place of death is not known. His father was Felix[7] [Enoch[6], "Captain" Enoch[5] {of Yadkin Valley,

Rowen County, North Carolina}, Ephraim[4] {of Essex County, New Jersey}, Ephraim[3] {of East Hampton, Middlesex County, Connecticut}, Ephraim[2], John[1] {of Ashford, Kent, England}, Thomas[1a], Jeremy[2a], Thomas[3a]] Osborne of Grayson County, Virginia. His mother was Lydia Dixon of North Carolina. Mary Jane[6] and Alexander[8] had six children: William R.[9], Alexander[9], John Sherman[9], Enoch S.[9], Lydia E.[9] and Nancy[9].

c. Enoch Livesay[6] Osborne
born on July 1, 1836 in Grayson County, Virginia. He died sometime after 1900 in Bosque County, Texas. He married Margaret Malinda "Peggy" Phipps in May 1860 in Grayson County, Virginia. They were divorced on November 2, 1875 in Livingston County, Illinois. She was born on December 27, 1843 in Grayson County, Virginia. She died on September 22, 1905 at Denver, Denver County, Colorado. Her father was Hugh [John, Benjamin {of Orange County, Virginia}, Joseph {of Philadelphia County, Pennsylvania}, Isaiah] Phipps of Fox Creek, Grayson County, Virginia. Her mother was Edith [John H. {of Wilkes County, North Carolina}, Nathan {of Woodbridge, Middlesex County, New Jersey}, Nathan {of New York}, Recompence {Stansbury of Long

246

Island, New York}] Stansberry of Grayson County, Virginia. Enoch[6] and Margaret had five children: Felix W.[7], Hugh Alexander[7], John Andrew[7], Anna Polly[7] and Arthur Augustus[7].

Margaret married, second, Quincy Adams Gorbet on November 7, 1875 in Livingston County, Illinois. He was born on February 4, 1832 in Claremont County, Ohio. He died on February 4, 1892 in Denver County, Colorado. His father was Henry David [Peter] Gorbet of Berks County, Pennsylvania. His mother was Sarah "Sally" Robinson of Franklin County, Maine. Margaret and Quincy had three children: Edwin Quincy, Ida May and Martha E.

Quincy had married, first, Rebecca C. Holland on March 23, 1854 at Ottawa, LaSalle County, Illinois. She was born on March 24, 1839 in Clermont County, Ohio. She died in 1870 at Pontiac, LaSalle County, Illinois. Her father was Edward C. Holland of Clermont County, Ohio. Her mother was Eva Catherine [Benjamin] Hess of Pennsylvania. Quincy and Rebecca had four children: Peter, Orlando Fidelious, Pruella and Alice.

S

JAMES STURGILL Sr c1725 — 1803
ANN GALLOWAY STURGILL WIFE OF JAMES

FRANCIS STURGILL Sr c1755 — 1807
REBECCA HASH STURGILL c1758 — 1841

REBECCA STURGILL WEAVER 1791 — 1828
WIFE OF WILLIAM WEAVER Jr

ANN STURGILL PERKINS 1793 — 1819
WIFE OF TIMOTHY PERKINS

SEVEN GRANDCHILDREN OF FRANCIS & REBECCA

The Life and Times of
James[4] Stodgill/Sturgill

PATERNAL ANCESTRY: [STURGILL/STODGILL: James[3], John Daniel[2], John[1] {of North Petherton Parish, Somersetshire, England}, Richard[1a], George[2a]]

MATERNAL ANCESTRY: [BLACKSTONE: Ann Williams[4], Argyle[3], Argyle[2], Thomas[1] {of England or Scotland}]

[EDITOR'S NOTE: The spelling STURGILL begins with this ancestor and continued through his direct descendants. On the Montomery County Virginia tax list for 1782 there were three Sturgills: Francis, Ambrose, and one with first name not given; also there is a James Sturgill in early Ashe County, North Carolina records. The name has variant spelling: Sturgis, Sturgeon, Stodgill and Stoggell. The family history has been researched tracing its route back up the Wagon Road to Orange County Virginia, where the will of James Stodgill left an estate including a "pair of old bagpipes" [1753]. Before that the name is found in Pennsylvania and New Jersey records, and an Ebenezer Sturgis signed the Elizabeth Town, New Jersey petition, 1744. The name is Scots-Irish in origin. The James Sturgill of Orange County, Virginia had sons, including the James, and Ambrose named above who traveled into the New River Valley together.

Their descendants are traced in the genealogy by David Sturgill, Sturgill: A Family History; the original Sturgill home place in the New River Valley was halfway between the forks of New River and Mouth of Wilson, on the north side of the river, 25 miles from Sturgills, North Carolina. Also see Allegheny County {North Carolina} Heritage 1983 (454-59).]

JAMES[4] was born circa 1730 in Orange County, Virginia. He died circa 1803/1804 in Ashe County, North Carolina and was buried in the Old Sturgill Cemetery, Piney Creek, Allegheny, North Carolina. His father was James[3] Stodgill of Essex County and later Orange County, Virginia. His mother was Ann Williams[4] Blackstone of Essex County, Virginia.

JAMES[4] married Susannah Ann[3] Calloway [another researcher calls her Ann Murphy Calloway] circa 1748 in Orange County, Virginia. Susannah[4] was born circa 1722/1725 in Essex County, Virginia. She died circa 1789 in Grayson County, Virginia. Her father was Joseph[3] [Joseph[2], Edmund[1] {of England}, William[1a]] Calloway of Caroline County and later of Essex County, Virginia. Her mother was Catherine Ann[2] [Joseph[1] {of England}] Brown of Lunenburg County, Virginia.

JAMES[4] and his brother Ambrose[4] had disposed of their land in Orange County by 1768 and were probably living in Montgomery County, Virginia. Both brothers deliberately changed the name to STURGEON and it appeared this way in Virginia records for many years. However, in later years, in an attempt to change back to the original spelling of STODGILL, they became known as STURGILL [probably by clerks spelling the name phonetically from the mouths of illiterate mountain men with thick accents]. In 1777 James[4] refused to take the oath of allegiance to the Commonwealth of Virginia before the clerk of Court of Montgomery County and he was described in the court records as an ". . . old and inoffensive man."

JAMES[4] was granted 70 acres of land in 1782. The property was on New River in Montgomery County, Virginia and, while it has not been precisely located, it appears to have been near the forks of the New River in what is now Allegheny County, North Carolina [Editor's Note: Before the Revolutionary War many people living in the mountains were little concerned about deeds, but after independence was won, many of them obtained legal deeds so they could leave the land to their heirs without contest, and James[4] may have been interested in new land to be sure his heirs had property willed to them].

The Children of
James[4] Stodgill/Sturgill
and Susannah Ann[4] Calloway

1. Ambrose Abraham[5] Sturgill
   born circa 1750 at Standardsville, Swift Run Creek, Orange County [in the part of Orange County that later became Greene County], Virginia. He died sometime after 1810 in Hayward County, North Carolina. He married Sarah Crostwait in 1770 in Allegheny County, North Carolina. She was born in 1750 in Orange County, Virginia. Her date and place of death is not known. The name of her father and mother is not known. Ambrose[5] and Sarah had at least one child:

   a. William[6] Sturgill [afa Stargel and Stockdell] born circa 1773 in Grayson County, Virginia [other researchers say circa 1770 in Allegheny County, North Carolina]. He died circa 1835 in Haywood County, North Carolina. He married Delphia Roszel [afa Roszell and Russell] on January 23, 1793 in Orange County, Virginia. She was born in 1775 in Orange County, Virginia. She died at Versailes, Woodford County, Virginia. Her father was Nehemiah [Peter of Weschester County, New York}] Roszell of Monmouth County, New Jersey and later of Davidson County, Tennessee. Her mother was Sarah Collins of Montgomery County, New York. William[6] and Delphia had four children: Hannah[7], Jacob[7], Mary[7] and John Jones[7] [who later became a Reverend].

2. Mary[5] Sturgill
born circa 1753 at Standardsville, Swift Run Creek, Orange County [in the part of Orange County that later became Greene County], Virginia. Her date of death in Hayward County, North Carolina is not known. She married John Jones circa 1770 in Orange County, Virginia. He was born circa 1750/1753 in Orange County, Virginia. His date and place of death is not known. The name of his father and mother is not known. Issue, if any, is not known.

3. **Francis[5] Sturgill**
born on circa 1755 at Standardsville, Swift Run Creek, Orange County [in the part of Orange County that later became Greene County], Virginia. He died in December 1807 at Piney Creek, Ashe County, North Carolina. He married Rebecca[3] Hash of Montgomery County, Virginia circa 1776 in Virginia. She was born circa 1758/1760 in Virginia. She died in 1841 at Piney Creek, Ashe County, North Carolina. Her father was John[2] "Old John," [John[1] {Hache of England}, Thomas[1a] {born circa 1602}] Hash of Grayson

County and later of Montgomery County, Virginia. Her mother was Rebecca [Jacob] Anderson of Fincastle, Grayston County, Virginia. Francis[5] and Rebecca had twelve children: Lydia[6], John[6], James[6], Francis[6], William[6], Joel Cass[6], David[6], Rebecca[6], Jane[6], Ann[6], Elizabeth[6] and Nancy[6].

4. Ruth[5] Sturgill
   born on January 9, 1758 at Standardsville, Swift Run Creek, Orange County [in the part of Orange County that later became Greene County], Virginia. She died in 1822 in Greene County [another source says Hardin County], Kentucky. She married Thomas[3] Hash in 1776 in Orange County [another source says Wythe County], Virginia. Thomas[3] was born on February 13, 1756 in Virginia. He died on 25 December 1848 at Mt. Vernon, Lawrence County, Missouri. His father was John[2] "Old John," [John[1] {Hache of England}, Thomas[1a] {born circa 1602}] Hash of Grayson County and later of Montgomery County, Virginia. Her mother was Rebecca [Jacob] Anderson of Fincastle, Grayston County, Virginia. Ruth[5] and Thomas[3] had ten children:

   a. Elizabeth[4] "Betsy" Hash
      born in 1778 Wythe County, Virginia. Her date and place of death is not known. She married James[4] Gaddie on October 9, 1798 in Greene

County, Kentucky. He was born in 1773 in Virginia. His date and place of death is not known. His father was George[3] [George[2] {of Bisland, New Kent County, Virginia}, William[1] {of Cupar-Burgh, Fife, Scotland}, Hendri[1a], John[2a] {of St. Andrews and St. Leonards, Fife, Scotland}] Gaddy of Bedford County, Virginia. His mother was Susannah Morris Kerr of Virginia. Elizabeth[4] and James[4] had two children Melinda[5] and John[5].

b. Jane[4] Hash
    born circa 1782 Wythe County, Virginia. She died in 1870 in Green County, Kentucky. She married Samuel[6] Combs on October 15, 1804 in Greene County, Kentucky. He was born on January 8, 1772 in Nelson County, Kentucky. He died on May 2, 1842 at Rock Creek, Menard County, Illinois. His father was John Davenport[5] [Joseph J.[4] {of Coomes Purchase, Charles County, Maryland}, Thomas[3], Richard T.[2], Richard[1] {of Stratford-on-Avon, Warwickshire, England}] Combs [afa Coomes] of Loudoun County, Virginia. His mother was Alice Nelson[2] "Elsie" [Samuel[1] {of Londonderry, Derry, Ulster, Ireland}] Jolly of Bucks County, Pennsylvania. Jane[4] and Samuel[6] had eleven children: Elizabeth[7], Thomas[7], Asa[7], Martha[7], Ruth[7], John[7], Alice[7], Jane[7], Nelson[7], Samuel R.[7] and

Sarah J.[7].

c. Nancy[4] Hash
circa in 1782/1784 in Wythe County, Virginia. She died on October 7, 1847 at Newmansville, Cass County, Illinois. She married James Fletcher on November 6, 1809 in Green County, Kentucky. He was born circa 1786 in Virginia. His date and place of death is not known. His father was Spencer [William {of Prince William or Stafford County, Virginia}] Fletcher of Faquier County, Virginia. His mother was Frances "Fannie" (Unknown) of Virginia. Nancy[4] and James had a child: Joseph C.

c. James[4] Hash
born in 1786 in Montgomery County, Virginia. He died in 1816 in Muhlenberg County, Kentucky. He married Sarah "Sally" Martin on October 20, 1807 in Greene County, Kentucky. She was born circa 1789/1795 in Virginia. She died in 1812 in Green County, Kentucky. Her father was Hartwell [Martin {Martin of St. Peters Parish, New Kent County, Virginia}] Martin of Charles City, Charles County, Virginia and later of Greene County, Kentucky. Her mother was Sallie [Edward Elias {of Fairfax, Fairfax County, Virginia}, John, Thomas {of Westmorland County, Virginia}] Porter of

Virginia and later of Greene County, Kentucky [another source says her mother was Nancy Skaggs]. James[4] and Sarah had at least five children: Alfred[5], Nancy[5], Joel[5], Thomas[5] and Sarah[5] [other researchers list five other children: Mary Ann[5], Reuben[5], Frances[5], Joseph[5] and Franklin[5]].

[Editor's Note: It is purported that Sally married, second, (Unknown) Scott, but no further record has been found]

e. Phillip[4] Hash
born on January 31, 1790 at Fincastle, Botetourt County, Virginia. He died on August 5, 1849 at Mount Vernon, Lawrence County, Missouri and was buried there on August 7th in the Old Taylor Graveyard. He married Sarah "Sally" Nance on January 10, 1809 at Charles City, Charles County, Virginia. She was born on October 24, 1791 near Richmond, Henrico County, Virginia. She died on February 24, 1897 in Lawrence County, Missouri and was buried there at Mount Vernon in the Old Taylor Cemetery. Her father was Zachariah Nance of Charles City County, Virginia. Her mother was Jane Wilkins of James City County, Virginia. Philip[4] and Sarah had sixteen children: Jane[5], Zachariah[5], Thomas[5], Martha[5], John[5], Caroline[5],

Polly[5], James[5], Robert[5], Henry[5], William[5], Philip Anderson[5], Nancy[5], (child)[5], (child)[5] and (child)[5].

f. Sarah[4] "Sally" Hash
born in 1791 in Wythe County, Virginia. She died on January 7, 1831 at Newmansville, Cass County, Illinois.

g. Mary[4] "Polly" Hash
born in 1793 in Greene County, Kentucky. She died in 1860 in Grundy County, Illinois. She married Eaton Nance sometime before 1826 [when their first child was born] in Illinois. He was born on September 14, 1794 in Virginia. He died in December 1880 in Grundy County, Illinois. His father was Zachariah Nance of Charles City County, Virginia. His mother was Jane Wilkins of James City County, Virginia. Mary[4] and Eaton had six children: Elizabeth, Robert, Ruth, Charles, Malinda and Caroline.

h. Ruth Sturgill[4] Hash
born in 1794 [another record says 1791] in Virginia. She died in 1822 in Greene County, Kentucky. She married Robert Nance on January 1, 1811 in Greene County, Kentucky. He was born on February 22, 1788 in Charles City County, Virginia. He died on November

14, 1853 in Lawrence County, Missouri. His father was Zachariah Nance of Charles City County, Virginia. His mother was Jane Wilkins of James City County, Virginia. Ruth[4] and Robert had seven children: Philip, Samuel, Thomas Hash, Elias, John, Henry and James Hansford.

Robert married, second, Mary Blunt on November 28, 1833 in Morgan County, Illinois. She was born in 1797 in Lawrence County, Missouri. Her date and place of death is not known. The name of her father and mother is not known. Robert and Mary had two children: Otway and Sarah.

   i. William[4] Hash
born in 1797 in Virginia. His date and place of death is not known.

   j. Martha[4] Hash
born in 1801 in Virginia. Her date and place of death is not known.

5. James[5] Sturgill
born in 1761 at Standardsville, Swift Run Creek, Orange County [in the part of Orange County that later became Greene County], Virginia. He died sometime after 1834 in Morgan County, Kentucky.

He married Rebecca (Unknown) [Editor's Note: Some researchers confuse her with the Rebecca Cordille {also found as Cordill and Caudill} who married a James Sturgill born in 1832 in Harlan County, Kentucky] circa 1776/1780 in Orange County, Virginia. She was born circa 1764 [another researcher says 1761] in Orange County, Virginia. Her date and place of death is not known. The name of her father and mother is not known. James[5] left Orange/Grayson County, Virginia for Morgan County, Kentucky circa 1815/1820.

[Editor's Note: Several researchers claim James[5] and Rebecca's children were later found as Sturgeon, particularly those who were supposed to have migrated to other states; however, further research indicates these Sturgeons are not of this family and, in fact, makes this list of children as suspect]

James[5] and Rebecca had twelve children:

a. David[6] Sturgill
   born circa 1784 in Grayson County, Virginia. His date and place of death is not known.

b. (daughter)[6] Sturgill
   born circa 1786 in Grayson County, Virginia. Her date and place of death is not known.

c. (daughter)[6] Sturgill
   born circa 1788 in Grayson County, Virginia.
   Her date and place of death is not known.

d. (daughter)[6] Sturgill
   born circa 1790 in Grayson County, Virginia.
   Her date and place of death is not known.

e. Jeremiah[6] Sturgill
   born circa 1793 in Grayson County, Virginia.
   His date and place of death is not known.

f. Elisha[6] Sturgill
   born circa 1796 in Grayson County, Virginia.
   His date and place of death is not known.

g. (daughter)[6] Sturgill
   born circa 1800 in Grayson County, Virginia.
   Her date and place of death is not known.

h. James[6] Sturgill
   born circa 1804 in Grayson County, Virginia.
   His date and place of death is not known.

i. Thomas[6] Sturgill
   born circa 1806 in Grayson County, Virginia.
   His date and place of death is not known.

j. (daughter)[6] Sturgill
born circa 1808 in Grayson County, Virginia.
Her date and place of death is not known.

k. (daughter)[6] Sturgill
born circa 1810 in Grayson County, Virginia.
Her date and place of death is not known.

l. John[6] Sturgill
born circa 1812 in Grayson County, Virginia.
His date and place of death is not known.

6. Theodocia[5] "Docia" Sturgill
born circa 1762/1765 at Standardsville, Swift Run
Creek, Orange County [in the part of Orange
County that later became Greene County],
Virginia. She died circa 1830 in Washington
County, Arkansas. She married John[3] Hash in 1784
in Orange County, Virginia [another record says
Ashe County, North Carolina]. He was born circa
1763/1764 in Orange County, Virginia. He died
circa 1842/1845 in Madison County, Arkansas. His
father was John[2] "Old John," [John[1] {Hache of
England and later of Montgomery County, Vir-
ginia}, Thomas[1a] {born circa 1602 of Tenterden,
Kent, England}] Hash of Grayson County and later
Montgomery County, Virginia. His mother was
Elizabeth[4] [James[3], John Daniel[2], John[1], Richard[1a],
George[2a]] Sturgill, Hash's second wife [his first

wife being Rebecca Anderson]. Theodocia[5] and John[3] had nine children:

a. William Wesley[4] Hash
born in 1783 in Grayson County, Virginia. He died, age 68, on October 1, 1851 at Rock Island, Warren County, Tennessee.

b. Nancy[4] Hash
born on February 11, 1790 in Grayson County, Virginia. She died on October 7, 1847 at Newmansville, Cass County, Illinois.

c. Thomas[4] Hash
born on April 2, 1792 in Grayson County, Virginia. He died, age 72, in 1865 at Rock Island, Warren County, Tennessee. He married Drucilla Howell in 1809 at Rock Island, Warren County, Tennessee. She was born in 1794 in Grayson County, Virginia. She died in 1863 at Rock Island, Warren County, Tennessee. Her father was George [James {of North Carolina}] Howell of Grayson County, Virginia. Her mother was Mary "Polly" [Enoch {of Rowen County, North Carolina}] Osborne of Grayson County, Virginia. Thomas[4] and Druscilla had nine children: Ewing A.[5], Malinda[5], Susan C.[5], Avary Melvin[5], Adaline Euphrates[5], Nancy[5], Tabitha Starr[5], Louisa[5] and George Howell[5].

d. John[4] Hash

born on April 16, 1794 in Grayson County,
Virginia. He died on March 20, 1828 at Spring-
field, Sagamon County, Illinois. He married
Mary[2] "Polly" Cole on January 15, 1812 in
Jefferson County, Kentucky. She was born on
September 15, 1794 in Grayson County,
Virginia. She died in September 1862 in Pike
County, Iowa. Her father was James[1] Cole of
Peterborough, Northamptonshire, England. Her
mother was Elizabeth [John {of Amherst
County, Virginia} John] Isom of Wythe County,
Virginia. John[4] and Mary[2] had seven children:
Nancy[5], Martha Ann[5], James Henderson[5], Alvin
Galinton[5], Teodocia Emmaline[5], John Isom[5] and
William Thomas[5].

Mary[2] married, second, David Ketchum in 1828
at Springfield, Sagamon County, Illinois.

Mary[2] married, third, Daniel Ketchum in 1835
at Springfield, Sagamon County, Illinois. He
was born on April 11, 1796 in Virginia. He died
in 1862, presumably in Pike County, Iowa. The
name of his father and mother is not known.
Mary[2] and Daniel had two children: Christopher C. and Mary Elizabeth.

e. Phoebe[4] Hash
    born circa in 1796 in Green County, Kentucky.
    Her date and place of death is not known [she
    may have died young].

f. Tabitha[4] Hash
    born on December 3, 1799 in Grayson County,
    Virginia. She died on March 1, 1885 in Grayson
    County, Virginia. She married Zachariah Ward
    on January 29, 1818 in Grayson County, Virg-
    inia. He was born on April 13, 1792 in Grayson
    County, Virginia. He died on November 18,
    1878 in Grayson County, Virginia. His father
    was Nathan [Wells Nathan {of Queen Anne's
    Parish/County, Maryland}] Ward of Coal
    Creek, Grayson County, Virginia. His mother
    was Sarah "Sally" Canoe of Lee County,
    Virginia Tabitha[4] and Zachariah had four
    children: Rosamond, Stephen, Silas and
    Zahcariah.

g. Alvin Josh[4] Hash
    born on March 18, 1800 in Ashe County, North
    Carolina [another researcher says Washington
    County, Kentucky]. He died on August 18, 1844
    at Richland, Washington County, Arkansas. He
    married Esther Elizabeth Drake in 1821 in
    Warren County, Tennessee. She was born on
    October 12, 1803 in Warren County, Tennessee.

She died on August 23, 1878 in Washington County, Arkansas. Her father was Jacob Drake of Juniata River, Bedford County, Pennsylvania. Her mother was Mary Esther "Polly" Nolen of Somerset County, Pennsylvania. Alvin[4] and Esther had fourteen children: Alvin G.[5], Salina[5], Livonia[5], Mary[5] "Polly," Fielding[5], Phoebe[5], Martha Melinda[5], Caroline[5], Emeline[5], Susan[5], Alvin[5], Viola[5], Benjamin[5] and Esther Elizabeth[5].

h. Mary[4] Hash
born in 1801 in Ashe County, North Carolina. She died in 1865. Her place of death is not known.

i. Lucinda[4] Hash
born in 1803 in Ashe County, North Carolina. She died in 1880 in Fayette, Calhoun County, Arkansas. She married Ralph[7] Lucas in 1823, possibly in Arkansas. He was born on June 12, 1802 at Boone, Hawkins County, Tennessee. He died on June 19, 1867 at Fayetteville, Washington County, Arkansas. His father was John[6] [John[5], Charles[4] {of Spotsylvania County, Virginia}, William[3] {of Brunswick County, Virginia}, William[2] {of Surry County, Virginia}, William[1] {of Saltash, Cornwall, England}, William[1a], William[2a], Roger[3a] {of Woodchurch, Kent, England}, Robert[4a], William[5a], Thomas

Houchon[6a] {of Sachum Parva, Suffolk, England}, "Sir" John Fitz[7a], Edmund Fitz[8a], John Fitz[9a], Edmond Fitz[10a], John[11a] {FitzLucas}, Edmund[12a] {born circa 1300 of St. Edmunds, Suffolk, England}] Lucas of Montgomery County, Virginia. His mother was Mary Kelly of Grayson County, Virginia. Lucinda[4] and Ralph[7] had nine children; Nancy[8], Mary[8] "Polly," Docia Elinor[8], Lucinda C.[8], Catherine[8], Sarah[8], William F.[8], Ralph L.[8] and William[8].

j. Fielding Henry[4] Hash
    born in 1805 at Pottoe Creek, Ashe County, North Carolina. He died in December 1849 at Clear Creek, Washington County, Arkansas. He married Elizabeth Katherine Russell on May 2, 1829 at Louisville, Jefferson County, Kentucky. She was born on August 9, 1811 at Louisville, Jefferson County, Kentucky. She died on June 17, 1880 at Bolivar, Polk County, Missouri. His father was Thomas [Nicholas] Russell of Pennsylvania. His mother was Charity [Solomon {afa Cornell}] Cornwell of Dutchess County, New York. Issue, if any, is not known.

7. John[5] Sturgill
    born in 1763 at Standardsville, Swift Run Creek, Orange County [in the part of Orange County that later became Greene County], Virginia. He died in

1820 in Grayson County, Virginia [another source says he died before 1830 in Crawford County, Indiana] and is buried there in the Sturgill Cemetery. He married Rebecca Ann Baldwin circa 1780, presumably in Grayson County, Virginia. She was born circa 1752 in Orange County, Virginia. She died in 1804 in Floyd County, Kentucky. Her father was Elijah Baldwin of Orange County, Virginia. The name of her mother is not known. John[5] and Rebecca had at least three children and maybe others:

a. John W.[6] Sturgill
   born in 1780 in Grayson County, Virginia. He died in 1839 in Floyd County, Kentucky. He married Amy Hall in 1798 in Grayson County, Virginia. She was born in 1780 in Ash County, North Carolina. She died in 1870 in Floyd County, Kentucky. Her father was Jesse [Thomas, John] Hall of Johnson Creek, Lunenburg County, Virginia. Her mother was Candacia Dicy[3] [John[2] "Old John," John[1] {Hashe of England}, Thomas[1a]] Hash of Grayson County, Virginia. John[6] and Amy had five children: Elijah[7], Jesse Jasper[7], Amy[7], Edith[7] and William[7].

b. Joseph Sturgeon[6] Sturgill
   born 1784 in Grayson County, Virginia. He

270

died in 1840 in Johnson County, Kentucky.

c. James[6] Sturgill
date of birth in Grayson County, Virginia is not known. His date and place of death is not known.

8. Lewis[5] Sturgill
born in 1765 at Standardsville, Swift Run Creek, Orange County [in the part of Orange County that later became Greene County], Virginia. He died in 1835 in Hawkins County, Tennessee. He married, first, Sarah[6] Hanks circa 1785 in Grayson County, Virginia. She was born circa 1765 in Orange County, Virginia. She died in 1840 in Hawkins County, Tennessee. Her father was Abraham[5] [Richard[4], William J.[3], William J.[2], Thomas[1] {of Shropshire, England}] Hanks of Virginia. The name of her mother was Sarah[3] [George[2], William[1] {of Scotland}] Harper of Campbell County, Virginia. Lewis[5] and Sarah[6] had six children:

a. Mary[6] "Polly" Sturgill
born in 1786 in Ashe County, North Carolina. She died on February 21, 1863 in Floyd County, Kentucky. She married Nimrod Rodden Hall in 1802 in Ashe County, North Carolina. He was born in 1784 in Ashe County, North Carolina. He died on June 2, 1875 at Lanesville, Floyd

County, Kentucky. His father was Jesse Hall of Jonathan Creek, Lunenburg, Halifax County, Virginia. His mother was Candacia Dicy Hash of Lunenburg, Halifax County, Virginia. Mary[6] and Nimrod had a child: Nimrod Sturgill.

b. John[6] Sturgill
born in 1787 in Grayson County, Virginia. He died in 1864 in Washington County, Virginia. He married Nancy Robbins in 1820 in Washington County, Virginia. She was born in 1790 in Grayson County, Virginia. Her date and place of death is not known. The name of her father and mother is not known. John[6] and Nancy had a child: Minerva[7].

c. Fielding[6] Sturgill
born in 1789 in Grayson County, Virginia. He died in 1864 in Lawrence, Lawrence County, Ohio. He married Phoebe[7] Sturgill on December 2, 1829, probably in North Carolina. She was born in 1809 in North Carolina. Her date of death in Gallia County, Ohio is not known. Her father was William[6] [Francis[5], James[4], James[3], John Daniel[2], John[1] of {North Petherton Parish, Somersetshire, England}, Richard[1a], George[2a]] Sturgill of Grayson County, Virginia. Her mother was Sophia[7] ["Doctor" David[6], Job[5], David[4], John[3], Phillip[2] {of Weymouth, Norfolk

County, Massachusetts}, John[1] {of Sherborne, Dorsetshire, England}, John[1a]] King of Ashe County, North Carolina. Fielding[6] and Phoebe[7] had seven children: William[7], Susan A.[7], Armand[7], James W.[7], Mary[7], Malinda[7] and Elvery[7].

d. Samuel[6] Sturgill

born in 1794 in Grayson County, Virginia. His date of death in Hawkins County, Tennessee is not known. He married Sarah (Unknown) in 1818 in Hawkins County, Tennessee. She was born in 1800 in Hawkins County, Tennessee. She died in 1860 in Hawkins County, Tennessee. Samuel[6] and Sarah had four children: (a daughter)[7] and three others whose names are not known.

EDITOR'S NOTE: On the following child, Alvin[6] Sturgill, there a lot of differences with researchers as to his marriages and dates thereof. The children are sorted out based on their year of birth. What follows is the best this editor can determine]

e. Alvin[6] Sturgill

born in 1800 in Grayson County, Virginia. He died on June 18, 1904 at Pickering, Nodaway County, Missouri. He married Pearl Lena Fraley on February 14, 1830 in Hawkins

County, Tennessee. She was born in 1813 in Hawkins County, Tennessee. She died in 1909 in Elliott County, Kentucky [Editor's Note: Apparently, they had a child prior to their marriage as Mary Lucinda[7] was purportedly born in 1828]. Apparently, they were divorced as he married second when Pearl was still living. The name of her father and mother is not known. Alvin[6] and Pearl had at least three children: Mary Lucinda[7], Elizabeth[7] and Isaac Lewis[7], and possibly a fourth child named America[7].

Alvin[6] married, second, Nancy Jane Fraley [this editor wonders if they were sisters or cousins] on January 14, 1841, supposedly in Ashe County, North Carolina [which seems odd as he was living in Elliot County, Kentucky and their first child was born there in 1843; the place of marriage is probably incorrect]. She was born on October 15, 1834 in Hawkins County, Tennessee. She died in 1909 in Elliott County, Kentucky [which makes this editor wonder if Alvin[6] left her, as he died in Missouri in 1904]. The names of her father and mother is not known. Alvin[6] and Nancy had five children: Virginia[7], Dianah[7], Alexander[7], Sarah D.[7] and Abigail F.[7].

f. William[6] Sturgill

born in 1802 [another researcher says 1808] in Grayson County, Virginia. He died in 1850 at Hendricks Mills, Russell County [another researcher says Scott County], Virginia. He married Rebecca (Unknown) in 1827 in Scott County, Virginia. She was born in 1807 in Scott County, Virginia. Her date of death in Lee County, Virginia is not known. William[6] and Rebecca had five children: Morgan[7], (boy)[7], (girl)[7], William[7] and Henry[7].

[Editor's Note: Some researchers claim Lewis[5] married second, Sarah Cole circa 1785/1787 in Virginia, but the date of marriage does not equate to that of his marriage to Sarah Hanks.]

The Life and Times of
James[3] Stodgill

PATERNAL ANCESTRY: [STURGILL/STODGILL: John Daniel[2], John[1] {of North Petherton Parish, Somersetshire, England}, Richard[1a], George[2a]]

MATERNAL ANCESTRY: [FRANKS: Ann, Daniel, Daniel]

JAMES[3] was born circa 1695 near Tappahannock in Essex County, Virginia. He died in 1753 in Orange County [another researcher says Rappahannock], Virginia. His father was John Daniel[2] Stodghill of Essex County, Virginia. His mother was Ann Franks of Rappahannock County, Virginia.

JAMES[3] married Ann Williams[4] Blackstone in 1723 in Essex County, Virginia. She was born in 1700 in Essex County, Virginia. She died in 1763 at St. Thomas Parish, Orange County, Virginia. Her father was Argyle/Argoll[3] [Argyle[2], Thomas[1] {of Scotland}] Blackstone of Essex County, Virginia. Her mother was Elizabeth[2] [Robert[1] {of Scotland and later of Rappahannock County, Virginia}] Armstrong of Essex County, Virginia.

JAMES[3] first appears in the records of Spottsylvania County, Virginia in 1732 when he was appointed overseer of a section of road. He served on the first jury called after Orange County was formed in 1734. He appears on a taxt list in the precinct of Thomas Calloway in 1735.

JAMES[3] of St. Marks Parish, Spottsylvania County, purchased from Zachariah Taylor of Drysdale Parish, Caroline County, for 20 pounds [sterling] 200 acres in St. Marks Parish on the branches of the James River near the foot of Parker Mountain, adjoining David Williams' property. The deed was witnessed by Daniel[3] Stodghill, Thomas Calloway and John Zachary and recorded by John Waller, Clerk of Court [1732 SPOTTSYLVANIA COUNTY DEED BOOK B:346-347].

JAMES[3] was sued by William Callaway on July 17, 1735 [CALLAWAY VS. STOGHILL] for trespass. Damages of 10 Pounds Sterling was asked. Callaway complained that James Stoghill, with force and arms, did shoot, kill and destroy a dog belonging to him. The case was dismissed as agreed.

JAMES[3] was indebted to Jefferey Croley for 260 pounds of tobacco for land bought of Croley in 1731. A petition was filed by Croley on July 19, 1735 and summons was sent to John Garrell in Caroline County [Virginia] to testify. Robert Dudley, Deputy Sheriff of Caroline County, reported the summons came into his hands too late to be executed and the action was dismissed [ORANGE COUNTY VIRGINIA DEED BOOK AND JUDGMENTS: CROLEY VS. STODGILL, August-September 1735].

JAMES[3] filed an action against Jeffrey Croley and Ella, his wife, complaining that they uttered false, scandalous words by means whereof he is not only fallen into discredit with his neighbors, but is also become liable to be prosecuted as a felon. The case was dismissed, as agreed [Same Court Session].

JAMES[3] bought 200 acres of land in 1741 in St. Thomas parish of Orange County from Thomas Calloway.

JAMES[3] Stodghill's will was filed on February 22, 1753 in the Orange County, Virginia Court House. The inventory's total valuation was 88 pounds, $18.10^{1/2}$ pence, including money due from Thomas Morris, George Berrie, John Lankford, Margaret Duglas, Moses Standley, William Standley, Darby Haney, Thomas Burbag, James Berry, Amb. Stodgill, William Hensley, James Stodgell, Thomas Morris, Eliza Bird, John Williams, John Love, Joseph Davis, Mr. Mosias Jones and John Lester. The witnesses were William Bell, Samuel Estis and Francis Williams. [WILL BOOK 2, 1744-1778 — Pages 185-186]

The Children of
James³ Stodgill
and Ann Williams⁴ Blackstone

1. **James⁴ Sturgill**
   born circa 1725 in Orange County, Virginia. He died circa 1803/1804 in Ashe County, North Carolina and was buried in the Old Sturgill Cemetery, Piney Creek, Allegheny, North Carolina. He married Susannah Ann⁴ Calloway circa 1748 in Orange County, Virginia. Susannah was born circa 1722/1725 in Essex County, Virginia. Her date and place of death is not known. Her father was Joseph³ [Joseph², Edmund¹ {of England}, William¹ᵃ] Calloway of Essex County, Virginia. Her mother was Catherine (Unknown). James⁴ and Susannah Ann⁴ had nine children: Ambrose⁵, John⁵, Mary⁵, Francis⁵, Ruth⁵, James⁵, Theodocia⁵ "Docia", John⁵ and Lewis⁵.

2. **Ambrose⁴ Stodgill**
   born circa 1727/1728 in Essex County, Virginia. He died in 1805 [another source says 1787 but he was still living in Grayson County, Virginia then and later moved to Kentucky] in Mercer County, Kentucky. He married Sarah Crostwait circa 1750/1753 in Orange County, Virginia. She was born circa 1733 in Orange County [another researcher says Essex County], Virginia. She died, pres-

280

umably by 1763 in Orange County, Virginia, when Ambrose[4] remarried. The name of her father and mother is not known. Ambrose[4] and Sarah two children:

[EDITOR'S NOTE: There is a lot of confusion about the children of Ambrose[4] Stodghill/Sturgill with both Sarah Crostwait and his second wife, Susannah Denton. I have listed all children reported by various researchers, even though some of the dates for the births of different children are in question. Further research is needed to sort out this issue.]

a. John[5] Sturgill [afa Stodghill]
born circa 1757 in Orange County, Virginia. His date of death in Mercer County, Kentucky is not known.

b. Samuel[5] Sturgill [afa Stodghill]
born circa 1760 in Orange County, Virginia. He died in 1836 in Jackson County, Indiana. He married Martha Elkins on January 1, 1799 in Clark County, Kentucky. She was born in 1781 in Montgomery County, Virginia. She died in 1854 in Jackson County, Indiana. Her father was Drury Elkins of Virginia. Her mother was Margaret (Unknown) of Virginia. Samuel[5] and Martha had seven children: Mary[6] "Polly,"

Drury[6], Nellie Renee[6], Margaret[6], William Sherman[6], Thoams[6] and Rebecca[6].

Ambrose[4] married, second, Susannah Denton on January 24, 1763 in Goochland County, Virginia. She was born circa 1745 in Essex County, Virginia. She died in 1824 in Fluvanna County, Virginia. Her father was William Hudson [William {of Brunswick County, Virginia}] Denton of Essex County Virginia. Her mother was Elizabeth [James] Dunman of Essex County, Virginia. Ambrose[4] and Susannah had eleven children:

   c. Cecilia[5] Sturgill [afa Stodghill]
      born circa 1763 in Albemarle County, Virginia. Her date and place of death is not known.

   d. Izell[5] Sturgill [afa Stodghill]
      born circa 1764 in Orange County, Virginia. His date of death in Orange County, North Carolina is not known.

   e. Ambrose[5] Sturgill [afa Stodghill]
      born circa 1765 in Orange County, Virginia. He probably died young as another child named Ambrose[5] was born in 1780.

   f. Jacob William[5] Sturgill [afa Stodghill]
      born in April 1768 in Orange County, Virginia.

His date of death in Mercer County, Kentucky is not known. He married Sally Duvall in 1786 in Orange County, Virginia.

Jacob[5] married, second, Kesiah West on November 25, 1794 in Kentucky. Jacob[5] and Kesiah had three children: (girl)[6], Reuben[6], (girl)[6].

g. William[5] Sturgill [afa Stodghill]
born on April 6, 1770 in Albemarle County, Virginia. He probably died young [another researcher says he died later in Highland County, Ohio; however, in 1773, there was another William[5] born].

h. Dorshee[5] "Docia" Sturgill [afa Stodghill]
born circa 1771 in Orange County, Virginia. Her date of death in Garrand County, Kentucky is not known. She married Jessee Liverston in 1799 in Garrand County, Kentucky. She married, second, James Lasley in 1845.

i. James[5] Sturgill [afa Stodghill]
born on July 5, 1772 in Albemarle County, Virginia. His date and place of death is not known.

j. William[5] Sturgill [afa Stodghill]
born in 1773 in North Carolina. He died in 1817 [another researcher says 1835 in Kentucky] in Harwood County, North Carolina. He married Delphia Roszel [afa Russell] in 1792 in Orange County, Virginia. She was born in 1775. She died on July 17, 1842. William[5] and Delphia had a child: John Jones[6].

k. Mary[5] Sturgill [afa Stodghill]
born circa 1775 in Albemarle County, Virginia. Her date and place of death in Prince Edward County, Virginia is not known.

l. Ambrose[5] Sturgill [afa Stodghill]
born on August 26, 1780 in Fluvanna County, Virginia. He died on July 5, 1812. His place of death is not known.

m. David[5] Sturgill [afa Stodghill]
born on May 23, 1883 in Fluvanna County, Virginia. His date of death in Stark County, Illinois is not known.

3. Mary[4] Sturgill
born circa 1730 in Orange County, Virginia. Her date and place of death in Orange County, Virginia is not known. She married William[5] Herring circa 1750 in Orange County, Virginia. He

was born circa 1730/1732 in Orange County, Virginia. He died in 1786 in Greene County, Virginia [another researcher says he died in White County, Tennessee]. His father was Alexander[4] [Alexander[3], Jan Pieterse[2] {Haring of Hoorn, Nord-Holland, The Netherlands}, Peter Janse[1] {of Nieunenhuysen, Noorn, Nord-Holland, The Netherlands and later of Tappan, Rockland County, New York}] Herring of Sussex County, Delaware. His mother was Abigail[2] [Isaiah[1] {of Brierly Hill, Yorkshire, England}, Richard[1a] {of West Kirby, Cheshire, England}, Richard[2a], Richard[3a] {born circa 1550 of Staffordshire, England}] Henison of Long Island City, Queens County, New York. Mary[4] and William[5] had eight children:

a. Henry[6] Herring
   born in 1750 in Orange [another researcher says Albemarle] County, Virginia. He died in July 1798 in Surry County, North Carolina. He married Morning Massey in 1771 in Wake County, North Carolina. She was born in 1751 in Wake County, North Carolina. She died in 1772 in Orange County, North Carolina. Her father was Abraham Massey of Orange County, North Carolina. Her mother was Gwendolyn Lewis of Orange County, North Carolina. There was no issue.

Henry[6] married, second, Frances "Franky" Creed in 1775 in Orange County, North Carolina. She was born in 1756 in Surry County, North Carolina. She died circa 1800 in Surry County, North Carolina. Her father was Matthew Creed of Virginia. Her mother was Margaret [John, John] McKinney of Orange County, Virginia. Henry[6] and Frances had at least one child: Margaret[7].

b. Sarah[6] Herring
born in 1752 in Orange County, Virginia. Her date and place of death is not known.

c. Elizabeth[6] Herring
born in 1754 in Albemarle County, Virginia. Her date and place of death is not known.

d. James[6] Herring
born circa 1755/1756 in Orange County, Virginia. He died on June 16, 1845 in Albemarle County, Virginia. He married Judah[6] Cofer [afa Cater] on April 2, 1784 in Orange County, Virginia. She was born in 1764 in Orange County, Virginia. She died in 1847 in Albemarle County, Virginia. Her father was James[5] [Thomas[4] {of Maryland}, John[3], Thomas[2] {of Charles County, Maryland}, John[1] {of England}] Cofer of Culpeper County, Virginia. Her mother was

Parthenia [John {of Frederick County, Virginia}] Linville of Orange County, Virginia. James[6] Herring was a Revolutionary War veteran. James[6] and Judah[6] had a child: Sally[7].

e. George[6] Herring
born on March 26, 1759 in Albemarle County, Virginia. He died on December 19, 1835 at Shelbyville, Shelby County, Indiana. He married Elizabeth Creed in 1795 in Surry County, North Carolina. She was born on August 7, 1771 in Virginia. She died on September 7, 1850 in Shelby County, Indiana. Her father was Matthew Creed of Virginia. Her mother was Margaret [John, John] McKinney of Orange County, Virginia. Issue, if any, is not known.

f. Thomas[6] Herring
born in 1764 in Orange County, Virginia. He died in October 1819 in Garrard County, Kentucky. He married Elizabeth[4] Rucker in Orange County, Virginia. The date of their marriage is not known. She was born in 1766 in Orange County, Virginia. She died on July 30, 1837 in Garrard County, Kentucky. Her father was Peter[3] ["Captain" John[2] {of Essex County, Virginia}, Peter[1] {from England; but possibly originally from Germany}] Rucker of Orange

County, Virginia. Her mother was Elizabeth[3] [Robert[2] {Terrell of St. Peters, New Kent County, Virginia}, Timothy[1] {of Staines, Middlesex, England}, Richmond[1a], Robert[2a], William[3a] {Tyrell of Thornton, Rockinghamshire, England}] Terrill of Orange County, Virginia. Thomas[6] and Elizabeth[4] had nine children: Mary[7] "Polly," Nancy[7], Sally[7], Augustine[7], Catherine[7] "Kitty," Jane[7], Elizabeth[7] "Betsy," George[7] and Terrill[7].

g. David[6] Herring
born in 1766 in Orange County, Virginia. He died sometime after 1838 in McNairy County, Kentucky. He married Virginia "Jennie" Ramsey on March 23, 1791 in Albemarle County, Virginia. She was born in 1770 in Orange County, Virginia. Her date and place of death is not known. The name of her father and mother is not known. David[6] and Virginia had two children: Nancy[7] and Mary[7].

h. William Fielding[6] Herring
born in 1776 in Surry County, North Carolina. He died in 1850 at Jefferson, Clinton County, Indiana. He married Wineford Creed in 1792 in Orange County, North Carolina. She was born in 1768 in Orange County, North Carolina. She died after 1850 in Shelby County, Indiana. Her

father was Matthew Creed of Virginia. Her mother was Margaret [John, John] McKinney of Orange County, Virginia. William[6] and Wineford had at least two children: Susan[7] and Nancy[7].

4. Elizabeth[4] Sturgill
born in 1735 in Orange County, Virginia. Her date and place of death is not known. She married John[2] Hash [afa Hache] in 1763 [other records say 1759] in Orange, Virginia. He was born on April 13, 1732 in Orange County, Virginia. He died on April 13, 1784 in Montgomery County, Virginia and his will proven on May 27, 1784. His father was John[1] [Thomas[1a] {born circa 1602 of Tenterden, Kent, England}, Arthur[2a] {Hatch of Aulers, Devonshire, England}] Hash of England and later of Montgomery County, Virginia. His mother was Elender[2] ["Lt." Ephraim[1] {of England and later of Williamsburg, James City County, Virginia}] Osborne of England. On December 16, 1774, John[2] Hash received a grant for 450 acres located on both sides of the Bridle Creek Branch of the New River in Fincastle County, Virginia.

"Old" John[2] Hash left a will on April 2, 1784 in Montgomery County, Virginia, recorded there in Will Book B, Page 63 and reads as follows:

In the name of God, Amen.

I, John Hash, being very sick and weak in body but of perfect mind and memory, thanks be given to God for it, and therefore calling to mind the mortality of my body and knowing that it is appointed unto all men once to die, do make and ordain this my last will and testament. And first, I give my soul into the hands of God who gave it and my body to ye earth, to be buried in a Christian manner at ye discretion of my executors. And as concerning such worldly estate as God hath given me I give and bequeath in ye following manner:

Item, I give and bequeath to my loving wife my manshun house and ye sole benifit of all ye land on ye north side of ye creek as long as she lives; with one black horse and a black mare, and two twin cows, one yew and a lam, and a wheather vane, a bed and all ye furniture thereunto belonging; one large pot and a frying pan, one puter dish, one beason, and six spoons; with 2 spinning wheels, and 2 pair of cords and a hackle, one rideing saddle with a box iron and heaters and 2 pleats.

Item, I give and bequeth to my son John who I had by my first wife, five shillings.

Item, I give and bequeath to my son William a full and equall share with all my children of all ye remaining part of my estate, except one cow to Enoch Osborn and one to Francis Sturgen, or ye price of a cow each of them.

Item, I give and bequeath to my son Thomas all my land lying on ye upper side of ye creek so far as to a small run that emties in ye creek above ye ford.

Item, I give and bequeath to my son John, who I have had by my second wife, all my land on ye Lower side of ye above sd creek after ye deceas of his mother whom I leve ye sole executer of this my last will and testiment.

I give Richard Hall my grand son a 2-year-old red heafer.

Signed, sealed, ratified and confirmed in ye year of our Lord 1784 and in ye presence of Test. Enoch Osborn, Thomas Vaughn (and) Robert Baker.

[Signed by mark] John Hash
[Will proved 27 May 1784]

Elizabeth[4] and John[2] had at least one child:

a. John[3] Hash

born in 1764 in Orange County, Virginia. He died in 1842 in Madison County, Arkansas. He married Theodocia[5] "Docia" Sturgill in 1780 in Ashe County, North Carolina. She was born in 1765 in Orange County, Virginia. She died in 1830 in Washington County, Arkansas. Her father was James[4] [James[3], John Daniel[2], John[1] {of North Petherton Parish, Somersetshire, England}, Richard[1a], George[2a]] Sturgill/Stodgill of Orange County, Virginia. Her mother was Susannah Ann[4] [Joseph[3] [Joseph[2], Edmund[1] (of England), William[1a]] Calloway of Essex County, Virginia. John[3] and Theodocia[5] had seven children: William Wesley[4], Nancy[4], Thomas[4], John[4], Tabitha[4], Alvin[4] and Fielding Henry[4].

[Editor's Note: Some researchers list the following children for Elizabeth[4] and John[2]; however, there are no further records found and it is doubtful they were married long enough to have more children: William, Mary "Polly," Elizabeth and Nancy. There is a lot of confusion about the children of Hash and his two wives.]

John[2] had married, first, Rebecca Anderson circa 1750 at Fincastle, Grayson County, Virginia. She was born in 1720 at Fincastle, Grayson County, Virginia. She died in 1763 in Grayson County, Virginia. Her father was Jacob Anderson of Montgomery County, Virginia. Her mother was Rebecca (Unknown). John[2] and Rebecca had at least four children and possibly others:

b. Jane[3] Hash
born in 1751 in Montgomery County, Virginia. She died on April 12, 1822 in Grayson County, Virginia and was buried in the Osborne Fort Cemetery. She married Enoch Osborne in 1765 in Montgomery County, Virginia. He was born in 1750 in Rowan County, North Carolina. He died in 1880 in Grayson County, Virginia. His father was Ephraim Osborne of North Carolina. The name of his mother is not known. Jane[3] and Enoch had two children: Enoch and Rebecca.

c. Mary[3] "Polly" Hash
born circa 1753 in Montgomery County, Virginia. Her date and place of death is not known.

d. Thomas[3] Hash
born on February 13, 1756 in Shenandoah
County, Virginia. He died on December 25,
1848 at Mt. Vernon, Lawrence County,
Missouri. He married Ruth[5] Sturgill in 1776
in Orange County, Virginia. She was born on
January 9, 1758 at Swift Run Creek, Orange
County, Virginia. She died circa 1822 in
Kentucky. Her father was James[4] [James[3],
John Daniel[2], John[1] {of North Petherton
Parish, Somersetshire, England}, Richard[1a],
George[2a]] Sturgill/Stodgill of Orange
County, Virginia. Her mother was Ann
Susannah Ann[4] [Joseph[3] [Joseph[2], Edmund[1]
(of England), William[1a]] Calloway of Essex
County, Virginia. Thomas[3] and Ruth had ten
children: Elizabeth[4] "Betsey," Sarah[4] "Sally,"
William[4], Jane[4], Nancy[4], James[4], Phillip[4],
Ruth[4], Mary[4] and Marsha[4].

e. Rebecca[3] Hash
born circa 1758 in Montgomery County,
Virginia. She died in 1841 Helton Creek,
Allegheny County, North Carolina.

5. John[4] Sturgill [afa Stodghill]
born circa 1740 in Orange County, Virginia. He
died in 1770, probably in Greenbriar County
[which later became Morgan County, West

Virginia], Virginia. John[4] married, first, Elizabeth Harvey circa 1760/1765 in Orange County, Virginia. She was born circa 1749 in Orange County [now Green County], Virginia. She died in 1824 in Monroe County, Virginia. Her father was John E. [Thomas {of Perquimans County, North Carolina}, Thomas {of Albemarle County, North Carolina}] of St. Thomas Parish, Orange County, Virginia. Her mother was Margaret Burke of Virginia. John[4] and Elizabeth settled and lived in Greenbriar County, Virginia [now Morgan County, West Virginia]. John[4] and Elizabeth had nine children:

a. Joel[5] Sturgill
born in 1765 in Monroe County, Virginia [later West Virginia]. He died on October 4, 1844 in Greenbriar County, Virginia [later West Virginia]. He married Elizabeth[2] Graham on January 15, 1793 in Greenbriar County, Virginia [which later became Morgan County, West Virginia]. She was born on March 29, 1770 in Greenbriar County, Virginia. She died on March 22, 1858 in Monroe County, West Virginia. Her father was James[1] [William[1a], Christopher[2a] {of Scotland}, Thomas[3a]] Graham of Donegal County, Ireland. Her mother was Florence[2] [John[1] {of Londonderry, Ireland}, Christopher[1a] {of Scotland}, Thomas[2a]] Graham

of Augusta County, Virginia. Joel[5] and Elizabeth[2] had nine children: William Graham[6], Rhoda S.[6], Elizabeth[6], John[6], Florence[6], James[6], Samuel[6], Nancy[6] and Joel[6].

b. Rhoda[5] Sturgill
born in 1768 in Orange County, Virginia. She died in 1846 in Giles County, Virginia. She married Hugh[2] Caperton on September 21, 1785 in Greenbriar County, Virginia [which later became Morgan County, West Virginia]. He was born in 1751 in Rockbridge County, Virginia. He died in 1816 in Monroe County, Virginia [later West Virginia]. His father was John[1] [Richard[1a] {of England}] Caperton of Ireland. His mother was Mary[1] [Adam[1a]] Thompson of Ireland. Rhoda[5] and Hugh[2] had nine children: James[3], Thompson Hugh[3], John Stodghill[3], Elizabeth[3], Mary[3] "Polly," Augustus William[3], Green C.[3], George Washington[3] and Overton Harrison[3].

c. Winifred[5] Sturgill
born in 1770 in Greenbriar County, Virginia [which later became Morgan County, West Virginia]. She died in 1850 in Ohio. She married Lively[5] McGhee on August 30, 1797 in Greenbriar County, Virginia. He was born in 1774 in Albemarle County, Virginia. He died in

1843 in Jackson County, Ohio. His father was William[4] [James[3], William[2] {Mackgehee of New Kent County, Virginia}, William[1] {Mackgayhe of Scotland}] McGehee of Hanover County, Virginia. His mother was Elizabeth Lively of Virginia. Winifred[5] and Lively[5] had six children: James Mayfield[6], Mary[6], Augustin[6], Elizabeth[6], Nancy Ann[6] and Allen[6].

d. William[5] Sturgill
born in 1772 in Greenbriar County, Virginia [which later became Morgan County, West Virginia]. His date and place of death is not known. He married Rebecca[2] Dinsmore in 1771 in 1799 in Augusta County, Virginia. She was born in 1771 in Goochland County, Virginia. Her date and place of death is not known. Her father was James[1] [Adam[1a], Laird {of Achenmead, Scotland}] Dinsmore of Belfast, Ulster, Parish of Ballywattick, Ireland and later of Canton, Washington County, Pennsylvania. Her mother was Rebecca Walker of Washington County, Pennsylvania. William[5] and Rebecca[2] had two children: Sarah[6] and William[6].

e. Elizabeth[5] Sturgill
born in 1776 in Greenbriar County, Virginia [which later became Morgan County, West Virginia]. She died in 1846 in Greenbriar

County, Virginia. She married John[3] Henderson in 1792 in Greenbriar County, Virginia [later West Virginia]. He was born circa 1776 in Greenbriar County, Virginia. His date and place of death is not known. His father was "Colonel" John[2] [James[1] {of Fordell, Fifeshire, Scotland}, William[1a], John[2a], John[3a], James[4a], William[5a], George[6a], James[7a], Robert[8a], John[9a], Thomas[10a] {born 1360 of Inverkeithing, Scotland}] Henderson of Augusta County, Virginia. His mother was Anne[2] [John[1] {of Antrim, Ireland}, Samuel[1a]] Givens of Augusta County, Virginia. Elizabeth[5] and John[3] had three children: Rhoda[4], Angelina[4] and Emily[4].

f. Millie[5] Sturgill
born in 1777 in Greenbriar County, Virginia [which later became Morgan County, West Virginia]. She married (Unknown) Bratton.

g. Nancy[5] Sturgill
born in 1779 in Greenbriar County, Virginia [which later became Morgan County, West Virginia]. Her date and place of death is not known [but before February 1813, when John[3] remarried] She married John[3] Arbuckle in 1799 in Monroe County, Virginia [later West Virginia]. He was born on October 2, 1771 in Greenbriar County, Virginia. He died on

September 30, 1845 in Madison County, Ohio. His father was Matthew[2] [James[1] {of Scotland}, James[1a]] Arbuckle of Augusta County, Virginia. His mother was Jane Lockhart of Lancaster County, Pennsylvania. Nancy[5] and John[3] had no issue.

John[3] married, second, Elizabeth[4] Bishop on February 2, 1813 in Champaign County, Ohio. She was born on September 9, 1788 in Greenbriar County, Virginia [later West Virginia]. She died on April 18, 1865 in Madison County, Ohio. Her father was Josiah[3] [Jonathan[2], Robert[1] {of Bridgeport, Dorset, England}] Bishop of Evesham, Burlington County, New Jersey. Her mother was Susanna[3] [James[2] {of Burlington County, New Jersey}, John[1] {of Gloucestershire, England}, John[1a] {of Staffordshire, England}] Inskeep of Gloucester County, New Jersey. John[3] and Elizabeth[4] had eight children: William[4], Matthew[4], Susan[4], Charles[4], Rebecca Rachel[4], Josiah[4], James[4] and Jacob Lockhart[4].

h. John[5] Sturgill
born in 1780 in Orange County, Virginia. His date and place of death is not known. He married Lucresia[7] "Lucy" Ballard on August 5, 1799 in Monroe County, Virginia [later West

Virginia}. She was born in 1780 in Orange County, Virginia. She died, age 100, in 1880 at Chestnut Hill, Monroe County, West Virginia. Her father was William[6] [Phillip[5] {of St. Ann's Parish, Essex County, Virginia}, William[4] {of James City, York County, Virginia}, Thomas[3], Thomas[2] {of Williamsburg, King James County, Virginia}, William[1] {of St. Mary's, Southwell, Nottinghamshire, England}, Henry[1a], Phillip[2a], William[3a] {born 1517] Ballard of St. Thomas, Orange County, Virginia. Her mother was Elizabeth Steppe of Monroe County, Virginia [later West Virginia]. John[5] and Lucy[7] had five children: Jesse[6], Joel[6], William[6], Mary[6] and Archibald[6].

Lucy[7] married, second, John Goodall on June 7, 1808 in Orange County, Virginia. He was born in 1780 in Monroe County, Virginia [later West Virginia]. He died in 1860 in Chestnut Hill, Monroe County, West Virginia. His father was James [John, Charles {of the Northern Neck of Tidewater, Caroline County, Virginia}] Goodall of Orange County, Virginia. His mother was Sarah "Sally" Harvey of Orange County, Virginia. Lucy[7] and John had six children: Sallie, Susan, Eleanor, John William, Fountain and James William.

John Goodall had married, first, Sarah Davis.

i. James[5] Sturgill
   born in 1781 in Morgan County, Virginia [later West Virginia]. His date and place of death is not known. He married Mary Dickenson on December 31, 1811 in Monroe County, Virginia [later West Virginia]. She was born in 1785 in Greenbriar County, Virginia [which later became Morgan County, West Virginia]. Her date and place of death is not known. Her father was John Dickenson of Greenbriar County, Virginia [later West Virginia]. The name of her mother is not known. Issue, if any, is not known.

j. Polly[5] Sturgill
   born in 1783 in Greenbriar County, Virginia [later West Virginia]. She died in 1836 in Greenbriar County, West Virginia [which later became Morgan County, West Virginia]. She married David[2] Graham on December 9, 1800 in Monroe County, Virginia [later West Virginia]. He was born on March 24, 1772 in Greenbriar County, Virginia [later West Virginia]. He died in 1836 in Greenbriar County, West Virginia. His father was James[1] [William[1a], Christopher[2a] {of Scotland}, Thomas[3a]] Graham of Donegal, Ireland. His mother was Florence[2] [John[1] {of

Londonderry, Ireland}, Christopher[1a] {of Scotland}, Thomas[2a]] Graham of Augusta County, Virginia. Polly[5] and David[2] had four children: James[3], Harrison[3], Sallie[3] and Sarah[3].

k. Sarah[5] Sturgill
born in 1785 in Morgan County, Virginia [later West Virginia]. Her date and place of death is not known. She married John Barrett on February 2, 1809 in Monroe County, Virginia [later West Virginia]. He was born in 1780 in Greenbriar County, Virginia [later West Virginia]. His date and place of death is not known. The name of his father and mother is not known. Issue, if any, is not known.

John[4] married, second, Mary Coffman on April 22, 1801 in Mercer County, Kentucky. Mary was born circa 1740 in Orange County, Virginia. Her date of death, presumably in Mercer County, Kentucky, is not known. Her father was Isaac Coffman of Orange County, Virginia. Her mother was Ann (Unknown). John[4] and Mary had no issue.

6. Joel[4] Sturgill
born circa 1744 in Orange County, Virginia [Editor's Note: He was bound to Elizabeth Harvey, his sister-in-law, about 1763 by the Wardens of the Church after his mother had died]. He died on

September 14, 1795 in Elbert County, Georgia. He married Martitia Oliver in 1781 in Orange County, Virginia. She was born circa 1763 in Orange County, Virginia. She died circa 1805 in Elbert County, Georgia. Her father was James Durrett [Nicholas "Nicholson", John {of New Kent County, Virginia}, Nicholas, John {of King William County, Virginia}] Oliver of Carolina County and later of Orange County, Virginia. Her mother was Tabitha Elizabeth[5] [Benjamin Minor[4] {of Virginia}, Minor[3] {of Westmoreland County, Virginia}, John[2], Owen[1] {of Llanrst, Caernarvonshire, Wales}] Winn [also found as Wynn] of Orange County, Virginia.

Joel[4]'s father died when he was three, his mother when he was thirteen. He was first bound to the guardianship of an older sister, Elizabeth, then four years later bound voluntarily to a neighbor, Joseph Davis, to learn the trade of a leather breeches maker. Joel[4] continued to live on his parent's homestead until 1790. After his marriage, in 1792, he and his wife, Martitia, along with his sons Durrett[5] and Willis[5], moved from Virginia to Elbert County, Georgia. At his death he left behind 250 acres of land, four slaves and personal goods worth $694.47.

Joel[4] and Martitia had four children:

a. Durrett[5] [afa Durrette] Sturgill
   born circa 1782 in Orange County, Virginia. He
   died on September 5, 1857 in Butts County,
   Georgia. He married Lucy[4] Higginbotham circa
   1804, probably in Elbert County, Georgia. She
   was born in 1798 in Wilkes County, Georgia.
   She died in 1862 in Butts County, Georgia. Her
   father was Francis[3] [Benjamin[2] {of Goochland,
   later Amherst, County, Virginia}, John[1] {of
   Phillip, Barbados}] Higginbotham of Amherst
   County, Virginia. Her mother was Dolly
   [Larkin {of King and Queen County, Virginia},
   Henry {of Essex County, Virginia}] Gatewood
   of Amherst County, Virginia. Durret[5] and Lucy[4]
   had eleven children: Joel[6], James M.[6], Martha
   Caroline[6], Mary[6] "Polly," William Francis[6], John
   Thomas[6], Malvana[6], Caroline[6], Henry B.[6],
   Catherine[6] and Sara Frances[6].

b. Willis[5] Sturgill
   born in 1784 in Orange County, Virginia. His
   date and place of death is not known.

[Editor's Note: There is no further mention on the
following two children, who probably died in
infancy]

c. Mary[5] "Polly" Sturgill
   date and place of birth and death not known.

d. Fanny[5] Sturgill
    date and place of birth and death not known.

7. William[4] Sturgill
    born circa 1746 in Orange County, Virginia. His
    date and place of death is not known.

The Life and Times of
John Daniel² Stodghill

PATERNAL ANCESTRY: [STURGILL/STODGILL/
STODGHILL: John¹ {of North Petherton Parish,
Somersetshire, England}, Richard¹ᵃ, George²ᵃ]

MATERNAL ANCESTRY: [(UNKNOWN)]

JOHN DANIEL² was born circa 1665 in Essex County,
Virginia. He died circa 1725 in Essex County,
Virginia. His father was John¹ Stodgill of North
Pemberton, Somersetshire, England and later of Essex
County, Virginia. The name of his mother is not
known.

JOHN DANIEL² married Ann Franks in 1690 in
Rappahannock County, Virginia. She was born circa
1675 in Rappahannock County, Virginia. She died
sometime after 1739 in Orange County, Virginia. Her
father was Daniel [Daniel] Franks of Rappahannock
County, Virginia. The name of her mother is not
known.

JOHN DANIEL² had a law suit between he and
Thomas Tinsley dismissed [1702 ESSEX COUNTY
DEED & WILL BOOK 10:145].

JOHN DANIEL[2] marks a hole and nick in the right ear, a crop and a slit and underkiel on the left ear. Daniel Franks marks a half spade and underkiel on the right ear, a crop and underkiel in the left ear. Sir, be pleased to record both these marks for me and the subscriber, but the latter in behalf of Daniel Franks to whom I gave a calf of the same mark with the female increase [Recorded later in 1703 ESSEX COUNTY DEED & WILL BOOK 11:20]. The gift of a calf to Daniel Franks was significant, not an everyday occurrence, and for the time, was valuable. It is thought that the gift was made at the time John[2] married Daniel's daughter, Ann Franks.

JOHN DANIEL[2] recorded another cattle mark for himself and Daniel Franks in 1704, to whom he had given a calf. Again, in those times a calf represented considerable wealth and this apparently was a gift to his father-in-law.

JOHN DANIEL[2] was deceased when his wife Ann appears [probably not long before her own death]. As the widow Ann Stodghill, she paid for two tithes on the 1739 Orange County, Virginia tithe records. Their property was in the precinct of James Pickett. They had purchased property in 1718 from a William and Sarah Pickett. The next available tithe record for the area in 1747 no longer showed a Stodghill name.

[EDITOR'S NOTE: Many researchers have this Ann as Ann Madison. However, research shows that while they were neighbors with the Madison family, that family did not have a daughter Ann or anyone else who married this John Daniel[2] Stodghill. There may have been confusion with his son, Daniel[3] who married Jean[3] Madison.].

The Children of John Daniel[2] Stodghill and Ann Franks

1. **James[3] Stodgill**
   born circa 1695 at Piscataway Creek, Essex County, Virginia. He died intestate in 1753 in Orange County, Virginia. He married Ann Williams[3] Blackstone in 1723 in Essex County, Virginia. She was born in 1700 in Essex County, Virginia. She died in 1763 at St. Thomas Parish, Orange County, Virginia. Her father was Argyle/Argoll[2] [Argyle[1] {of Scotland} Thomas[1a]] Blackstone of Essex County, Virginia. Her mother was Elizabeth[2] [Robert[1] {of Scotland}] Armstrong of Essex County, Virginia. James[3] and Ann[3] had seven children: Ambrose[4], James[4], Elizabeth[4], John[4], Joel[4], Mary[4] and William[4].

2. Susannah[3] Stodghill
   born circa 1696/1697 at Piscataway Creek, Essex

County, Virginia. She died sometime after 1769 in Essex County, Virginia. She married John "Thomas" Smith circa 1720 in Essex County, Virginia. He was born circa 1700 in Essex County, Virginia. His date and place of death is not known. The name of his father and mother is not known. Susannah[4] and Thomas had two children: one whose name is not known, and:

a. Alice Smith
   born circa 1725 in Essex County, Virginia. Her date and place of death is not known. She married (Unknown) Baughn. Alice and (Unknown) Baughn had two children: Otis and Thomas Smith.

3. Daniel[3] Stodghill
   born circa 1705 at Piscataway Creek, Essex County, Virginia. He died sometime after 1769 in Essex County, Virginia. He married Jean[4] Madison circa 1730 in Essex County, Virginia. She was born circa 1710/1712 at Piscataway Creek, Essex County, Virginia. She died sometime after 1808 in Essex County, Virginia. Her father was John[3] [John[2], John[1] {of England}, Isaac[1a]] Madison of St. Stephen's, King and Queen County, Virginia. Her mother was Isabella Minor Todd of King and Queen County, Virginia [Editor's Note: Some researchers have her marrying a man named

David Roach {1700-1761} with a child by him named Reuben {1732-1795}, but the dates don't match up with the marriage date and dates of birth of her children with Daniel³ Stodghill]. Daniel³ and Jean⁴ had a child:

a. James⁴ Stodghill
born in 1730 in Essex County, Virginia. He died on July 21, 1783 in Essex County, Virginia. He married Mary⁴ Croxton in 1760 in Essex County, Virginia. She was born in 1750 in Essex County, Virginia. Her date of death at Madisonville, Hopkins County, Kentucky is not known. Her father was Thomas³ [John Carter² {of Stratton Major, King and Queen County, Virginia}, (Unknown)¹ {the immigrant ancestor of England}] Croxton of Tappahannock, Essex County, Virginia. Her mother was Mary Ann Haile of Beaver's Hill, Essex County, Virginia. James⁴ and Mary⁴ had six children: Catherine⁵, Thomas⁵, Elizabeth⁵, John⁵, Thomas⁵ and Catherine⁵ [presumably the first two children died early].

4. John³ Stodghill
born circa 1710 at Piscataway Creek, Essex County, Virginia. He died on May 16, 1773 in Goochland County, Virginia. He married Elizabeth³ Miller circa 1735 in Essex County, Virginia. She was born

on November 8, 1700 at Christchurch, Middlesex County, Virginia. Her date and place of death is not known. Her father was John[2] [Symon[1] {of Bristol Parish, Gloucestershire, England}, "Captain" Symon[1a]] Miller of Middlesex County, Virginia. Her mother was Mary[2] [John[1] {of Slapton, Devonshire, England}, John[1a], Richard[2a], John[3a], William[4a], John[5a], Andrew[6a], Osbert[7a]] Hawkins of Middlesex County, Virginia. John[3] and Elizabeth[3] had four children:

a. Keziah[4] Stodghill
born in 1737 at Goochland, Goochland County, Virginia. She died in 1765 in Essex County, Virginia.

b. Ambrose[4] Stodghill
born in 1740 at Goochland, Goochland County, Virginia. He died circa 1789/1790 in Fluvanna County, Virginia. He married Susannah Denton sometime before 1763 [when their first child was born], probably in Albemarle County, Virginia. She was born in 1745 in Essex County, Virginia. She died in 1824 in Fluvanna County, Virginia. Her father was William Hudson [William {of Brunswick County, Virginia}] Denton of Virginia. Her mother was Elizabeth Dunman of Virginia. Amborse[4] and Susannah had ten children: Cecelia[5], Charles[5], William[5],

James[5], Mary[5], Celia[5], James[5], Ambrose[5], Joanna[5] and David[5].

c. Sarah[4] Stodghill
born in 1742 in Essex County, Virginia. She died in 1805 at Goochland, Goochland County, Virginia. She married James[5] Jordon on February 27, 1761 at St. James Northam Parish, Goochland County, Virginia. He was born in 1736 in Goochland County, Virginia. He died in October 1771 in Goochland County, Virginia. His father was Charles[4] [Samuel[3] {of Chuckatuck, Nansemond County, Virginia}, Thomas[2], Thomas[1] {of Wiltshire, England}, Samuel[1a] {of Burnham, Buckinghamshire, England}, Robert[2a] {of Melcomb, Dorset, England}] Jordon of New Kent County, Virginia. His mother was Hellenah (Unknown) of Virginia. Sarah[4] and James[5] had a child: James[6].

d. Mary[4] Stodghill
born in 1745 at Goochland, Goochland County, Virginia. She died in 1805 at Goochland, Goochland County, Virginia. She married to Matthew[5] Jordon on October 10, 1763 at St. James Northam Parish, Goochland County, Virginia. He was born in 1741 in Goochland County, Virginia. He died in 1777 at St. Georges Parish, Accomac County, Virginia. His father

was Charles[4] [Samuel[3] {of Chuckatuck, Nansemond County, Virginia}, Thomas[2], Thomas[1] {of Wiltshire, England}, Samuel[1a] {of Burnham, Buckinghamshire, England}, Robert[2a] {of Melcomb, Dorset, England}] Jordon of New Kent County, Virginia. His mother was Hellenah (Unknown) of Virginia. Mary[4] and Matthew[5] had a child: Benjamin[6].

The Life and Times of
John[1] Stodgell

PATERNAL ANCESTRY: [STURGILL/STODGILL/
STODGHILL/STOGELL: Richard[1a], George[2a]]

MATERNAL ANCESTRY: [(UNKNOWN)]

JOHN[1] was christened on April 10, 1615 at North
Petherton Parish, Somersetshire, England. He died
sometime before 1704 [when the Quit Rent Rolls were
taken] in Essex County, Virginia. His father was
Richard[1a] Stodgell of North Pemberton, Somersetshire, England. The name of his mother is not
known.

JOHN[1] married an unknown wife circa 1653 in
Rappahannock County, Virginia.

JOHN[1] requested in 1650, at the age of 35, and was
granted permission from the church in England to
"go beyond the seas." He was from Saint Stokes
Parrish, Somerset County, England, apparently still
unmarried. Under the "headright" system of Virginia,
each person coming over would receive 100 acres for
himself and for each person for whom he paid
passage. In 1650, John[1] Stodgell was one of eight
people whose passage was paid by James Heard
[Hurd]. The ship may have been the *Benjamin*

Harrison, which may have embarked from Bristol. Once in Virginia, John[1] first appears in the tithe [tax] records of Rappahannock County in 1659 and continues through 1669 where he paid tax on 100 acres located on the Potomac River.

[EDITOR'S NOTE: The headrights system encouraged wealthy individuals to pay to transport indentured servants to Virginia. In theory, the servants would work five to seven years clearing new land and moving the edge of English settlement further west into the North American continent. The indentured servants did not acquire title to land through their work during their term of service. At the end of their term of indenture, they were given some basic clothing and equipment, and expected to move to the unsettled frontier. They could purchase unimproved land there, "improve" it by cutting down the trees and preparing fields suitable for growing crops such as corn and tobacco. As the forested frontier was converted into farms, indentured servants were transformed into land owners who could provide their children a better opportunity at gaining wealth.]

JOHN[1] owned 100 acres on Piscataway Creek, then part of Rappahannock County, Virginia, now near Tappahannock in Essex County. This land continued in the family for several generations.

The Children of
John[1] Stodgell
and an (Unknown Wife)

1. James[2] Stodgell

   born circa 1660 in Essex County, Virginia. He died
   sometime after 1704 when he is last found in York
   County, Virginia. It is thought that those of the
   same or similar surname who migrated from there
   up the Delmarva Peninsula and on into New
   Jersey and Pennsylvania may have been his
   descendants.

2. **John Daniel[2] Stodgill**

   born circa 1665 [another source says 1655] in Essex
   County, Virginia. He died circa 1725 in Essex
   County, Virginia. He married Ann[2] Franks in 1690
   in Rappahannock County, Virginia. She was born
   circa 1675 in Rappahannock County, Virginia. She
   died sometime after 1739 in Orange County,
   Virginia. Her father was Daniel[1] Franks of England
   [he came to America on a ship out of South-
   ampton] and later of Rappahannock County,
   Virginia [Editor's Note: he was condemned circa
   1622/1624 for being a cattle thief]. The name of her
   mother is not known. John[2] and Ann[2] had four
   children: James[3], Susannah[3], Daniel[3] and John[3].

The Life and Times of
Richard[1a] Stodgell

PATERNAL ANCESTRY: STURGILL/STODGILL/ STODGHILL/STOGELL/ STOGGELL: George[2a]]

MATERNAL ANCESTRY: [(UNKNOWN)]

RICHARD[1a] was christened on October 11, 1579 at North Petherton, Somersetshire, England. He died on October 5, 1655 at North Petherton, Somersetshire, England. His father was George[2a] Stoggell of North Petherton, Somersetshire, England. His mother was Edith Walford of North Petherton, Somersetshire, England.

RICHARD[1a] married an unknown wife. She was born in 1581, presumably in Somersetshire, England. She died on August 4, 1668 at North Petherton, Somersetshire, England.

[EDITOR'S NOTE: Records of this family are found in the Shire of Somerset in the Parish of North Petherton, England]

The Children of
Richard[1a] Stodgell
and an (Unknown Wife)

1. **Richard[1] Stodgell**

   christened on October 16, 1608 at North Petherton Parish, Somersetshire, England. He died on December 1, 1690 at North Petherton Parish, Somersetshire, England. The name of his wife and the date and place of his marriage is not known. Issue, if any, is not known.

2. **Nicholas[1] Stodgell**

   born in 1612 at North Petherton Parish, Somersetshire, England. He died in 1660 in Somersetshire, England.

3. **John[1] Stodgell**

   christened on April 10, 1615 at North Petherton Parish, Somersetshire, England. He died sometime before 1704 [when the Quit Rent Rolls were taken] in Essex County, Virginia. He married an unknown wife circa 1653 in Rappahannock County, Virginia. John[1] and the unknown wife had two children: James[2] and John Daniel[2].

4. Elizabeth[1] Stodgell

 born circa 1626 at North Petherton Parish, Somersetshire, England. Her date and place of death is
 not known.

5. Ann[1] Stodgell

 born circa 1626 at North Petherton Parish, Somersetshire, England. Her date and place of death is
 not known.

The Life and Times of
George²ª Stoggell

PATERNAL ANCESTRY: [STURGILL/STODGILL/ STODGHILL/STOGELL/STOGDELL/STOGGELL: (UNKNOWN)]

MATERNAL ANCESTRY: [(UNKNOWN)]

JOHN²ª was born circa 1546 at North Petherton Somersetshire, England. He died on March 28, 1620 at North Petherton, Somersetshire, England. The name of his father and mother is not known.

JOHN²ª married Edith Walford on November 8, 1576 at North Petherton, Somersetshire, England. She was born circa 1556, presumably at North Petherton, Somersetshire, England. She died in 1604 at North Petherton, Somersetshire, England. The name of her father and mother is not known.

[EDITOR'S NOTE: Records of this family are found in the Shire of Somerset in the Parish of North Petherton, England]

The Children of
George[2a] Stoggell
and Edith Walford

1. Peternell Henry[1a] Stoggell

   born in 1577 at North Petherton, Somersetshire, England is not known. She died in 1668. Her place of death is not known.

2. **Richard[1a] Stoggell/Stodgell**

   christened on October 11, 1579 at North Pethetron, Somersetshire, England. He died on October 5, 1655 at North Petherton, Somersetshire, England. He married an unknown wife. She was born in 1581, presumably in Somersetshire, England. She died on August 4, 1668 at North Petherton, Somersetshire, England. Richard[1a] and his unknown wife had five children: Richard[1], Nicholas[1], John[1], Elizabeth[1] and Ann[1].

3. Roger[1a] Stodgell

   christened on September 24, 1580 at North Petherton, Somersetshire, England. He died [either at birth or as an infant] in 1580 at North Petherton, Somersetshire, England.

4. John[1a] Stodgell

born in 1585 at North Petherton, Somersetshire, England is not known. He died [either at birth or as an infant] on May 20, 1585 at North Petherton, Somersetshire, England.

5. Mary[1a] Stodgell

born circa 1589 at North Petherton, Somersetshire, England is not known. Her date and place of birth is not known.

5. Alice[1a] Stodgell

born circa 1590 at North Petherton, Somersetshire, England is not known. She died [either at birth or as an infant] on May 8, 1804 at North Petherton, Somersetshire, England.

ADDENDA PAGE

Pg Ref #   Comment/Correction/Addition/Etc.

_____

_____

_____

_____

_____

_____

_____

_____

_____

_____

_____

_____

_____

_____

_____

_____